Found Wanting

A new series of books from Cassell's Sexual Politics list, Women on Women *provides a forum for lesbian, bisexual and heterosexual women to explore and debate contemporary issues and to develop strategies for the advancement of feminist culture and politics into the next century.*

COMMISSIONING:
Roz Hopkins
Liz Gibbs
Christina Ruse

Found Wanting

Women, Christianity and Sexuality

Alison R. Webster

Foreword by Sara Maitland

CASSELL

Cassell
Wellington House, 125 Strand, London WC2R 0BB

215 Park Avenue South
New York, NY 10003

First published 1995

**British Library Cataloguing-in-Publication
Data**
A catalogue record for this book is available from
the British Library.

ISBN 0–304–32848–0 (hardback)
    0–304–32850–2 (paperback)

The poem 'Four years on – what's left?' on
pp. 85–7 is © the author, and is reprinted here
with her permission.
The excerpt from *Sappho's Reply* on p. 181 is
reprinted here by kind permission of Rita Mae
Brown.

Typeset by York House Typographic Ltd
Printed and bound in Great Britain by Biddles Ltd,
Guildford and King's Lynn

contents

For Elaine, and in honour of all the other women who are 'warriors who came before'.[1]

1. A phrase from Phyllis Chesler, quoted in Sue Wilkinson, 'Women and madness: a reappraisal', *Feminism and Psychology Journal*, vol. 4, no. 2, May 1994, p. 264.

For those who know Alison Webster's work, this book will come as no surprise: the clarity of concept, of analysis and of the writing itself is what you will expect. Even so it is a remarkable book. In the first place it is a paradigm of how feminist theory claims research should be done: the data of the book are the experiences of women concerned with what I will call for shorthand 'living on the margins' of organized Christianity, but these data are analysed in their relationship both to the women's movement more widely and to Christian ecclesial politics. That analysis is done from a clearly declared personal base, and yet manages to treat the data with respect, even with tenderness.

There is a crisis in the relationships between women and institutional religion. This can be seen most clearly in the Roman Catholic Church because of the high-profile interventions from the Vatican: in the last year we have seen the publication of the new Catechism delayed because the Vatican-chosen translator was unable to produce an acceptably sexist version of the text. We have also seen an extraordinary, because totally unnecessary, papal encyclical telling us we should not even think about the ordination of women. Meanwhile the Church of England has decided to ordain women to the priesthood, but – just in case this should give them fancy ideas – specifically to exclude them from the episcopacy.

These pressures have also led to a polarization among Christian women, with an increasingly noisy conservatism on the one hand (the American New Right and fundamentalist movements here at home) and a radical disengagement not just from church attendance but from the entire methodology of Christian theology – especially the theology of ethics – on the other. This latter is not a drift into agnosticism, quietism, or indifference; it is rather an angry and often highly articulate protest driven by a profound religious need and a sense of disillusionment: Christianity's reaction to feminism has often been totally bizarre.

At the statistical level all this has been talked about extensively; what has not been discussed enough, or certainly with enough care and attention, is the emotional and intellectual specifics that drive individual women to alter their religious posture and how they feel about it once that is done. This attention has not been paid, I suspect, because too many commentators really do not want to take the oppression of women, as women, seriously. The experience of sexism, of discrimination on grounds of gender, once it has been made conscious through feminist discourse, is extremely hard to bear. Because she takes sexism seriously, and because she can bring a feminist analytical discourse to bear on it, Alison Webster is not only sensitive to what women are saying, she is also very intelligent about it.

This book is descriptive rather than programmatic. It describes a set of circumstances rather than prescribing for them. It is not even clear whether the case calls for a doctor or not. But if all the people (of both genders, and all political positions) who want to prescribe for us will read this book they will not only know very clearly what Christian feminists are 'on about' and why, they will also find themselves much better informed – as well as being entertained, angered, touched and I hope grateful. I am.

Sara Maitland

*a*cknowlegements

I would like to thank all of the hundreds of women with whom I have come into contact in the course of my work on sexuality issues over the last few years. It is my discussions with them – conference and workshop participants; colleagues on committees and commissions; friends and friends of friends – which culminated in the idea of putting together a book like *Found Wanting*.

In converting that idea into reality, the written and verbal contributions of over forty women were crucial. These women responded to my invitation to write down their experiences, or to be interviewed by me about their lives. I have included material from most of them and I am profoundly thankful for their cooperation and creativity. Those whose actual words are not reproduced in the book should be assured that their contributions were nevertheless extremely valuable in informing the work. The categories of analysis, according to which the book is structured, were generated from a careful reading of *all* the contributions which I received, although it was impossible to use all the material in an illustrative way.

Of those whose material is included, many prefer to remain unnamed. For some this is a direct result of the realities of institutional discrimination which *Found Wanting* aims to illuminate and to challenge. Contributors who are in a position to be acknowledged by name are as follows: Jan Berry (see her 'letter to God', pp. 155-8), Polly Bluck, Ann Collins, Kathleen Cross, Liz Ford, Jutta Ried, Anne Pounds, Jane Robson, Margaret Trivasse and Sue Vickerman.

I would also like to thank those who supported my work on the book in other ways. Ros Hunt, Elizabeth Stuart, Mary Hunt, Carol Adams and Elaine Willis read and offered comments upon various bits of the manuscript. They are joined by many other friends and colleagues who contributed, perhaps without even realizing it! Conversations over dinner and at parties, on aeroplanes and trains rank alongside speeches at conferences, books, articles and correspondence in providing the inspiration and critical resources which I have utilized in this work.

A final thank you must go to Sara Maitland for her foreword to *Found Wanting* and for her advice and support in the book's pre-contract stage.

Alison Webster, September 1994

introduction

The churches don't seem to have noticed it yet, but members of their primary constituency (women) are deserting them in droves, largely because of current Christian attitudes towards gender, sexuality and personal relationships. I should make it clear from the start that my main concern in this book is not what this means *for the churches*; I do not lose sleep over their survival prospects. This book is not written for them, but for the women who leave. Having said that, it would do some churchmen no harm to read what they have to say.

Christianity has been a significant component in the personal histories of many women. Some have left it behind; others continue to find meaning within it; some have attempted to expunge Christianity from their lives, only to find that spirituality is an inescapable part of their identity. It is often issues of sexuality and gender which bring us into conflict with our inherited Christian values, forcing us to reassess and sometimes to reject them.

In my experience, once a woman finds herself on the margins of Christianity, she has few choices about where 'to go' in order to make sense of her situation. If she remains committed to Christianity itself she may find Christian feminism an inspiration; but if she is a lesbian she may not feel that this primary aspect of her identity is adequately addressed. If she is doubtful about Christianity she may find that secular feminism helps, but that any interest she retains in theology or spirituality must be suspended. If she looks to literature for accounts of experiences which echo her own, she will find a dearth of it. Since the 1970s, the Lesbian and Gay Christian Movement (formerly the Gay Christian Movement) has been successful in highlighting issues of anti-gay discrimination within the churches. Its work has been of particular interest and support to gay Christian men – particularly clergymen. But here again, lesbian women of

Christian heritage find themselves on the margins. In the 'lesbian and gay' Christian world women remain under-represented, not least because the implication of Christian commitment as a condition of membership is itself alienating to many.

In the course of my work for the Institute for the Study of Christianity and Sexuality I have encountered many women of Christian heritage who are questioning their sexuality and seeking resources for theological reflection. I have discovered that there is little reading I can recommend which is generated from the experiences of women in the UK. *Sex and God: Some Varieties of Women's Religious Experience*[1] is an exception. I have no hesitation in recommending the brilliant analytical work of certain American feminist theologians and ethicists on sexuality issues. Indeed, I draw upon much of it – particularly that of lesbian scholars – in this book. But women's experience of Christianity and sexuality in the UK is culturally specific, and it is difficult to identify fully with the quite different culture of the USA, particularly regarding religion. An exploration of quite *how* they are different, especially in feminist terms, has yet to be fully articulated. *Found Wanting* is an attempt to give voice to British women – particularly lesbians – of Christian heritage.

The women in this book offer perspectives on the dynamics of Christianity and therefore upon the dominant values that have shaped our culture for good or ill, and which continue to have an effect whether we like it or not. Although it includes assessments of certain theological ideas, *Found Wanting* is not primarily a theological work. Readers will find that remarkably little attention is given to those debates which are rehearsed endlessly by voices who argue about Christianity from *within* the Christian community: what it says in the Bible and what the Church has taught historically, for instance. This book begins in a difference place. Its focus is an exploration of the dynamics of institutional power. For that reason, women who live and work within other male-dominated and patriarchal institutions may well find it of interest, and its analysis helpful.

Methodology

Found Wanting is not intended to represent a quantitative study of women and their relationships with Christianity. If I had turned up outside a range of churches and interviewed women at random about their experiences of sexuality, I have no doubt that such a study would have revealed a very different picture.

In a sense, the women in this book selected themselves. A letter was sent out via various women's spirituality networks inviting contributions. Because the focus of the project was upon women who retain few links with organized religion, I also relied upon informal networks to reach contributors. Women were invited to make contributions in any form, of any length and in response to any of the issues outlined in the following synopsis:

Part One: will be a feminist critique of Christian sexual ethics, drawing upon theological and church documents for illustrative material.

Part Two: will explore the impact of these ethics on the lives of women, exploring a range of issues and their interrelationship: e.g. the exclusion and misrepresentation of single women (including those who are parents, and those whose partners have died); the invisibility of and discrimination against lesbians; suspicion and hatred of women's sexuality in general; women's experiences of marriage and heterosexuality; the use of sexuality as an instrument of violence against women and girls; attitudes towards women who are in heterosexual relationships outside of marriage.

Part Three: will be an exploration of alternative ways of understanding sexuality, spirituality and relationships, in order to construct new models for the future. I would like to find out from those women for whom Christianity has been important whether they consider themselves still to be 'religious' or 'spiritual'. What do such concepts mean to them, and how are they expressed? If they have left Christianity behind, do they miss being part of the Christian community, and if so, what do they miss? How do they understand sexuality and desire? Where do they look for inspiration in making decisions about their sexuality and relationships? Do they recognize any forms of 'authority'? What do they consider makes a good sexual relationship?

Over forty women replied, some at great length, either in writing or via an interview. About half of the women were lesbian. Confidentiality was assured, so in the contributions which have been reproduced all names and places have been changed.

All of the contributors to this book have clashed in a direct or indirect way with Christianity or church institutions, to such an extent that they felt the need fundamentally to rethink their identity as religious persons – and indeed whether 'religious' is an identity they wish to retain at all.

I do not know all the women personally, so it is not my place to label or define them. In general, they have histories of participation in the mainstream denominations in this country. For this reason, Found Wanting does not promise a *universal message* about women, Christianity and sexuality. The factors which restrict participation within the mainstream churches in this country (particularly classism and racism) will inevitably have had an impact upon the contributors to this book. The nature of the project itself will also have been important in this respect, as the women in this book find themselves on the periphery of Christianity *primarily* because of issues of sexuality and gender. I recognize that a completely different set of issues would have emerged from a group who saw race as the primary cause of their marginalization, rather than sexuality and gender. This is not to underestimate the importance of the project undertaken, just to be clear that, as I say in the introduction to Part Two, I cannot guarantee that every woman will find her experience reflected here.

I do not believe that we can be objective when reflecting upon the lessons which arise from women's experience; neither can we be exhaustive. My own 'situatedness' has undoubtedly been important in compiling, editing and analysing the contributions to this book.

My perspective

I am a white, Protestant, University-educated lesbian woman, aged 28. I was brought up with a liberal and exploratory kind of Christianity, in a family where Methodism formed a central focus (my father is a Methodist minister). I have been consciously interested in theology and religion from the age of 13 or 14, when the questions of 'ultimate meaning and value' began to fascinate me. I began my religious questioning by assuming that the point was to find 'an answer'. I even thought that I'd found it for a few months when I was 16 or 17 and engaged in a brief flirtation with the more evangelical kind of Christianity. However, this soon came to an abrupt end when I discovered the rigid nature of the beliefs that accompanied the rock music and the holiday camps.

I moved on to a faith centred upon 'political and social action' when I began a course of theology and religious study at university. Before beginning my theology degree I encountered the philosophical idea that God does not actually exist 'out there' but is a human creation – an idea which seemed to make a lot of sense, and which I found attractive. This precipitated something of an 'unconversion' from Christianity, the precise nature of which I have yet to work out. Neither discovering feminism nor becoming lesbian caused a 'crisis of faith' for me, because by this time I didn't really have a 'Christian faith' in the conventional sense. For this reason, perhaps, I have always found 'secular' feminism rather more inspiring and relevant than 'Christian' feminism, but wished that there was a more determined effort to span the gap between the two.

I remain committed to the pursuit of theological ideas but (for the moment at least) 'changing the church' remains on my agenda only tangentially, if at all. It dwells in my consciousness as a possible by-product of work which I am doing for other more important reasons. Unlike many of the women in this book, I have little experience of outright rejection at the hands of church institutions. However, this is largely because I have had low expectations about the possibility of full acceptance of my theological perspectives and sexual choices, and have exercised the appropriate degree of self-censorship in church circles when it was necessary.

I now go to church very rarely, but I maintain a commitment to my Christian roots, which I consider to be an inescapable part of my cultural heritage. It is my inexplicable ambivalence towards Christianity which convinces me that negotiating change in our religious commitments and identities is not a straightforward matter. Hence the focus in the final part of this book upon the meaning, or otherwise, of the question which often preoccupies women on the periphery of Christianity: should I stay or should I go?

One final point deserves to be made by way of introduction. Some people may question the wisdom of including this book in a secular publisher's lesbian, gay and sexual politics list. In a multicultural and predominantly secular Britain, is it not a form of collusion with Christian imperialism to focus on Christian attitudes to sexuality in this way? I have some sympathy with this perspective. I would be the first to ignore the more repressive manifestations of Christianity in this country if I thought that their influence would thereby be undermined. But history and political reality persuade me otherwise. Although only a tiny minority of the population admits to being 'practising Christians', clergymen enjoy a privileged access to the media, 'morality' is still largely equated with 'Christian morality' and the Establishment of the Church of England grants it disproportionate political power.

Britain in the 1990s is in the grip of a form of conservatism which would annihilate 'difference' – in particular, sexual difference – in pursuit of a 'golden age' of stability and uniformity. The justification, if not the origin, of this conservatism is establishment Christianity. This is not to say that all those who promote conservative values also espouse the Christian faith, or that all those who espouse Christianity will also be conservative. The picture is far more complex than that. Nevertheless, when it comes to sexuality, there is a correlation between theological and political conservatism, and each movement works against sexual justice and equality in the widest sense of both terms. In so far as the belief system of Christianity underpins such conservatism, it deserves to be deconstructed via a rigorous analysis of its effects. *Found Wanting* represents a contribution to that task.

NOTE

1. Linda Hurcombe (ed.), *Sex and God: Some Varieties of Women's Religious Experience*. Routledge & Kegan Paul, London, 1987.

I

Christian
Sexual Ethics

introduction

To begin, I'd like to offer a deliberately tendentious overview of Christian sexual ethics. I have chosen not to attempt a systematic exploration of the various denominational positions on sexuality, since this would be tedious and unnecessary. Those within the Christian community tend to lapse into esoteric discussions comparing, for example, the Anglican approach with the Methodist approach, or assessing Roman Catholic teaching in the light of that of the Plymouth Brethren or the Baptists, the United Reformed Church or the Society of Friends, the Church of Scotland or the Presbyterian Church. This kind of discussion has its place – but not in this book. Having read and explored many denominational documents, I am convinced that it is not necessary for others to do likewise in order to understand 'Christian sexual ethics'. It is possible to draw various lessons from these documents about how contemporary church people deal with sexuality. That is what I aim to do here, assessing these approaches from an unapologetically lesbian and feminist perspective.

Two broadly defined approaches to sexuality are usually identified among Christians – the 'liberal' and the 'conservative'. The former, it is said, has taken significant strides towards the acceptance of lesbian and gay sexuality (which tends to function as the defining issue), while the latter remains tied to a rigid and exclusive sexual morality.

Conservatives are easy to spot. They espouse marriage as the only fully correct and ideal context in which an intimate sexual relationship may be conducted. Extramarital sex and premarital sex are therefore outlawed, as are same-sex relationships. The message is simple, and it's the same whoever the audience. 'Liberals' are rather harder to pin down – largely because they make some attempt to tailor their message to its recipients, i.e. they 'take account of people's experience'. When pushed, however, they usually stand by the ideal of 'Christian marriage', although the consequences for those who do not adopt it will vary according to the extent of liberality being expressed.

As Part One will aim to show, my own perspective is that conservatives and liberals share more in common than they might think. Far from being 'polarized', they differ only on peripheral issues. This idea would be deeply unsettling to many church people who perceive the differences between conservatives and liberals to lie at the heart of Christian conflicts about sex. The real difference as I see it, however, is between the liberals and conservatives on the one hand, and the 'radicals' (for want of a better word) on the other. Radicals are those who seek a fundamental rethink of Christian concepts of sexuality and gender. They do not make much of an appearance in this section because they have not, as yet, gained a significant input into those church bodies which make the rules. Their insights will be important in Part Three.

One other category of Christians which does make an appearance in this section is that of the 'pseudo-radicals'. They propose what *look like* radical changes in Christian sexual ethics, but on closer examination these turn out to be rather disappointing rehashes of 'liberal' sentiment. Pseudo-radicals are usually men, who omit to declare anything about their own sexuality and therefore about the starting point for their argument.

*m*ade for *e*ach *o*ther? *a*ssessing *c*omplementarity

The key concept which is pivotal in making sense of Christian sexual ethics is that of 'complementarity': the idea that male and female are somehow 'made for each other'. This is adequately summed up for us in the Methodist Church's report on marriage and the family: 'It is man and woman together, as a single whole, who are described as being "made in the image of God".'[1] The origins of the idea of complementarity are unclear. The creation story in Genesis is often cited as its biblical foundation, in particular the sentence 'male and female created he them'.[2] That such a bald statement of fact could have come to be imbued with such a definite value-laden perspective leads me to suspect a misuse of biblical evidence. 'Male and female created he them' says nothing to me about how men and women might or should be expected to behave towards one another, either in the Garden of Eden or subsequently. What is more, the apparently contradictory tenet of the New Testament that 'in Christ there is neither Jew nor Greek, slave nor free, male nor female'[3] is, of course, rarely cited in the same context. Christian teaching usually considers New Testament teaching to take priority over the Hebrew scriptures but not, it seems, in this case. The implication that gender differences are or should be transcended is ignored.

It is possible that influences other than the Bible are important. Religious professionals specializing in pastoral care draw upon the insights of modern psychology and various therapeutic methodologies. An assimilation of Jungian theory and Christian theology has resulted in calls for a balance between 'masculine' and 'feminine' principles within the psyche of individuals and of institutions. This has been extrapolated in a haphazard way to apply to one-to-one relationships. It is assumed that a good and healthy relationship also requires a balance of 'male' and 'female' input – and that this is most likely to be achieved in a relationship between one man and one woman. This is well illustrated by a Church of Scotland report on human sexuality:

> within each of us there is an underlying component of our personality which is complementary to our conscious selves: thus the 'anima' (in Jung's terminology) is the unconscious feminine component of the male psyche, the 'animus' the masculine component within the female psyche. In an ideal marriage, the unconscious male within the woman would be complementary to her partner's unconscious feminine element; in such a union, two would indeed become one. To be whole people, we must be able to give expression to all facets of our personhood: to deny the feminine is a false attempt to be 'manly'. To accept the 'female within' as a complement to the masculine self, and vice versa, gives recognition to the integrated self. In this mature person, body, mind and spirit are in harmony within the self, in relation to others and to God.[4]

Greek thought might also be implicated in the origin of the theory of complementarity. I have been struck by parallels between church documents and a myth recounted in Plato's *Symposium*. In that work, Zeus decides to undermine the strength of humanity (as is the wont of jealous deities) by punishing them with bisection. Our current state as human beings is therefore a pathetic diminution of what it once was.

> It is from this distant epoch, then, that we may date the innate love which human beings feel for one another, the love which restores us to our ancient state by attempting to weld two beings into one and to heal the wounds which humanity suffered.[5]

The Christian concept of complementarity, however, is predictably something of a parody of the myth, which goes on to say:

> Those men who are halves of a being of the common sex, which was called, as I told you, hermaphrodite, are lovers of women, and most adulterers come from this class, as also do women who are mad about men and sexually promiscuous. Women who are halves of a female whole direct their affections towards women and pay little attention to men; Lesbians belong to this category. But those who are halves of a male whole pursue males, love men throughout their boyhood, and take pleasure in physical contact with men.[6]

COMPLEMENTARITY AND GENDER

Whatever the origins of complementarity, it is very closely tied in with concepts of gender – particularly of gender differentiation. Conservative and liberal approaches are virtually indistinguishable in their wholehearted acceptance of complementarity as the basis for relationships between men and women. Compare these two excerpts:

> [women and men] do live that common humanity in different ways which make the distinctive contributions of each essential for the fullness of human kind as a whole; and it is important for the mature development both of individual men and women and of society that each person should come to understand and to value this complementarity. The place where people normally begin to do this is in the family, headed by a father and a mother.[7]

And:

> A man looks at spiritual truths differently from a woman. Put together the male and female viewpoints and you have a rich whole. The relationship becomes, not like a flabby lettuce which has no heart, but one which is firm at its centre, healthy, satisfying, growing.[8]

The first is from the most recent report from the Church of England bishops, *Issues in Human Sexuality*, widely classified as a 'liberal' document. The second is from a book by a conservative Christian writer, Joyce Huggett, famed for writing books about sex for students and teenagers. I will be quoting her again. Notice that both are clear that there is a difference between men and women, and both see wholeness as consisting in some combination of these two distinctive natures. Curiously, when it comes to defining the *exact nature* of the difference, most writers fall silent or speak in euphemisms and deliberately ambiguous language. This helps to head off any accusations of overt sexism from outsiders, while ensuring that insiders will draw the correct conclusions, according to the teaching they have received. For example, another conservative writer (Derek Wood) has this to say:

> Jesus treated women as people on the level with men, talked to them in public, valued their care and fellowship and signalled to the world that God, at least, did not regard them as in any way inferior to men, but different in function and approach. Thus he did not appoint women among his twelve

storm troopers for the kingdom, but he did reveal himself first after the resurrection to a woman.[9]

This is qualified later: 'in complementarity both come off best if they can work out proper submission-love and responsible-love towards each other.'[10]

We might assume from the first passage that Derek Wood does not consider the ordination of women to the priesthood (or indeed any kind of leadership role) to be in line with a woman's 'function', whereas a man is presumably well qualified to be part of that particular divine task force. One is obviously supposed to draw conclusions about the female role from the fact that Christ saw fit to 'reveal himself first' to a woman after the resurrection. This is tricky for one not versed in conservative evangelical language, but my own conclusions are that a woman's role is to be 'done to' rather than to 'do'. Any passive role is permissible.

As for the qualification about complementarity, this would commonly be interpreted by conservative Christians to mean that women must learn submission, and men must learn responsibility. I can confirm this, having seen the belief system in action. During the wedding of a friend at a conservative evangelical church, I was stunned when she promised to 'love, honour and obey' her husband. I asked her in a letter why she opted to obey, since it is no longer a compulsory part of the service. In her reply she explained that it was her conviction that she and her husband were equal members of 'a team', although the ultimate authority lay with him. I also witnessed this same avowal of obedience in the wedding video of another friend. Again, I asked why. Apparently, she feels sure that it will not become an issue: 'I know that he loves me, so he would never call upon me to obey him in anything which I didn't want to do'!

Many women will testify that love can be a poor guarantor of their safety. It is not uncommon for Christian women who are subjected to battering by their Christian husbands to be told by clergy that this is an inevitable part of their submissive role. This is the case whether or not the husband's behaviour is construed as 'responsible'. Historically, wife beating has been considered a responsible exercise of a man's marital rights – sometimes even a compulsory part of it. A more modern interpretation is that battering is unacceptable, but allowances are made for men on the grounds that they are not aware of what they are doing (because of stress, drunkenness, jealousy, fear, or one of a hundred other reasons). In such situations, when women are called upon to 'remember their marriage vows' and stand by their men (not an uncommon occurrence), their part of the bargain is being enforced while the husband reneges upon his. This is a common Christian double standard.

Both of my friends were married within the evangelical Anglican tradition. In each case one senses a recognition that a relationship of equality could be built only upon the gaps between the vows taken, rather than upon the vows as they stood. This is hardly surprising given that the vows themselves were not designed as the foundation for a relationship of equality but for one of ownership. It is significant, therefore, that these women were discouraged from disregarding the vow – a fact which confirms my suspicion that 'complementarity' in this context is a veiled form of inequality.

There are, therefore, some very confused and confusing messages at large in contemporary Christianity about the nature of men and women. Are they equal, or aren't they? One priest, violently opposed to women's ordination, recently called women priests transvestites. Another called them bitches who should be burned. How do we make sense of the absurdity that both men might simultaneously have put their hands on their hearts and expressed the belief that men and women are 'equal before God'? The key to this is the idea that women and men are 'equal but different' – a tenet which is popular among conservative and liberal alike. While the cosmetic effect may be egalitarian, the reality is definitely not so, for in the 'small print' there lies a catch-22 for women. Crucially, it is assumed that part of the essential God-given character of *masculinity* is to define the nature of men and women and the difference between them.

COMPLEMENTARITY AND HETEROSEXUALITY

The first important conclusion to draw about this key concept of complementarity is that it is implicated in notions of gender which are male-defined and which perpetuate inequality. Now I would like to return to the first passage I quoted from the Church of England report, *Issues in Human Sexuality*. It was said to be important that 'each person *should come to understand and to value* [this] complementarity'[11] (my italics). There is just a *hint* of coercion here: people are under a social and moral obligation to value complementarity, and the implication is that they will be *made* to value it. The reason becomes clear later in the same paragraph:

In heterosexual love this personal bonding and mutual self-giving happen between two people who, because they are of a different gender, are not merely physically differentiated but also diverse in their emotional, mental and spiritual lives, their way of experiencing and responding to reality.[12]

Thus, the logical outcome of imposed complementarity is compulsory heterosexuality.

Heterosexual normativity, endemic in the Christian community, rests on the concept of complementarity. Clearly, if it is God's plan, his (sic) creative intent that human beings pair off with someone of the opposite (sic) gender, then any relationships other than heterosexual ones are bound to be classified as 'falling short' of the ideal. Again, there is common ground here between liberal and conservative Christians. The Gloucester Report, a Church of England document shelved in 1979 because it was too liberal, had this to say:

> In a homosexual relationship ... the deep biological complementarity of the partners is lacking altogether. Hence the ideal of sexual love as deeply personal, which many thinkers today rightly insist upon, is not readily detachable from its roots in the sexual polarity of men and women.[13]

It therefore concluded:

> Thus we believe that Anglicans should continue to teach that the norm for sexual relationships is one of mutual love, expressed and nurtured in life-long and exclusive marriage, based on the givenness of biological and psychological potential.[14]

This perspective changed little between 1979 and 1990, when Issues in Human Sexuality had this to say:

> The fact that heterosexual unions in the context of marriage and the family are of such primary importance for the fostering of true man–woman complementarity seems to us to confirm their essential place in God's providential order.[15]

The bishops show no indication of having taken account of any developments in the theory of gender which might distinguish the context in 1990 from that of 1979. Rather, they fall back on a kind of unsophisticated biological and psychological determinism in order to explain 'the difference' between men and women. They demonstrate no sense that there may be (actually or potentially) as much difference between individuals within gender categories as between individual men and women.

Two very different forms of conservative Christianity agree wholeheartedly with the assumptions inherent in these Anglican pronouncements. Firstly, Roman Catholic teaching is summed up by a Vatican letter published in 1986:

> He [God] fashions mankind, male and female, in his own image and likeness. Human beings, therefore, are nothing less than the work of God Himself; and in the complementarity of the sexes, they are called to reflect the inner unity of the Creator. They do this in a striking way in their cooperation with him in the transmission of life by a mutual donation of the self to the other.[16]

It continues:

> To choose someone of the same sex for one's sexual activity is to annul the rich symbolism and meaning, not to mention the goals, of the Creator's sexual design. Homosexual activity is not a complementary union, able to transmit life … when they engage in homosexual activity they confirm within themselves a disordered sexual inclination which is essentially self-indulgent.[17]

Secondly, conservative evangelical theology is, in many ways, directly opposed to Roman Catholicism. Indeed, Protestant conservatives often deny that Roman Catholics are Christian at all. But the two traditions are remarkably similar when it comes to the relationship between 'correct' gender identity and its implications for sexual relationships. Out of Egypt: Leaving Lesbianism Behind is (unintentionally) a tragicomedy by Jeanette Howard which graphically illustrates the conservative Christian view that lesbianism is a rejection of one's true (God-given) womanhood. In the book she describes how she came to be 'healed' of her lesbian feelings, and how she now counsels other women with a similar 'problem'. The therapy consists of learning to embrace one's true femininity, an important part of which is learning to wear dresses and make-up: 'I found that as I began putting on dresses and experimenting with make-up, I created a framework in which God could work.'[18] 'Nothing in my healing process has come naturally to me', she confides. 'I still prefer to wear trousers rather than a dress.'[19] At one point she mentions how difficult it was for her to feel comfortable when people at church complimented her new 'feminine' appearance: 'The breakthrough occurred when I was able to receive God's name for me, Woman. Since that point, I've made a conscious effort to embrace their compliments.'[20]

When it comes to the task of defining what God's design for true femininity actually is, she makes a telling comment: 'one crucial concept involves having a gentle and quiet spirit.'[21] Her friend, with whom she counsels other lesbians, echoes this:

> When I first joined a church, it particularly irritated me to find men seemed to run the show. I resolved to overcome my attitude towards men as soon as possible so that I could fully enter into church life.[22]

These women learned variously that: 'self-determination was detrimental to my Christian walk';[23] that by 'attaining "equality" with men, we entomb our gentle, vulnerable and trusting qualities under a guise of toughness, independence and suspicion'.[24] At the same time they perceive God to be male and, consciously or unconsciously, as an initiating sexual partner:

> Because it required submission, listening to God did not come easily. He was calling me to yield to him when I wanted to assert myself. God desired that I get in touch with the feminine, responsive part of me. A frightening prospect.[25]

This 'theological' version of 'all she needs is a good screw' is terrifying indeed. For what has been built here is a hierarchical cosmos in which God is 'on top'; his will carried out by authoritative male figures to whom these women admit that they look for guidance. Obviously, lesbianism represents a thoroughly awkward and subversive threat to this order of things, so it is deemed to result from bad gender-programming. Interestingly, the culmination of Jeanette's healing was the curtailment of a recurrent dream in which she saw herself as a traveller bound for the land of the 'Faulty Feminine'.

Heterosexual normativity

We might sum up the concept of complementarity as the foundation, the *theological structure* by which Christianity justifies its suppression of all expressions of same-sex love. Although the restrictions officially only rule out 'sexual contact', the ultimate effect is to undermine all forms of friendship. Feminist scholar Janice Raymond defines 'hetero-reality' as 'the world view that woman exists always in relation to man'.[26] And theologian Mary Hunt explains the effects of this:

> With heterosexual marriage touted as every woman's goal, friendships with other women become way-stations on the road to the perfect match with Mr Right ... The power of women's friendships is amazing in a cultural context that makes them a relational also-ran.[27]

If women are not supposed to exist outside of relationships with men, then we are not supposed to live in relationships with other women. And if it is unthinkable that we should find one another attractive to be with as friends, then it is certainly unthinkable that we should become one another's lovers. This is what Mary Daly calls the 'Terrible Taboo'[28] – a taboo held in place by the theological construct of complementarity.

The conditions under which lesbians and gay men can gain partial acceptance are also determined by the theological structures of complementarity. For instance, it is said in *Issues in Human Sexuality* that 'Christian teaching about marriage offers ... a direction to which other sexual relationships can and should move'.[29] As lesbian and gay people, we are called by the church to recognize the applicability of the ideal of marriage to our own lifestyles. And we are to measure the success of our relationships by the extent to which they approximate happy heterosexual marriages (assuming we can locate one to emulate).

This is a peculiarly 'liberal' phenomenon, since the vital precursor to this is the recognition that lesbian and gay people do actually exist, and do enter into relationships. But it is here that our first 'pseudo-radical', Jeffrey John, makes his entrance. In a pamphlet entitled *Permanent, Faithful, Stable*, he argues for the full acceptance of monogamous (lesbian and) gay partnerships by the church. Along with similar calls from Bishop Jack Spong this step has been widely perceived as a radical way forward – particularly since both men include priests among those who may enter such relationships. Jeffrey John expresses the hope that his pamphlet will 'persuade gay Christians that this [the traditional Christian] theology of sex and its implications apply to all human beings made in God's image, not just heterosexuals'.[30] He observes that:

> Much has been said and written about the need to find a theological model for gay relationships, but there has been a marked reluctance to apply the obvious one, perhaps because of the negative image of marriage among some gay people (particularly among many lesbians for whom it often carries connotations of male dominance).[31]

Having acknowledged the ambivalence which many women feel towards the institution of marriage, this is never mentioned again. Rather, lesbians and gays are exhorted to embrace traditional Christian teaching on marriage and sexuality as though it were drawn up with us in mind and were relevant to our needs. The deal, presumably, is that in exchange for this we will gain a grudging acceptance from the minority of men in ecclesiastical power who are liberal enough to grant it – with, if we are male, more chance of an unfettered career in the ecclesiastical hierarchy which might otherwise have eluded us. Jeffrey John does not go any way towards undermining the theological structures of compulsory heterosexuality which I have outlined in my exploration of complementarity. Indeed, the dangers of appropriating heterosexual relationship models is demonstrated in his adoption of the work of Ben Fletcher on stress in the clergy, from which he quotes the following:

> It is surely now necessary for the church to change policy. Evidence shows that committed relationships provide partners with a protective buffer against stress and illness ... What is needed surely is a positive ethic for committed and stable homosexual relationships analogous to heterosexual marriage.[32]

Ben Fletcher's gender-free language obscures the painful reality which the stories in this book will help to highlight. Women who have been married to clergymen, and have thereby provided this esteemed 'protective buffer' from stress and illness, have done so at inestimable cost to themselves. Their experience demonstrates the dangers in lesbian and gay clergy adopting without critique heterosexual models in their relationships. Jeffrey John's approach also demonstrates the dangers of assuming that church teaching must be, in essence, correct – with the fault lying in our interpretation of it.

WORSHIP OF 'THE FAMILY'

Fletcher's oversight is just one illustration of how heterosexual normativity tends to encourage an unquestioning idealization of marriage and family life. Church reports are particularly culpable in this regard. It is not insignificant that these reports are usually written by men whose ecclesiastical careers would be seriously impaired if they did not have wives to take care of all their practical needs. Women's experiences of 'Christian marriage' are seldom the primary concern of such documents. Indeed, they are rarely of concern at all.

There is little recognition within churches of the immense suffering to which women and children have been subjected within families. Physical, sexual, emotional, psychological and economic violence against women and children have had little coverage in church reports which glorify and romanticize married life. The church was not a noticeable force in the campaign to end the legality of rape within marriage. Those working towards a recognition of the fact that violence occurs just as commonly within Christian families as within any other kind of family are meeting much resistance. Even to put up a flyer in a church porch advertising a support group for Christian survivors of sexual abuse proved difficult for one woman, who discovered that it was immediately torn down.

Focusing on what churchmen and their reports do *not* say can be as enlightening as an assessment of what they do say. Equally, their utterances on seemingly tangential issues can also teach us much. Recently, many churchmen, Anglican bishops in particular, had no hesitation in speaking out against an equal age of consent for gay men. Many Christians argued against an equal age of consent on the grounds that it would encourage predatory behaviour by older men against younger men and boys. This argument is harmful in several ways. Firstly, it adds to the devastating confusion which already exists in our society between consenting sexual behaviour and sexual abuse. The age of *consent* means exactly that. Coercing people into sex is a serious offence, but it is totally irrelevant when considering a law about consenting sexual behaviour. The question of what constitutes *authentic consent* is, however, a pressing one when submission and acquiescence in situations of coercion are often taken as consent. But I submit that this is a question of more relevance to heterosexual relationships than to gay ones.

Secondly, the hidden implication of the argument is that young women do not matter. It should not escape our attention that all talk of the need to protect 'vulnerable young people' is only ever voiced when it is young men who are perceived to be at risk. Finally, Christians opposing the equal age of consent for the reasons outlined above are reinforcing the falsehood that gay men are the primary perpetrators of sexual violence. This in turn obscures the fact that most sexual violence is committed by heterosexual men who prey upon those to whom they are closest – their immediate family members.

No doubt some Christians will protest that they did not mean to advocate any of the above in opposing equality before the law for gay men on this issue. But this is part of their active refusal to recognize the full practical implications of particular moral positions, and a refusal to see connections between issues. It may be that a 'liberal' Church of England bishop wishes to subscribe to the Church's current worship of male–female complementarity. If that is the case, however, he must recognize that such a position effectively denigrates lesbian and gay relationships, reducing them to the status of 'making the best of a bad job'. The problem with such bishops, in my experience, is that they are not willing to take responsibility for the latter as a necessary consequence of the former. They want to worship male–female complementarity, and at the same time appear affirmative of lesbian and gay sexuality. They will not make the necessary choice between the two positions. Sometimes lesbians and gay men are even consulted at this stage, forced into the role of helping the bishop with his political problem!

Other problems with complementarity

The extreme popularity of the theory of complementarity among modern Christians may be put down to its politically expedient function. It allows negative feelings about same-sex relationships free rein. These feelings are transformed into the indirect by-products of a seemingly positive theory of human sexuality and relationships rather than the malign and deliberate results of prejudice or discrimination. Theology which originates in political expediency, however, is seldom without its problems. Two recent examples will serve as illustrations here.

Firstly, when the bishops of the Church of England published *Issues in Human Sexuality*, their primary task was to prevent the acceptance of openly lesbian and gay people as clergy in that denomination, a prospect which would have been potentially damaging to church unity. This had to be achieved without obviously giving ground to the forces of extreme conservatism, the rantings of which would in turn be damaging to the Church's image as a compassionate and inclusive institution. Their answer was to introduce a distinction between the behaviour which is acceptable for clergy, and that which is acceptable for lay people. The report effectively gave the go-ahead to gay lay Anglicans to be sexually active, but denied that 'privilege' to clergy. What was not fully appreciated at the time, I think, was the gravity of this statement for that Church's theology of priesthood. Likewise with the ordination of Anglican women to the priesthood. The politically expedient move to allow women to be deacons but not priests forced some rapid theologizing after-the-event about the 'distinctive role' of deacons, a role which it had hitherto been assumed was akin to an apprenticeship for the priesthood, rather than a valid end in itself. Similarly, the recent decision to ordain women did not include the possibility of women becoming bishops, thereby introducing for the first time a qualitative difference between a priest and a bishop.

The theory of complementarity raises similar fundamental theological problems rarely appreciated by those under its spell. The first is the absurd implication that being of only one gender is somehow to fall short of our full potentiality as human beings. This makes God appear even more ham-fisted in 'his' creative work than the usual run-of-the-mill questions of theodicy (the vindication of 'divine mistakes' such as evil and suffering in the world) have hitherto recognized.

Some theologians have been led to the rather extreme lengths of inventing a new concept of humanness which overcomes God's basic oversight – the androgynous person. I would define one such theologian, Paul Avis, as a 'pseudo-radical'. In his book, E*ros and the Sacred*, his stated aim is 'to overcome "masculine"/"feminine" stereotypes in theology and in the church, and to explore the possibilities of a merely human, *androgynous* theology and practice' (italics his).[33] He advocates androgyny as 'the antithesis of those stereotypes that bedevil character development and social integration whether it be the macho male or the insipid female',[34] and goes on to say:

> Androgyny ... is directed towards the creation of whole, balanced and integrated persons who, psychologically and in their character, are able to combine so-called masculine attributes such as courage, leadership, competence, rational decision making with so-called feminine attributes such as gentleness, compassion, understanding and the ability to foster human relationships.[35]

He deserves three cheers for his recognition, unlike the Church of England bishops, that essential psychological and intellectual differences between women and men are so difficult to pin down as to be non-existent, and he is correct to identify social forces as the root of male–female inequality. However, I would take issue with his proposed remedy, for sticking 'so-called' before 'feminine/masculine' hardly represents a radical challenge to the all-pervasive, socially reinforced habit of gender stereotyping. What looks like a tiny inconsistency becomes a huge one when, in the last chapter he undertakes a swingeing attack upon lesbian and gay relationships, while indulging in some characteristically sickly sweet Christian eulogizing about marriage:

> When a woman's point of view begins to undermine the assumptions of
> patriarchy, the possibility emerges of a new interpretation of the erotic in
> personalist terms, emphasising its potential for consummating and cementing
> the most absolute of human relationships – marriage.[36]

It seems to me that his aim is to blur gender stereotypes just enough to benefit men a bit more (e.g. by allowing them to have a more fulfilling emotional life), but not enough actually to change anything. This is plainly illustrated by the book's grand finale: 'No society ... can allow itself to indulge for long the illusion that homosexual relationships are as valid, normal and natural as heterosexual relationships, or that they are an acceptable alternative to marriage.'[37] It is interesting that feminist women find nothing remotely deficient in being *only* women. In general, the human reality which restricts us to one gender is only perceived to be a problem by male theologians. This is part of their wish to have their gender-cake and eat it by 'rethinking' masculinity in such a way that they experience no pain, only gain. Social trends have long proved that married men are physically and psychologically healthier than their unmarried counterparts, while the opposite is true for women. There is no suggestion by men such as Avis that they might surrender the privileges which their masculinity and heterosexuality afford them. These are the vested interests at stake for those men who would breathe new life into the old vision of complementarity.

NOTES

1. The Methodist Church, A *Christian Understanding of Family Life, the Single Person, and Marriage.* Methodist Publishing House, Peterborough, 1989, para. II 46, p. 16.
2. Genesis 1:27.
3. Galatians 3:18.
4. The Board of Social Responsibility of the Church of Scotland, *Report on Human Sexuality.* Church of Scotland, Edinburgh, 1994, para. 3.1.8.
5. Plato, *The Symposium.* Penguin Classics, Middlesex, 1985, p. 62.
6. *Ibid.*
7. A Statement by the House of Bishops, *Issues in Human Sexuality.* Church House Publishing, London, 1991, para. 4.17, p. 37.
8. Joyce Huggett, *Just Good Friends: Growing in Relationships.* Inter-Varsity Press, Leicester, 1986, p. 116.

9. Derek Wood, *The Adam and Eve Agenda: Male and Female – Who's in Charge?* Inter-Varsity Press, Leicester, 1992, p. 154.
10. *Ibid.*, p. 155.
11. House of Bishops, *Human Sexuality*, para. 4.17, p. 37.
12. *Ibid.*
13. *Homosexual Relationships: A Contribution to Discussion* (otherwise known as The Gloucester Report). CIO Publishing, London, 1979, para. 160, p. 50.
14. *Ibid.*, para. 161, p. 50.
15. House of Bishops, *Human Sexuality*, para. 4.17, p. 37.
16. Joseph Cardinal Ratzinger and Alberto Bovone, *Letter to the Bishops of the Catholic Church on the Pastoral Care of Homosexual Persons.* Congregation for the Doctrine of the Faith, Rome, 1986, para. 6, p. 3.
17. *Ibid.*, para. 7, p. 4.
18. Jeanette Howard, *Out of Egypt: Leaving Lesbianism Behind.* Monarch Publications, Eastbourne, 1991, p. 194.
19. *Ibid.*, p. 195.
20. *Ibid.*, p. 196.
21. *Ibid.*, p. 191.
22. *Ibid.*, p. 34.
23. *Ibid.*, p. 184.
24. *Ibid.*, p. 186.
25. *Ibid.*, p. 184.
26. Janice Raymond, *A Passion for Friends: Toward a Philosophy of Female Affection.* The Women's Press, London, 1986, p. 3.
27. Mary E. Hunt, *Fierce Tenderness: A Feminist Theology of Friendship.* Crossroad, New York, 1991, p. 28.
28. Mary Daly, *Outercourse: The Be-Dazzling Voyage.* The Women's Press, London, 1993, p. 144.
29. House of Bishops, *Human Sexuality*, para. 3.20, p. 27.
30. Jeffrey John, *Permanent, Faithful, Stable: Christian Same-sex Partnerships.* Affirming Catholicism, London, 1993, p. 2.
31. *Ibid.*, pp. 1–2.
32. *Ibid.*, p. 25.
33. Paul Avis, *Eros and the Sacred.* SPCK, London, 1989, p. x.
34. *Ibid.*, p. 30.
35. *Ibid.*, p. 31.
36. *Ibid.*, p. 124.
37. *Ibid.*, p. 152

2 **perceptions of perversity: outside of complementarity**

'Making the best of a bad job'

As we have seen, complementarity is utilized to rule out lesbian and gay lifestyles as anything other than 'making the best of a bad job'. There is more to be said, however, about the strategies developed by those in power within the Christian community for dealing with sexualities and lifestyles which fall outside of prescribed manifestations of heterosexual normativity.

The first of these is the yawningly obvious attempt to make a distinction between behaviour/practice and feelings/orientation. The whole spectrum from liberal through to conservative Christianity adopts this strategy, although there are various degrees of rigidity in application. Interestingly, the obvious rejoinder has seldom been made, which is to draw a parallel between religious faith and sexuality. Most Christians are rather keen on the fact that their faith is all-embracing: 'God is for life, not just for Christmas' pops up periodically on fluorescent pink and yellow posters around Britain at Christmas time. Any suggestion that 'being a Christian' consists only of participating in worship on a regular basis is sternly rejected. Faith, it is said, imbues the way you do everything from peeling carrots to earning a living, to playing the church organ. There is a close parallel between this concept of spirituality and a concept of sexuality which locates its influence way beyond what happens in the bedroom. To argue that gay orientation is acceptable but gay sexual activity is wrong is equivalent to the proposition that private religious beliefs are acceptable only in so far as they involve no practical outworking. Just as Christians would say that religious beliefs without practical application are worthless, so lesbians and gay men are justified in arguing that the term 'sexual orientation' has no meaning outside of a relational context.

'Relational context' is used here to signify the whole network of personal and social relationships with which we are all involved – not just those involving sex. In other words, we are not lesbian or gay only when we are in bed with someone of the same gender.

The 'orientation'/'practice' split is helpful in salving the consciences of Christians of all types. It allows conservatives to condemn same-sex relationships, but at the same time to appear loving, so inducing in the 'sinner' a dependence upon the goodwill of a small and closely knit community of faith. For the fence-sitting liberal bishop who is not inclined to undertake a radical rethink of received teaching about sexuality (which might damage his career prospects), the idea allows him to be seen to be taking some notice of the world as it is. It may also offer some kind of a way forward for the lesbian and gay clergy in his diocese, who need only to be secretive about 'what they do' and not about 'who they are'. This means, incidentally, that they are forced to acquiesce in the bishop's construction of reality in return for a stipend and the opportunity to fulfil their perceived call from God to the priesthood. The questions and difficulties this raises differ according to gender, a subject to which I will return later in this book.

A second strategy, with which gay men are particularly prone to collude, is that of the deprivation of moral agency. The starting point for Christians is that lesbians and gay men 'can't help the way we are'. This explains the preoccupation with the 'causes of homosexuality', which is common in most Christian denominations as they struggle to come to terms with the existence of lesbian and gay people. Conservatives tend towards the hope that it will eventually be proved that 'homosexuality' is a wilfully perverse choice; in which case lesbians and gay men can be straightforwardly condemned as sinners. Alternatively, they believe that a biological or genetic cause will be discovered which will vindicate their search for effective 'treatment' or eradication. Liberals, on the other hand, prefer to highlight those theories which point to the mysterious 'fixing' of sexual orientation at an early age. If the cause remains a mystery, then treatment becomes a waste of time, and if sexuality is fixed early on, then people cannot be held responsible for it.

Neither conservatives nor liberals make any attempt to assess the value-laden starting point of biological and psychological explanations for homosexuality. Those with only theological training are easily overwhelmed by those trained in the sciences. General practitioners and psychiatrists are usually disproportionately represented on denominational commissions on human sexuality, and are perceived as guarantors of objective truth. The few who are skilled in both theology and the physical sciences are held in awe if they maintain the status quo (e.g. John Habgood) or vilified if they become too radical (e.g. Don Cupitt).

The deprivation of moral agency is also a factor in considerations of singleness. A clear distinction is often made between those who are single by misfortune (e.g. death of a partner) and those who are single by choice. This distinction determines how a person is assessed. Those in the first category are pitied as 'victims of circumstance', and those in the second are feared as threatening and perverse (if they are female), or their choices are ignored (and sometimes envied) if they are male. Special condemnation is reserved for single women who become mothers by choice (thereby contaminating a future generation by their bad example). In a recent article on this theme, John Habgood made the following distinction:

> there is in my view a major moral difference between those who are single parents as a result of misfortune – death, desertion or divorce – and those who deliberately choose it as a way of life. The latter group ranges from naive young girls who think that by becoming pregnant they can gain some significance for themselves and perhaps even get on a housing list, to self-sufficient career women who want babies but not men.

(This last statement proves that he knows not the first thing about the effect child-bearing has upon a woman's career prospects.) He continues: 'self-chosen single parenthood ... should be firmly discouraged as deliberately representing an inadequate image of what a family should be.' Here we return to the central theme of complementarity and its link with the promotion of particular gender-roles:

> To suppose that it does not matter when a child is consciously and willingly deprived of the presence of a father ... is to ignore also the importance to a child's emotional maturing of learning from parents of both sexes, and of having role models on which to form adult relationships with both sexes.[1]

The denial of moral agency takes two forms with regard to lesbian and gay people. The first is the extreme 'demon possession' option, as evidenced in Jeanette Winterson's *Oranges Are Not the Only Fruit*. Here, one's attraction to, and sexual intimacy with, someone of the same sex are the fault of external forces, demons which must be defeated by exorcism. Less obviously barbaric, but ultimately also as traumatic, is the 'sickness' option. The idea that homosexuality can be cured forms the focus for numerous so-called 'ex-gay' ministries with an international appeal. Proponents of this view tend to work on laughably simplistic theoretical bases, combining pop-psychology with Freud (inter alia), to come up with explanations for same-sex attraction which are as vague and universally applicable as the horoscope in your daily newspaper. Such explanations are perfectly parodied by Gerd Brantenberg in her novel *What Comes Naturally*:

The father-bond with its subsequent Electra complex is not at all the only explanation [as to why one becomes a homosexual]. If you have a domineering mother and a pale shadow of a father, female dominance at home will easily lead to an admiration for women and – even more unfortunate – female identification, with a corresponding contempt for the male, represented by one's father, the hen-pecked husband. Very many lesbians have had domineering mothers.

If one grows up alone with one's mother, the male will become a distant and peculiar figure, whom one will later have inhibitions approaching ... Several lesbians have had no father.

If one grows up in a family with only sisters, the intimacy with them will easily lead to joint masturbation in the shared bedrooms ... It turns out that a lot of lesbians have had only sisters.

If one has only brothers, close contact with the male sex in the tender years will easily lead to the development of a nervous fear of all males, and one becomes a lesbian. A considerable number of lesbians have had only brothers.

If one grows up as an only child with one's father and mother, one will easily become spoilt, and therefore unsuited to the more mature role of women (which is that of self-sacrifice). It turns out that the typical lesbian woman grew up as an only child ...

It also turns out that parents may influence the development of lesbianism even before one is born. There are numerous stories of lesbians whose parents wanted a boy. When such parents have a girl, they do not face the truth and they pretend that they have a boy. And the poor innocent girl, of course, lives up to her parents' expectations, and becomes a lesbian ...

Apart from a couple of cases in which a girl grows up with a father and a mother and two brothers and a sister ... In such cases there is a tendency towards sex polarisation in the home, such that the sisters ... developed an unfortunate solidarity with their own sex, which has later unwittingly been turned into lesbian love ... an amazing number of lesbians ... spent their childhoods with two brothers and a sister.

But these are all exceptions. In all other cases little girls grow up to become heterosexual women. That is, of course, also the normal state of affairs.[2]

The affiliation of such simplistic theories with the status quo is enough to overcome any concerns that sensible 'liberal' mainstream church people might otherwise have had about their shortcomings. This can be clearly seen in the meteoric rise to fame of Elizabeth Moberly, who has become the doyenne of the Christian male establishment – conservative and liberal. Her name crops up with monotonous regularity as the token woman whose work churchmen read in their perfunctory studies of sexuality issues. This is hardly surprising given the substance of her argument:

The homosexual – whether male or female – has been unable to meet the normal developmental need for attachment to the parent of the same sex ... Needs for love, dependency and identification that are normally met through this relationship, remain unfulfilled. If the attachment-need later emerges from repression, it seeks fulfilment in a renewed same-sex relationship – a so-called 'homosexual' relationship.[3]

Churchmen love her because, to quote Patricia Duncker:

She carefully avoids any analysis of heterosexual relationships beyond asserting that this is the normality to which we all aspire as mature God-fearing adults ... With a stealthy flick of the pen Moberly ... casts out of court all possible questioning of the present structure of heterosexuality as an institution; sexual violence against women and children by men, also an institution; and any critical analysis of the difference between female and male sexuality.[4]

Racism is also an institution which is exploited by those who would exclude lesbian and gay people from the Christian community. In the sexuality debates within Methodism some conservative Christians have argued that to affirm lesbian and gay people would alienate Black men and women in the denomination. This is damaging in two ways. Firstly, it implies that all people of colour think in the same way, and that all are homophobic. Secondly, it gives the impression that there are no lesbian and gay people of colour. Both are clearly untrue. My experience of

Methodism is that churches where people of colour are in a majority also tend to be those most skilled at dealing creatively with human diversity.

'Valuing' the Bible and Christian history

It is not my intention to go into great detail about biblical and historical approaches to sexuality. But in the current context it is worth making some comments about how the evidence from both sources is used, taking the Bible first.

Debates about sexuality within the churches usually proceed as follows. Discussion of human sexuality becomes, within a matter of seconds, discussion of 'homosexuality'. Then an appeal is made to 'Holy Scripture'. The particular bits of this vast literary collection to which reference is made are almost always: the story of Sodom and Gomorrah (Genesis 19); a verse in Leviticus from the purity code (Leviticus 20:13); and two or three verses in Paul's letters which have been translated to refer, somewhat anachronistically, to 'homosexuality', when they could well have referred to two or three other issues (1 Corinthians 6:9; 1 Timothy 1:9, 10). It is perhaps worth noting that scholars are uncertain whether Paul actually wrote the latter letter. The conclusion is that the Bible states that 'homosexuality is wrong'. (Incidentally, this includes lesbianism, despite the fact that the Bible contains only one verse (Romans 1:26) which could possibly be construed as referring to it, and even this is debatable.) End of argument.

What's missing, as with other areas of our discussion in this section, is any appreciation by participants in such Bible study of the value-laden perspective which they bring to it. They know (unless they are complete literalists) that they need to take into account the context in which it was written in order to understand it. They also recognize that to work out its implications for today is a separate task. But the question they rarely ask is *why are they looking at these particular passages?* The assumption is that, objectively speaking, these are 'about' sexuality, whereas the other passages of the Bible are primarily concerned with different issues.

Let's briefly consider two examples. The story of Sodom and Gomorrah has become synonymous with homosexuality. Nobody seems much bothered by the gang rape of Lot's virgin daughters, or the fact that in an alternative version of the story (Judges 19:11–30) a traveller's concubine is battered and raped until she is dead, cut into twelve pieces by her 'owner' and dispatched to the twelve tribes of Israel. Why haven't these aspects of the story ever been the focus of Christian ethical discussions? And what about the Song of Songs? A prime example of erotic love poetry, one would have thought it represented a perfect scriptural resource for Christians seeking to understand human sexuality. However, when I run workshops on sexuality it is hardly ever mentioned as a text considered relevant in any way to 'sexuality debates'. Most importantly, Jesus is reported as having had nothing to say about 'homosexuality', and very little to say specifically about any other aspect of sexual ethics, apart from a couple of rather cryptic comments about marriage and eunuchs. There is a widespread assumption among Christians that Jesus was celibate, but there's very little evidence to prove this one way or the other. Its rationale lies with the need Christians have to believe that if someone was divine and therefore perfect, he must also have refrained from involvement in intimate sexual relationships.

The conclusion must be that Christians draw upon those aspects of Scripture which they have been taught are relevant to sexuality, and that those who are responsible for the teaching have chosen texts which accord with their own assumptions and ideals. The net result is that a small selection of verses condemning various 'sex acts' are decontextualized, universalized and misapplied to our situation in the twentieth century, 'proving' beyond reasonable doubt that 'homosexuality is incompatible with Christianity'. Again, conservative and liberal Christians share common ground in their failure to see that the values we bring to the biblical evidence determine the answers we take from it, particularly if we remain unconscious of those values in the first place because we assume them to be normative.

Christian history is likewise often deliberately over-simplified in order to demonstrate that the Church has taught consistently and without deviation for two thousand years that God's intent for Christian sexual ethics can be summed in one sentence: chastity before marriage and fidelity within it. What should be emphasized is the ambiguity and plurality evident in the history of Christian attitudes to sexuality and intimate relationships. An additional fascination is how these attitudes developed through a mixture of adoption, adaption and rejection of other philosophical and religious ideas, so that different ideals became fashionable in different eras. Once upon a time celibacy was considered to be the superior lifestyle – now it is 'marriage and family life'. Who knows what it might be in the future? The simplistic version of church history is nothing short of a selective reading-back in order to present today's Christian ideals as timeless and unquestionable. They are neither.

Choice

The net result of all that has been said so far is that the idea of *choosing* a same-sex relationship over and above heterosexual relationships is unthinkable to liberal and conservative Christians. Certainly, it could not be seen as a carefully thought out theological perspective, or a choice for which one is prepared to take full moral responsibility. The Church of England's pronouncements on bisexuality demonstrate this perfectly: 'The Church's guidance to bisexual Christians is that if they are capable of heterophile relationships and of satisfaction within them, they should follow the way of holiness in either celibacy or abstinence or heterosexual marriage.'[5] This reinforces a statement issued in an earlier report: 'In so far as they [bisexuals – termed 'ambisexuals' in this particular report] have what may be called a "real" choice, our whole argument suggests a straightforward answer. They should seek to restrain their homosexual inclinations and develop a heterosexual orientation.'[6]

This attempt to obliterate the sexual middle ground strengthens the tendency among Christians to polarize 'heterosexuals' and 'homosexuals' as two completely discrete groups which have nothing to say to one another. Notice that in the excerpts above no account is taken of the quality of the possible relationships being considered. Rather, the assumption is that heterosexual relationships will be better precisely because they are heterosexual. Personally, I choose lesbian relationships because I deem them to be (for me) qualitatively superior to heterosexual ones in terms of mutuality, equality, intimacy, communication and sexual pleasure. My perspective has no place in the church's world-view. I concede that I am perfectly capable of forging 'satisfactory' relationships with men, but my own ethical analysis has led me to a commitment to aim higher than that. Women like me are profoundly dangerous to mainstream Christian theology; much more of a threat than the 'self-confessed homosexual man' who readily admits that he can't help being gay and would much rather be straight. We are taking full moral responsibility for our sexuality and for our choices in making relationships. However, we are often forced to keep quiet about this both for our own safety, and lest we disturb the partial and fragile acceptance possible for gay Christian men who admit to being so through no fault of their own.

NOTES

1. John Habgood, 'Why deliberate single parenthood is dangerous', *Church Times*, London, date unknown.
2. Gerd Brantenberg, *What Comes Naturally*. The Women's Press, London, 1987, pp. 31–3.
3. Elizabeth Moberly, *Counselling the Homosexual*. Pamphlet published by Turnabout, London, n.d., p. 3. First published as an article in *The Expository Times*, T. and T. Clark, 1985.
4. Patricia Duncker, 'Confronting the angel', in Pearlie McNeill, Bea Freeman, Jenny Newman (eds), *Women Talk Sex: Autobiographical Writing on Sex, Sexuality and Sexual Identity*. Scarlet Press, London, 1992, p. 148.
5. A Statement by the House of Bishops, *Issues in Human Sexuality*. Church House Publishing, London, 1991, para 5.8, p. 42.
6. *Homosexual Relationships: A Contribution to Discussion* (The Gloucester Report). CIO Publishing, London, 1979, para. 263, p. 78.

straight and narrow: christian concepts of sexuality

Concepts of sexuality

It is worth making some general comments now about the concepts of sexuality which underlie attitudes towards same-sex relationships and singleness, and which bolster heterosexual normativity.

Modern Christians talk a lot about the need to 'celebrate sexuality as given by God'. This is in contrast to the bad old days of Christian history, when sexuality was perceived as basically evil. A direct consequence of 'the fall', sexual desire was considered to be that which tied humanity firmly to earth and frustrated our heavenly and spiritual aspirations. Denigration of the body and sexuality are now thought of as damaging, and even as an insult to God's creative achievements. Nevertheless, there remains ambiguity. Conservative Christians place so many restrictions upon exactly how sexuality can qualify as a God-given activity that one wonders whether the attitude of celebration is not just a little disingenuous. Liberals also display an uneasiness with sexuality, though their anxieties are more likely to be revealed in unguarded moments. Let's look again at *Issues in Human Sexuality*, and one particularly revealing passage:

> The Christian vision for human sexuality looks beyond life in this world to its fulfilment in the world to come ... What will no longer be needed ... is the physical expression of sexuality, which is required now because of our mortality in order that human life may continue.[1]

I detect here a distinct eagerness among these bishops to be rid of their bodies! Sexuality is something from which we will thankfully escape when we reach paradise. This is not the only option open to them. For instance, they could have chosen to conceive of heaven as the place where all that is *left* is our sexuality, closely akin to our spirituality, engaged in a constant worship of God which is one eternal orgasmic experience.

The bishops maintain a generally pessimistic view of human beings: 'All three ways of life which we have described – the married, the single and the celibate – are ones which by the grace of God can help to transform our fallen human nature.'[2] They continue:

> This impulse [to transcend human mortality] is part of a sexuality which is in various ways defective or distorted or corrupted, because it is linked at a profound level with our whole personality and identity. In theological terms we are fallen creatures. The 'image of God' in us is not wholly defaced, but there is nothing in us which is not in some degree marred, disordered, out of true.[3]

I am left wondering what exactly is the difference between this and the old-fashioned view that sex and sexuality originated with 'the fall'. If we are so hopelessly corrupted, how can we hope to regain any sense of our sexuality as being a gift from God? The problem here is that much of Christian teaching seems to be aimed at encouraging a belief in oneself as the smallest and most worthless of beings, in order that God can be the most worthy and great of beings – 'O Lord, I am not worthy even to gather up the crumbs under your table …' This does not sit easily with the body-positive, self-valuing perspectives which lie at the heart of most sexuality-affirming philosophies.

The language of sex and sexuality

The perceptions of sexuality which are most common in Christian discourse about sex are very narrow and male-defined. Consequently, the language employed lacks imagination, pluralism and sophistication. Dominant are phrases like 'the sex act' (as though there were only one), and 'intercourse' is clearly understood to mean penile penetration of the vagina with male ejaculation. This is the 'end' of a process (both temporally and teleologically), and represents its completion. For instance, *Issues in Human Sexuality* states that 'full sexual intercourse requires total commitment'.[4] I wonder what 'full sexual intercourse' might mean for lesbians, and whether the bishops would entertain it? Presumably, any sex which does not involve penetration of a vagina by a penis is only 'partial'.

The Church of Scotland's report on sexuality illustrates the potential dangers of such narrow definitions of proper sexual activity. A section considering the sexuality of people with physical disabilities states: 'In the event of marriage taking place, further assistance might be necessary to facilitate the accomplishment of full penetrative sexual intercourse.'[5] There is no appreciation of the myriad other possibilities which are open to those who wish to express intimacy through their sexuality; or of the fact that plenty of people, with or without disabilities, may consider penetrative hetero-sex to be inappropriate and unnecessary. The statement is preceded, predictably, by the heterosexist assumption that 'People with learning difficulties are attracted to members of the opposite sex in exactly the same way as those who do not have handicaps'.[6] In this report and others, a limited awareness of the diversity of relationship possibilities is coupled with a severely restricted imagination as to how intimacy might be expressed in those relationships.

A distinct preoccupation with genitalia is in evidence in much Christian writing. Here is another example from *Issues in Human Sexuality*:

> It is true, of course, that there is a continuum of physical manifestations or erotic feeling from first attraction to full arousal, and that genital pleasure may play its part in this from an early stage. But deliberate genital contact does nevertheless represent the crossing of a significant boundary.[7]

The more conservative Christian voice of Joyce Huggett insists: 'The Bible knows of only one context for *genital fusion* and that is the marriage relationship'[8] (my italics).

In debates about same-sex relationships a morbid fascination with anal sex between men often eclipses more important issues. I have witnessed highly qualified (male) doctors and theologians avidly debating the divine purpose for the lining of the rectum in their quest to discover God's opinion of 'homosexuality'. Protestations that anal sex is not exclusively a gay male preserve, and that equal consideration is seldom given to the condition of a woman's cervix in assessing hetero-sex are swept aside.

PROJECTION

The reports which result from such puerile discussions often make the most of pseudo-scientific language and abstract arguments in an attempt to appear objective. It is possible that the authors do not discern their own value-laden perspective, which is often much more obvious to the reader.

The language adopted and the assumptions made can both be instructive. In general, those who advocate equality for lesbians, gay men and bisexuals are immediately assumed to be 'libertarians' who think that 'anything goes':

> Failure to acknowledge these values [primacy of marriage] and to be guided by them or toward them is a plentiful source of disorder and suffering. The bogus philosophies of erotic freedom which have, for example, marked twentieth century European culture, and which have sought to justify every excess or deviation, stand condemned by the chaos and misery, disease and death they have brought into many lives.[9]

Thus, anyone who dares to challenge the primacy of heterosexual marriage is immediately assumed to be an advocate of a 'bogus philosophy of erotic freedom', since the authors can conceive of no other reason for challenging it. Exactly which philosophies they are criticizing is not clear. For whom do they reserve their disapproval, the Marquis de Sade or Alex Comfort; Claire Rayner or Wilhelm Reich? Or all of them? There is little awareness that while lesbian feminists, for instance, would resist some theories of so-called 'erotic freedom', the bishops' thinking does little to counteract the assumptions on which these are based. For instance, the simplistic biological and psychological determinism which underpins their theory of complementarity is utilized by others to justify the age-old double standard by which male promiscuity is held to be inevitable and natural, while that of women is considered the height of wickedness.

To the suggestion that marriage might not be the best model for lesbian and gay people, the same document has this response: 'The attack on permanent partnerships here described has nothing to do with such alternatives, but is simply a pretentious disguise for the evil of promiscuity.'[10] Like Jeffrey John they dismiss out of hand the possibility that there could be anything wrong with the pattern of heterosexual marriage as it has developed in our society.

Some of the worst incidences of projection are seen in the official documents of Roman Catholicism. Those who bring pressure to bear to 'accept the homosexual condition' (*sic*) are said by the Vatican letter of 1986 to reflect:

> a materialistic ideology which denies the transcendent nature of the human person as well as the supernatural vocation of every individual ... [they] seek

to create confusion regarding the Church's position, and then to use that confusion to their own advantage.[11]

Membership of this group is said to be:

restricted by and large to those who either ignore the teaching of the Church or seek somehow to undermine it ... she [the Church] is really concerned about the many who are not represented by the pro-homosexual movement and about those who may have been tempted to believe its *deceitful propaganda* [my italics].[12]

LANGUAGE AS VIOLENCE

The logical culmination of all this is that both the Church of England and the Roman Catholic Church documents blame lesbians and gay men for our own oppression – in effect, we bring it on ourselves. According to the Church of England it is we who cause polarization and conflict over our sexuality:

Other homophiles, who refuse to be trapped in these ways [of concealment] are driven to protest by taking up a *defiant stance,* demonstrating their pride in being gay or lesbian, and making *exaggerated claims and demands.* This further polarises what is already a situation of conflict, and leads others who were sympathetic, to be hostile [my italics].[13]

Similarly, according to the Vatican letter any violence we experience is understandable and only to be expected:

It is deplorable that homosexual persons have been and are the object of violent malice in speech or in action ... But the proper reaction to crimes committed against homosexual persons should not be to claim that the homosexual condition is not disordered. When such a claim is made and when homosexual activity is consequently condoned, or when civil legislation is introduced to protect behaviour to which no one has any conceivable right, neither the Church nor society at large should be surprised when other distorted notions and practices gain ground, and irrational and violent reactions increase.[14]

Both the Anglican and Roman Catholic documents (which represent a liberal and a conservative approach respectively) pay lip-service to the condemnation of violence against lesbians and gay men. However, they simultaneously condone such violence by implying that lesbian and gay people bring it upon ourselves by our extreme behaviour. In my experience 'extreme' behaviour can mean anything other than total secrecy coupled with a large dose of self-abasement.

While the Vatican letter deplores homophobic verbal violence, much of what is said within it could be said to constitute such violence, since it is potentially damaging, both directly and indirectly, to lesbian and gay people. Descriptions of lesbian and gay sexuality as, 'a more or less strong tendency towards an intrinsic moral evil'[15] and 'a disordered sexual inclination which is essentially self indulgent',[16] can hardly be calculated to promote understanding and respect. Together with the charge that the 'pro-homosexual' deals in 'deceitful propaganda' and puts the 'nature and rights of the family' in jeopardy,[17] the Vatican document could be described as nothing short of an incitement to homo-hatred.

There is no shortage of offensive language about lesbian and gay relationships in other Christian writings. Here are the words of John White, a particularly vicious conservative writer:

> Starving people in besieged cities of the past found their mouths watering for such delicacies as boiled rats. In the merciless grip of hunger their feelings changed about what was tempting and inviting and what was not. Though a homosexual's urge in one direction is blocked, his sexual appetite remains. When appropriate circumstances arise, it will affect him powerfully.[18]

The general lack of willingness to address and speak of same-sex relationships in terms which those in such relationships have chosen for ourselves is a further manifestation of discrimination and prejudice which is rarely recognized by the offenders. One member of the Methodist Conference Commission on Human Sexuality wrote of his experience: 'Until I served on the Commission on Human Sexuality I had only very rarely met a confessed homosexual person, and certainly not a confessed lesbian.'[19] As I am the woman to whom he indirectly refers, I can assure the reader that he never did, in fact, meet a 'confessed' lesbian! John White chooses to be offensive via this reductionist definition: 'A homosexual act is one designed to produce sexual orgasm between members of the same sex. A homosexual is a man or woman who engages in homosexual acts.'[20]

There is no appreciation in any Christian writing, liberal or conservative, of the dynamics of structural heterosexism and its parallels with other forms of oppression. Witness the Church of England's adoption of the quaint terminology of 'homophile'. Liberals have learned that lesbian and gay people do not like to be called 'homosexual', but they think that to adopt the terminology which we choose for ourselves would be 'biased' or partisan, so they come up with an alternative which is presumably designed to be 'neutral'. Then, just to add that extra dash of synthetic generosity, they take upon themselves the terminology of 'heterophile'.

It is interesting to compare this with other issues of political discrimination. Although the churches are far from exemplifying equal opportunities, official documents no longer refer to women as 'ladies'; to people of African and Asian descent as 'coloureds'; or to those with disabilities as 'handicapped'. Of course, there is still some impatience that the language of identity evolves and changes. As in the rest of society, when those of us who belong to normative groups assume that life should be made easy for us, we protest by saying things like: 'Why don't "those people" just make up their minds about what they want to be called and stick to it?' This is to assume, of course, that members of oppressed groups are of one mind and should all agree with each other. It is precisely this unwillingness to deal with the ever-shifting dynamics of prejudice and discrimination which has resulted in the popular invention of the rhetoric of Political Correctness as a bad thing. This is not to say that the oppression of women, Black people and people with disabilities is on the wane within the churches, but there is at least a partial acceptance that this is against the Christian gospel rather than a manifestation of it. When it comes to discrimination and prejudice against lesbians and gay men, however, the church juries are still out.

In summary, the elementary lesson that self-definition is crucial for members of such groups, and that we should be allowed the opportunity to speak for ourselves, has been deliberately ignored. As a result, while liberal Christians would perhaps never dream of describing same-sex loving as akin to an acquired taste for boiled rats, they do speak in euphemisms which can be almost as offensive. Take, for instance, the following statement made by the Anglican bishops:

> Those who are homophile can find themselves faced with specific difficulties . . . . There is, for example, a mismatch between their sexuality and their physical and often also their emotional capacity for parenthood. There may be for some a mismatch between their bodies and the ways in which they wish to express their mutual self-giving.[21]

I suggest that what is more likely is a mismatch between the requirement upon the bishops to speak knowledgeably about lesbian and gay sexuality, and their willingness and ability to seek out the most basic and necessary of authorities: lesbian and gay people themselves. It is worth noting here that I once heard a bishop (one who has written a book about 'homosexuality' and is therefore treated as something of an authority in these matters) wonder aloud whether or not it could be possible that lesbian women might want to have children. He said something like (and I paraphrase): 'I've never heard of it happening, but I expect that it isn't beyond the bounds of possibility'! From that day on I have viewed male clerical authority on any subject with a certain amount of cynicism.

'Sexual' versus 'non-sexual'

A further characteristic of Christian discourse about sexuality is the strict delineation of 'sexual' relationships from other forms of relationship – particularly from 'platonic friendship'. There is little understanding that our sexuality is important in all our relationships, because all relationships are mediated via our physicality. Indeed, any attempt to make this point is usually deliberately misconstrued as meaning that 'all relationships are sexual', which is not quite the same thing. There is great resistance to any renegotiation of the distinction between 'friendships' and 'sexual relationships', together with a yearning for the golden age when friends were 'only' friends and lovers were spouses. The Anglicans are particularly prone to such nostalgia:

> The word 'friend', like 'neighbour', used to have a much wider reference than it does today. Our own day is much too ready to interpret any intimate friendship as no more than a disguise for hidden homosexual or heterosexual involvement.[22]

And again, in the earlier Gloucester Report:

> The possibility of deep and close friendship between people, devoid for all practical purposes of any sexual connotation, is an extremely valuable aspect of the life of any society ... it would be unfortunate if the 'liberalisation' of society in regard to homosexuality resulted in close friendships being automatically interpreted as involving genital expression. If, in other words, it ever came to be assumed that every Sherlock Holmes and Dr Watson, or

even Starsky and Hutch were homosexually related, the value of friendship would be greatly damaged.[23]

Setting aside the irony in their choice of illustrative material, it seems strange that the most obvious solution seems to elude the bishops. For, if lesbian and gay relationships and singleness were affirmed on an equal basis with heterosexual relationships, the shame and innuendo which they argue surrounds same-sex friendship would be wiped out at a stroke.

As we might expect, Jeffrey John, our pseudo-radical, agrees with the fundamental distinction made by the bishops: 'Friendship in any normal use of the term does not imply sexual activity, still less does it in any theological use, and it is an abuse to try to force it to do so.'[24] The context of his comments is a critique of the writings of the only woman to make it into his bibliography, Roman Catholic lesbian theologian Elizabeth Stuart. She has suggested,[25] like Mary Hunt,[26] that taking up friendship rather than marriage as the starting point for relational ethics would be more inclusive and therefore more productive. She argues that there is a precedent in the Christian tradition for redefining relationships in terms of friendship and, indeed, that the only models of just, mutual, passionate relationships in the tradition are same-sex friendships (with the exception of the aforementioned Song of Songs).

It is worth pausing at this point to consider exactly what is at issue here. In asserting that sexuality is present in all our relationships, feminist and pro-feminist thinkers are calling our attention to the need to assess how our sexuality is appropriately expressed in these relationships. In other words, the question is not *whether* sexuality should be expressed in a particular situation, but *how*. Commitment, fidelity, mutuality, equality, and in particular issues of power and the dangers of exploitation and betrayal, will be considerations of utmost importance. The ultimate aim is *more* clarity about the nature of relationships, not less. On the other hand, the rigid distinction between 'lovers' and 'friends' which is defended by churchmen assumes that sexuality will automatically be excluded from some relationships and included in others. It recognizes no complexity, and discourages discernment. As with all such formulaic thinking, its usefulness is limited. When life throws up experiences which do not fit the expected mould (which is more often than not), people are left floundering with no analytical skills and no vocabulary to make sense of what is happening. Thus, the defenders of clarity and good order become (albeit unwittingly) the agents of chaos and confusion.

Sexuality as uncontrollable

Further common ground for otherwise conflicting Christian traditions is the tendency to see sexuality as an explosive, uncontrollable force:

> Because love-making is an authentically ecstatic experience, excluding everything else from consciousness, the Church has tended to see sexual attraction and activity as particularly hostile to God's due place as supreme object of human love and the proper controller of all human thought, feeling and conduct.[27]

The idea that love-making excludes everything else from consciousness is an interesting one. If my house caught fire while I was making love with my partner, I suspect that I would have no trouble becoming conscious of that. If the telephone rings, I'm conscious of that too. My decision about what to do in each case is dependent upon my will and my rationality: it makes sense to escape from a burning house – less sense, perhaps, to answer the telephone.

It is often said that the perspective represented in the above excerpt from the church report is a male one. That's true in the sense that men have acquiesced in this particular construction of their sexuality, usually in order to escape moral responsibility for their actions. But I suggest that men are not inherently sexually incontinent. In the film *Thelma and Louise*, a man caught in the act of rape is acutely conscious of a gun pointing at him; had he lived to tell the tale, however, we might anticipate that he would claim to have been unaware of his victim's protestations. He was therefore oblivious to some things, but acutely conscious of others. He was exercising selectivity in his self-awareness. In cases like this it's all a question of motivation. Of course, he was in the middle of perpetrating a sexual assault, not of 'love-making', but in a society that misconstrues rape as being primarily about sex, constructions of male sexuality such as that expressed in the Church of England document can have devastating implications. It would be more helpful to promote the virtues of self-possession and self-control in the midst of love-making, which in my experience are positive advantages. This is particularly true in a context where safer sex can be a matter of life and death. I suggest that men who can't help what they do when 'in bed' because their self-control has been obliterated make, at best, lousy lovers – at worst, abusive ones.

In order to dissuade young people from having sex, conservative Christians, in particular, emphasize the 'basic instinct', uncontrollable qualities of human sexuality. This is expressed in dramatic language in which sexual desire almost takes on the characteristics of demon possession. Here are three examples from the pen of Joyce Huggett:

> Our glandular urges, the biological tension that pulsates through our body, the sexual desire which surges through our minds and emotions threatening to devour our entire person, like a class of rowdy rebellious teenagers, can be controlled and disciplined.[28]
>
> Touch is dangerous. Petting is like a slippery slide. Step on it and your pace accelerates faster than you imagined it would. It's better to be cautious: 'Don't squeeze me till I'm yours'.[29]
>
> 'There's a tigress living inside me, and if you touch me there it will leap out at us.' [A correspondent. Huggett's response:] She was right. That tiger has to be tamed, not chained, nor mounted and ridden, but trained. Tiger-training becomes much more difficult with every new and exciting form of touch.[30]

This kind of approach may be amusing to those of us outside the genre. But when one explores it further, a perception of sexuality is revealed which is far from benign. In fact, it involves a misplacing of the responsibility for appropriate behaviour, resulting in the worst kind of victim-blaming:

> Provocative dress eggs people on. So we will avoid wearing jeans specially designed 'to make you sexy', perfume guaranteed to inflame the passion, see-through blouses which leave little to the imagination, or skin-tight tee-shirts. Girls won't go braless. We will recognize that nakedness or near-nakedness and any form of undressing are in themselves powerful stimuli; such dress – or state of undress – are not only unwise but unloving because they make self-control difficult for one's partner and Christians in general.[31]

Let's recall, for a moment, Jeanette Howard's anti-lesbian piece quoted earlier. This disallowed the wearing of any clothing which could possibly be construed as 'masculine' on the grounds that to don such apparel constitutes a rejection of one's God-given femininity. Clearly, women in the evangelical Christian tradition are being asked to negotiate a balancing act in which they will always be the losers. This resembles the Roman Catholic tradition where women are called upon to emulate Mary's example of true, ideal womanhood by taking on the role of virgin and mother. Huggett's writing is also profoundly dangerous, as it would be difficult for any survivor of sexual assault who read it not to blame herself. She would be encouraged to ask all the wrong kinds of questions: What was I wearing? Was I wearing enough? Did I smell too inviting? At the same time, the perpetrator is discouraged from taking any responsibility for his own behaviour. Later sections of this book will demonstrate the devastating impact which such misplaced advice can have upon young women.

Christian distinctiveness

There's a common feeling that society's rules are not good enough for Christians, who are called to be different. Both Jeffrey John and the Church of England bishops uphold the reality of this vocation:

> As 'aliens and exiles' Christians still understand themselves to be called, no less than the Jews in Babylon, to a distinctive morality and a distinctive holiness which will challenge the world in sexual matters as in all else.[32]

And:

> We recognise that it is increasingly hard today for the unmarried generally, and for young people facing peer group pressure in particular, to hold to this ideal, and therefore both the Church and its individual members need to be clearer and stronger in supporting those who are struggling against a tide of changing sexual standards.[33]

As one might expect, this call to separateness extends to draconian rules among conservatives, particularly in relation to the nature of a possible life-partner: the crucial element is that he/she must also be a Christian (a conservative one). According to Joyce Huggett: 'The Christian going out with a non-Christian suffers a kind of vitamin deficiency in the relationship.'[34] In order to steer people away from fraternizing with non-Christians, the latter are depicted in less than flattering terms: 'For many non-Christians, it seems, relationships with the opposite sex are about making sexual conquests or enjoying a series of sex thrills. Faith and morals do not come into it.'[35]

Morality is therefore equated with a particular narrow Christian version, and the possibility of other codes of conduct is anathema. However, the non-Christian may wonder at the ethical rectitude of the distinctiveness which is advocated. Take this example: 'The purpose of one-to-one relationships for the Christian, sandwiched as they are between the intimacy once provided by parental love and the intimacy of the hoped-for marriage relationship, are gap-fillers.'[36] One can imagine the relationship-vocabulary which might spring from this world-view: 'Hello, I'm Felicity, and this is my significant gap-filler, Raymond. He's keeping me company until I find a suitable husband.' A person's function is apparently more important than who they are in themselves. The 'amoral' secular person has a description for such behaviour: it's called using people.

The irony is that amid their claims to be 'distinctive', and their talk of courageous gestures of resistance to 'secular social trends' *vis-à-vis* sexuality, the vast majority of Christians succeed in achieving just the opposite. As we have seen in this section, Christians rarely offer a significant challenge to the most powerful social forces which shape our understanding of sexuality and gender: compulsory heterosexuality, and the homo-hatred and denigration of women which represent both its roots and its results. As a rule, Christianity compounds the effects of these forms of oppression by giving them supernatural justification via a divine stamp of approval.

Confidence in the knowledge of 'what God wants' is present in varying degrees in all manifestations of Christianity. Most effusive is the conservative evangelical who seems never to harbour doubts about what the Lord is telling her/him. Direct divine instruction is available (usually through Jesus) in all life decisions, from whether to choose Chicken McNuggets or a Big Mac through to whether or not to go to war and whether and with whom to have babies. No concern is too large or too small. More subtle, but nonetheless self-confident, are some of the 'statements of fact' found in church reports. Here are some examples:

> For all these positive reasons God's perfect will for married people is chastity before marriage, and then a lifelong relationship of fidelity and mutual sharing at all levels [my italics].[37]

> Sexual intercourse is intended by God to serve a profoundly unitive purpose . . . It establishes the 'one flesh union' [my italics].[38]

> [the family] is the primary form within which God intends his children to share in common life and experience.[39]

The big question is, of course, how do they know? This need not lead us into the realms of supernatural religious experience, for most Christians accept the word of other Christians, more powerful than themselves, as to 'what God wants'. Religious institutions are such that some people are invested with more power than others to mediate the divine will. Often, informal manifestations of this power in apparently egalitarian contexts (e.g. charismatic house churches) can be more damaging than its more overt and official forms, such as that represented by priests and bishops.

When a particular ideal is labelled 'God-given' the immediate effect is to discourage exploration of its origin and rationale. We are diverted from asking crucial questions about whose interests are served by it. In addition, moral responsibility for the enforcement of rules which spring from the ideal can be abrogated by those in power who are, after all, only 'following orders'. Throughout its history Christendom has invested men with ecclesiastical and theological authority, and excluded women from it. There is, consequently, a remarkable correlation between what 'God thinks' and that which is of benefit to men. Women, therefore, have cause to be suspicious of all forms of Christianity which maintain 'no-go' areas where received teaching may not be questioned. As the experiences of the women in this book demonstrate, Christian teaching on sexuality is one such no-go area, and the penalties for challenging it can be severe.

At the close of Part One it is worth reiterating, for the sake of clarity, my central point. Liberal Christians won't like to hear it, but still it has to be said – that liberal and conservative Christian perspectives on sexuality are not diametrically opposed but are cut from the same cloth. Insofar as they offer an uncritical endorsement of the doctrine of complementarity, they are implicated both in gender inequality and in unquestioning heterosexism. This insight helps us to reframe contemporary Christian debates, for it explains why the so-called liberal churches have been ultimately unhelpful and ineffective in the struggle for lesbian, bisexual and gay civil rights. From conservative Christians we expect rejection and incomprehension. From liberals we have expected better, but it seems that we are destined to be forever disappointed.

NOTES

1. A Statement by the House of Bishops. *Issues in Human Sexuality*. Church House Publishing, London, 1991, para. 3.26, p. 30.
2. *Ibid.*, para. 3.16, p. 25.
3. *Ibid.*, para. 3.17, p. 26.

4. *Ibid.*, para. 3.2, p. 19.
5. The Board of Social Responsibility of the Church of Scotland, *Report on Human Sexuality*, Edinburgh, 1994, para. 6.2.3.
6. *Ibid.*, para. 5.3.1.
7. House of Bishops, *Human Sexuality*, para. 4.10, p. 35.
8. Joyce Huggett, *Just Good Friends: Growing in Relationships*. Inter-Varsity Press, Leicester, 1986, p. 78.
9. House of Bishops, *Human Sexuality*, para. 3.16, p. 25.
10. *Ibid.*, para. 5.9, p. 42.
11. Joseph Cardinal Ratzinger and Alberto Bovone, *Letter to the Bishops of the Catholic Church on the Pastoral Care of Homosexual Persons*. Congregation for the Doctrine of the Faith, Rome, 1986, para. 8, pp. 4–5.
12. *Ibid.*, para. 9, p. 5.
13. House of Bishops, *Human Sexuality*, para. 4.8, p. 34.
14. Ratzinger and Bovone, *Vatican Letter*, para. 10, pp. 5–6.
15. *Ibid.*, para. 3, p. 2.
16. *Ibid.*, para. 7, p. 4.
17. *Ibid.*, para. 9, p. 5.
18. John White, *Eros Defiled: The Problem of Sexual Guilt*. Inter-Varsity Press, Leicester, 1993, p. 113.
19. Howard Marshall, 'The question of homosexuality – a personal comment', *Headline: Methodism and the Homosexuality Issue*, December 1990.
20. White, *Eros Defiled*, p. 105.
21. House of Bishops, *Human Sexuality*, para. 4.19, p. 38.
22. *Ibid.*, para. 3.12, p. 24.
23. *Homosexual Relationships: A Contribution to Discussion* (The Gloucester Report). CIO Publishing, London, 1979, para. 232, p. 70.
24. Jeffrey John, *Permanent, Faithful, Stable: Christian Same-sex Partnerships*. Affirming Catholicism, London, 1993, p. 18.
25. Elizabeth Stuart, *Daring to Speak Love's Name: A Gay and Lesbian Prayer Book*. Hamish Hamilton, London, 1992, pp. 2ff.
26. Mary E. Hunt, *Fierce Tenderness: A Feminist Theology of Friendship*. Crossroad, New York, 1991.
27. House of Bishops, *Human Sexuality*, para. 3.20, p. 27.
28. Huggett, *Just Good Friends*, p. 102.
29. Joyce Huggett, *Life in a Sex Mad Society*. Framework, Leicester, 1991, p. 13.
30. *Ibid.*, pp. 38–9.
31. *Ibid.*, p. 51.

32. John, *Permanent, Faithful, Stable*, p. 10.
33. House of Bishops, *Human Sexuality*, para. 3.8, p. 22.
34. Huggett, *Sex Mad Society*, p. 72.
35. *Ibid.*, p. 69.
36. Huggett, *Just Good Friends*, p. 73.
37. House of Bishops, *Human Sexuality*, para. 3.8, p. 22.
38. The Methodist Church, *A Christian Understanding of Family Life, the Single Person and Marriage*. Methodist Publishing House, Peterborough, 1989, para. III 53, p. 29.
39. *Ibid.*, taken from a shortened version of the report in *The Methodist Recorder*, Thursday 11 May 1989, p. 12.

II

The Impact of
Christian Sexual Ethics

In Part One I began to identify some common strands which characterize Christian teaching on sexuality and relationships, and which unite the diverse manifestations which Christianity takes in our society. That background gives us some idea of the *theoretical structures* which shape and underpin Christian teaching on sexuality. Having assessed Christian sexual ethics in the abstract, I would like to move on to the more important theme of the impact which such teaching has *upon the real lives of women*. Integral to this part of the book are the voices of women who have recounted to me their experiences and insights, either in writing or verbally. The substantial and valuable material which was generated has in large part determined the categories of analysis which I have chosen. More than half of the forty women who contributed their stories and insights currently identify as lesbian, and lesbian experiences provide the focus for the second half of Part Two. A significant proportion of contributors, however, spoke about their experiences of heterosexuality.

Finding the most useful method for categorizing women's experiences was difficult. One option would have been to refuse to categorize them at all, reproducing a random series of stories which would stand alone and 'speak for themselves'. But such were the overlapping and multiple connections between the experiences, that I felt it necessary to draw these out by means of commentary and analysis. That is not to say that I regard the women's contributions as 'raw experience', for which I provided the reflection and analysis. Far from it. Reflection *and* analysis were integral to the contributions I received. My aim has been to honour these perspectives, drawing out areas of commonality and difference in order to build a cohesive picture of the impact which Christian sexual ethics can have upon the lives of women.

Note that I have not divided the experiences of 'heterosexual women' from those of 'lesbian women', but that I have separated 'heterosexual experiences' from 'lesbian experiences'. There are political and practical reasons for this. To begin with, not all of the experiences of heterosexuality that were described to me came from women who now identify as heterosexual. Similarly, many of the lesbian experiences involve issues and questions which originate in the Church's failure adequately to address heterosexuality. Furthermore, to have divided 'lesbian women' from 'heterosexual women' would have been to fall into the trap of the very thought-structures which I criticized in Part One: the imposition of the binary opposition of 'heterosexual' and 'homosexual' as categories into which all human experience must fit.

Human experience quite clearly does not fit that model. But at the same time I strongly resist the proposal that we should avoid any categorization at all. This is sometimes advocated on the grounds that 'we are all the same', and our aim should be to do away with all labels that distract us from the fact that we are, first and foremost, just human beings. It did occur to me that an appropriate way forward could have been to choose a general category, 'women's experiences of sexuality', including lesbian and heterosexual experiences side by side to illustrate other themes. In the end, however, it became clear to me that heterosexual experiences and lesbian experiences require separate attention if the specificity of each is to be honoured, and the loss of important political insights avoided. As explained in Part One, unquestioned hetero-reality forms the social context within which all of us live our lives. This means that analytical explorations of heterosexuality are rarely undertaken, which in turn makes such work all the more crucial. Equally, employing the generic category of 'homosexual' or 'lesbian and gay' often means that the experiences of lesbians are eclipsed. Both these trends will be explored in more detail later. It is worth pointing out, at this stage, that the underlying purpose of homing in on the specificities of heterosexual and lesbian experiences is to help to build a whole picture of the context in which all women seek to understand our sexuality. Ultimately, the sections are not really separate at all; they inform each other.

On the theme of specificity and difference, it is worth saying that I make no claims to universality. While I hope that many women will find echoes of their own experience here, I cannot guarantee that every woman will. The contributors, as a group, encompass differences in age; denominational background and current religious affiliation; national, class and educational background. As I stressed in the Introduction, the substantial analytical input that I offer must be assessed bearing in mind the nature of my own subjectivity. There are undoubtedly themes which are not covered explicitly in this section, and which demand additional attention elsewhere.

4 *e*xamining *h*eterosexuality

Feminist theory tends to assume heterosexuality as a given, developing analyses with women's (and men's) heterosexuality as a taken-for-granted, but never explicitly addressed, substrate. Psychology similarly assumes heterosexuality, with lesbianism (and male homosexuality) as 'alternative lifestyles' at best, 'pathological perversions' at worst. In both feminism and psychology, heterosexuality disappears into the background, leaving lesbianism as the interrogative focus.[1]

This excerpt summarizes the rationale of the three (lesbian) editors of the *Feminism and Psychology Journal* in publishing a 'special issue' on heterosexuality. In Adrienne Rich's words: 'Heterosexuality is an enormous assumption to have glided so silently into the foundations of our thought.'[2] If heterosexuality is unquestioned in secular disciplines such as psychology, and in feminist critiques of such disciplines, it is hardly surprising that it is also unquestioned in theology. And if it remains unquestioned in theology, it is unlikely to be questioned by Christians. The construction of same-sex relationships in secular society as that which is 'other' – odd and fearsome – acts to discourage us from questioning the nature of heterosexual relating. Christianity adds to this the further disincentive of a religious thought-system built upon the fear and loathing of same-sex relationships. The consequences for lesbian and bisexual women, and those who are uncertain about their sexuality, are certainly negative, as we shall see later. But what is seldom recognized is that the refusal to examine assumptions about heterosexuality means that women often experience *heterosexuality itself* in damaging and harmful ways.

The 'discouragement' or 'disincentive' to question heterosexuality is, of course, so pervasive as to be invisible. This can be illustrated by an ecclesiastical example. A more or less acceptable report on human sexuality was put to the Methodist Conference (the governing body of that denomination) in 1993. This had been put together by a commission of some twenty-five people (of which I was one) over a period of two years, and at great expense to the denomination. The first significant point to note in the context of the current discussion is that although this report addressed sexuality in all its forms, the discussion which resulted from its publication was rapidly reduced to a debate about whether the ordination of 'practising' lesbian and gay Methodists should be 'allowed'. In other words, the 'interrogative focus' (as the editors of *Feminism and Psychology* so helpfully put it) was instantly and firmly shifted away from questions about heterosexuality (which formed a significant part of the report) towards the issue of lesbian and gay clergy (which had occupied only a minute proportion of the commission's time and energy). That there was little or no public recognition of this fact is proof enough of the invisibility of the refusal to discuss heterosexuality. This highlights the very important political role of 'homosexuality' as explained in a report of the Presbyterian Church of the USA:

> Homosexuality is typically invoked in a rhetorical, almost formulaic, way to signal that something has gone wrong. However, homosexuality often remains an abstraction, unrelated to – and uninformed by – real people. It functions primarily as a very powerful symbol carrier of people's fears and discomfort about sexuality in general.[3]

But let us return to the Methodist Conference of 1993, at which a rather extraordinary thing happened. The representatives were faced with a choice. On the one hand, there was a set of motions which represented a mild and ambiguous acceptance of the status quo where lesbians (potentially) and gay men (actually) can – with a lot of luck and in some local situations – become ordained and also be 'out' at the same time. On the other hand, a group of conservatives had put together a rigid and definite motion which unequivocally excluded lesbian and gay people, not only from ministry but also from membership of the Church. In the event, the conference threw out both options and accepted two completely new and apparently contradictory motions. These read as follows:

1. The Conference reaffirms the traditional teaching of the Church on human sexuality; namely chastity for all outside marriage and fidelity within it. The Conference directs that this affirmation is made clear to all candidates for ministry, office and membership ...

2. Conference recognises, affirms and celebrates the participation and ministry of lesbians and gay men in the church. Conference calls on the Methodist people to begin a pilgrimage of faith to combat repression and discrimination, to work for justice and human rights and to give dignity and worth to people whatever their sexuality.

Here is a possible explanation of what happened. The Methodist Church is a traditionally 'compassionate' Non-conformist denomination. An explicit and harsh rejection of lesbian and gay Christians would not have accorded with the Church's self-image. At the same time, like all beleaguered Christian denominations in a secular age, Methodism is clearly beset by a fear of change and of division. Members of the conference fell upon motion (1) as a Godsend, for it excluded lesbian and gay people *by inference only*, and they welcomed motion (2) even more enthusiastically because it expressed acceptance *while leaving the terms of that acceptance ambiguous*. This was further reinforced in 1994 when the conference voted by an overwhelming majority not to rescind motion (2), but simultaneously refused to approve a proposal to carry out research into discrimination against lesbian and gay people within Methodism. This would seem to confirm that the 'acceptance' expressed has its origins in political pragmatism rather than principle, with no practical implications envisaged.

Given that background, the main point to note is that while motion (1) has profound implications for heterosexual Methodists, these were not identified or considered in the debate, which was completely dominated by discussion of male homosexuality. The result was that the Church made a significant ruling, by default, about an issue which was not even the subject of its discussions – the status of heterosexual relationships outside of marriage. Even the Church of England has not yet gone so far as to exclude sexually active heterosexual people from membership and ministry. To this day I am aware of little public discussion of the implications of the measures for heterosexuals. Ironically, those most dismayed by the proceedings were unmarried sexually active heterosexuals, many of whom were present to lend their support to the lesbian and gay cause, and who were not expecting that they themselves would be excluded and their lifestyles outlawed. Of course, the irony is that it is unlikely that motion (1) will ever be enforced for heterosexuals. There is little doubt, however, that it will be applied to exclude lesbian and gay people, although the language utilized by the motion makes any application to lesbian and gay lifestyles highly inappropriate.

It is absurd that such a thing could happen, but unsurprising given the context of prevailing heterosexual normativity. As part of the overall strategy to undermine that normativity, it is essential for the second part of this book to explore the dynamics of heterosexuality by giving voice to those women who have encountered it via Christian sexual ethics. It is hoped that as a result we will be able to, in the words of Sheila Jeffreys, 'draw heterosexuality out of the protective camouflage of "nature" or "just the way things are", and into the spotlight of political analysis . . . '.[4] In this way, we place the choices of all women in a realistic context and perspective.

Messages about (hetero)sexuality

JOANNE

I grew up with the following basic attitudes to sex: men wanted as much as they could get; women did not initiate it – they were objects of worship for men, and held power over men because they could grant or withhold sex; it was acceptable for women to flirt but not to behave in an overtly sexual manner. In contrast, in terms of career and public life, men were held to be dominant.

To what extent were these attitudes Christian? With hindsight I can see within them the Christian ambivalence towards women's sexuality: woman as object of worship, but at the same time the holder of sexual power and threatening to men. There is also the attitude towards women's social role, deeply ingrained in the Church: the woman as dominant within the home, where the man is despised and helpless, but in public life the man in control, despising the woman's lack of practical business sense. Undoubtedly these were, at some level, Christian values, although I did not recognize them as such. However, in my family there was also a healthy tolerance of sexual diversity, and an acceptance that premarital and extramarital sex took place and were not automatically wrong.

I became a Christian at 19 through an evangelical conversion at university, and accepted the 'package' of beliefs at first, although I fairly soon began to question them. I embraced a naive and sickly attitude to sexuality: Christian marriage became my ideal, sex being a sacred act only permissible in marriage. I did not consciously condemn homosexuality at this time – I simply side-stepped the issue. But I did begin to have anxieties about relationships – I never had a boyfriend and did not seem to attract men. I believed that marriage was the only way in which I would become a whole person, and I was afraid I might end up alone. But my worries in themselves caused me guilt, because the image I wanted to live up to was that of the committed Christian, concerned only to do God's will, for whom relationships, and especially sex, were minor considerations.

After I graduated, I got married to a man to whom I was not suited, with the idealistic assumption that so-called Christian marriage would overcome the obvious difficulties in the relationship, and that sex would 'just happen'. I then discovered that my husband was repelled by sex and was, at first, impotent. During our four years of marriage we had very little in the way of a sexual relationship. I was appalled both by the situation and by my own reactions to it. I had been brought up to think that men were sexual initiators, and I could not cope with finding myself in that role. I also felt dreadfully guilty about the frustration I felt because I thought that as a Christian I should accept the situation 'for better or worse'. The level of my anger and resentment was quite frightening to me.

Looking back on this time, I can see that Christian assumptions about sex and marriage contributed to my naive expectations, to my guilt feelings, and to my husband's repressed attitude to sex (he had been brought up in a fairly austere Christian context). Neither of us had had any sexual experience and believed that sex should only take place in marriage, but we were completely unprepared for the fact that sex does not simply happen automatically for most people. I had no understanding of women's sexual needs – I think I knew that I had them, but had always assumed that when I was married those needs would be met, and that a man's sexual drive would always be the stronger force. The situation that I faced in my marriage left me floundering without any models to relate to, and I found I was too embarrassed to talk to anyone about what was (or was not) happening.

I do not feel confident, however, in laying blame at the door of Christianity or the Church in a generalized sense. That would be too simplistic. I came into a branch of Christianity that particularly fostered naive notions about relationships, and in my circle some very young and inexperienced people gained spiritual influence. There was a deep mistrust of 'theology' and of any critical approach to scripture. I grew out of this attitude quite quickly and began to study academic theology and to develop my own critical approach, but I was afraid to let go of my hope of Christian married bliss. Had I sought out more honest discussion about relationships and sexuality, I might have found it in other branches of the Church, but I saw no need to do so. My only Christian experience was evangelical and I knew no other way of being a Christian.

Overall, I think I have found little theological or more popular Christian literature (in my limited experience, that is), that addresses the situation I faced in my marriage. There is plenty of discussion about sex taking place where it shouldn't, but little about sex not taking place where it should. Christian teaching tends to concentrate on limiting sexual behaviour within certain limits, usually marriage, or in more liberal circles, a committed relationship, and sexual sin is seen as having too much, or the wrong kind, of sex. However, having my sexual needs denied by my partner was probably the most painful experience of my life – denial of sexuality can be sinful too. Of course, the Church affirms the importance of marital sex, often regarding it in rather high-flown terms as a sacred act of union, but I find that attitude rather pretentious. How true is it to most people's experience? It seems to me that the Church still presents the view that sex is basically 'bad' and that certain conditions and theological arguments have to be created in order to make it good. I feel more comfortable with the view that sex is basically good, but that for various practical and emotional reasons people may need certain boundaries to help them handle it.

JUDITH

I grew up in a Methodist family. My parents, both virgins when they married, considered this the only 'proper' status for an unmarried person, especially their children. I never questioned this whilst growing up, but accepted it all as biblical and hence right. Nice girls didn't have a sexuality (let alone a sexual experience!) until their wedding night, and if you weren't a 'nice girl', no decent man was ever going to marry you.

Even as a student at polytechnic my indoctrinated prudishness didn't really change. But by then I was doing some thinking for myself. After all, nowhere in the Bible is virginity demanded; and exploration of my own sexuality was very much on my personal agenda. I had gone so much further than hand-holding and a quick kiss on the first date that it was very much a question of when, rather than whether, I would explore further. Reading Nancy Friday's *My Secret Garden,* lent by some friends at polytechnic, started a lot of questions and self-exploration.

My first sexual experiences were not very positive. Even being touched for the first time was traumatic when sex had been instilled as a no-no. Any enjoyment was lost in a welter of guilt. At home the pressure was still on to be 'virgin pure'. It was that denial of my right to be me that I felt most deeply; the feeling that somehow my sexuality was something to deny, to be ashamed of, that I found hardest to live with.

HEATHER

The possession of a penis seemed to lead to important roles and respect, and lack of them meant we were assigned less important roles and less respect, for, most importantly, we could never be ordained. Even then, before my clergyman husband rubbed it in, I knew that ordination was special and different and, because it could only be done by men, I would never be special and different. This still had an effect, even if one never wanted to be ordained. The equation was: penis = man, penis = God, penis = ordination, penis = value, penis = worth. All these go together. The fact that sexual parts were never named or discussed made the irony, the mystery, the confusion, the lack of self-worth even more bitter.

And so, something there was that made ordination – and men – very special. It couldn't be sex, could it? Or sex as related to and defined by the male sex organ? But whatever it was, it was so special that only men could have it. My job as a teacher, and my enjoyment of sex in a female body, were definitely second-rate.

As special sex could only happen with a special man after a special ceremony in a special building by a special, ordained man, the effect on my valuing of my own, my woman's sexuality, was enormous. So much was denied and almost completely lost. Sex was male-dominated and church-dominated for many overlapping and complicated reasons.

First, to a Christian and a Methodist, particularly one with an ordained fiancé, sex was only allowed to happen and was only recognized (and, hopefully, enjoyed) after marriage. I had been well prepared for this by my strong Methodist upbringing before the fiancé insisted on its rightness and the impossibility of any other way. What was meant by this word 'sex' which could only happen after marriage was of course penetrative sex, penis–vagina.

Other 'foreplay', 'love-making' , was acceptable in this apparently logical code of conduct, but it was not real and therefore not sinful. That it might also be wonderfully satisfying, for me, until it was denied, was not allowed. It couldn't be, because 'real' sex hadn't happened yet and wouldn't until after marriage. My joyful claims to first orgasm were strenuously denied as impossible as we hadn't had 'real' sex yet. Later, similar experiences of mine went unacknowledged or denied.

So the penis was idealized, and made all the difference between married and unmarried sex, sex and not sex, real and pretend sex, fun and sin sex, bad and good sex. But worse, it made all the difference between the denial and acceptance of the woman, of her sexuality and what gave her pleasure. What was feared as emasculation of the male, the admission of pleasure without his specialness, led to the bitter irony of failure of real love and sharing.

All this, which I discover to have been a similar experience of many of my friends who are Methodists of a similar age, must have been one of the strongest reasons for so many failed wedding nights. We wives have shared stories and pain, and some self-mocking to hide the pain with laughter – wives whose sexuality had been denied became their husbands' sex therapists at great costs to themselves.

ANNE

I am afraid of my sexuality – its strength and power. It has lain dormant for so long. As a young woman I did not really acknowledge my sexuality. I felt unattractive, was not in popular demand – maybe I was too serious and intense, and lacking in confidence. I did not like myself, others seemed so much more talented. It was important to me to be in a relationship with a man/boy. And I was from the age of 15.

I have been married for almost 22 years. I have had sexual intercourse with only one man, have been in conventional terms 'faithful' to him. It was important to him, when we first met in 1968, that I was a virgin. So was he. A virgin – strange word. I had had two intense relationships before him, with men. Or were they boys?? We had kissed, been passionate and with one of them, Peter, I had experienced the joy and relief of clitoral climax. One occasion stands out – in his Mini. Not the most comfortable or convenient place to make love!, yet it was the setting of my first orgasm – aged 18 or 19. I had spent my first term at university, leaving Peter behind (I knew this relationship would eventually end, since study for me then took precedence). On my return, he collected me from the station, and on my way home we stopped in a secluded country lane, desperate for the comfort of each other's bodies. He gave me so much pleasure, but my overriding anxiety was that he might think I was used to doing this – allowing other men access to my special private places. It was a special and important event, and yet . . . disappointing. A sense of it not being quite right.

I guess from an early age I have wanted men to want me (yet I am only now being able to analyse this and acknowledge it, and it is quite painful). I also want to have power over men, yet ironically I often give power away to them. They disempower me. I find myself organizing my life around them.

As I suggested in Part One, the predominant view of sexuality among Christians is that it represents a rather narrow and discrete aspect of life, focused on genital sexual expression. Even men of a politically radical hue rarely challenge this construction, believing sexuality issues to be marginal in social justice terms: a luxury item on their shopping list of global economic and ecological ills. This reductionist perspective appears to have played an important role in all the experiences outlined above. Indeed, Heather goes further. For her, not only were definitions of sexuality restricted to genital expression alone, they also betrayed a clear phallocentric bias. She grew up with male definitions of sexuality: the penis made the difference between real and pretend sex; good sex and sinful sex. For all of the women, penile penetration of the vagina had been equated with 'sexual intercourse', which had in turn been equated with 'sex'/'sexuality'.

This is the construction of sexuality fuelling the controversy which still rages in many parts of the Christian community about cohabitation as 'living in sin'. Some conservative Anglican vicars have apparently instituted the requirement of a repentance clause in the wedding service for cohabiting couples who wish to get married in church. It is only the 'sex' aspect of cohabitation to which Christians object, because 'sex before and outside marriage' has been consistently condemned (they say) in the Christian tradition. Without an unambiguous definition of what 'sex' actually is, the prohibition is unworkable. It is therefore in the interests both of those who wish to maintain the prohibition, and of those who want to go as far as possible without actually transgressing it, to maintain the narrow and rigid definition of 'sexual intercourse'. The same is true, incidentally, of the definition of 'marriage'. As Adrian Thatcher points out in his book *Liberating Sex*,[5] the Church has never taught that it marries couples; rather, it stresses that two people marry each other, and the church service is just a symbolic celebration of that. Exactly when a marriage actually begins is therefore debatable, and can only be defined by the two people involved. It certainly does not necessarily begin when the priest pronounces his/her blessing. This makes 'sex before marriage' rather more difficult to identify.

In all four cases it was the women's life experience which caused them to question the messages they had received about sexuality, and in no case was this questioning a pain-free process. All of these women grew up comparing their own experience with a particular set of expectations. Sometimes these expectations took the form of an ideal which was explicitly spelled out, but sometimes they were communicated in more subtle ways by implication or suggestion. When we compare our own experience with expectations which have never been articulated, the result is likely to be confusion: a sense that something is 'not quite right', or that *we* are not quite right. 'Right' in this context may mean 'moral' or 'normal'. When an ideal has been articulated we are likely to feel that our experience 'doesn't live up to it' or that it falls outside of it, in which case the response is one of shame or denial.

The pain expressed in these stories results directly from such denial. This is summed up by Heather, for whom the enjoyment of sex in a female body was 'definitely second rate'; for Joanne: 'having my sexual needs denied ... was probably the most painful experience of my life'; and for Judith: 'it was that denial of my right to be me that I felt most deeply.' The link which is drawn by Heather between male genitals and ordination, God, value and worth gives us a clue as to the gravity of the denial of women's sexuality. We are not talking here of the denial of some peripheral accessory to our individual psyches. Rather, we are concerned with what provides the key to our self-worth, our social interactions and our expectations of ourselves. This is about *politics*, a fact that is borne out by Anne's experience. She highlights just one of the practical manifestations of the construction of heterosexuality: '[men] disempower me. I find myself organizing my life around them.'

It is worth making a more general comment at this point. Joanne counsels caution when it comes to apportioning blame to Christianity. It is impossible, she implies, to establish any definite 'cause and effect' between the cultural dynamics which have shaped us and the person we have become. It is true that each of us has been exposed to a complex cocktail of influences which are inextricably linked, and it would be impossible, for instance, to isolate the parts of our personality which are purely 'Christianity's fault'. Nevertheless, while it may be unhelpful to trace cause and effect on an individual level, it is crucial to assess the role of Christianity and Christian values in shaping and maintaining the structures of those institutions which hold power over us. First-hand experience of these institutions must form the bedrock of such analysis.

Experiencing reality

SARAH

> When my marriage broke down, I was a local preacher, and unofficial 'caretaker' at our church. I have painfully vivid memories that stay with me about how the church responded.

After the panicky 'we must get them back together, it can't be that bad' response by church people, and after they had realized we weren't going to get back together, the next response was a flurry of activity to 'get me off' with someone else! This was profoundly hurtful. Firstly, they seemed unable to live with the evidence of marriage breakdown (although, obviously, I had to live with that in its most acute form). They couldn't cope with my ability to survive in my new identity, i.e. as a single parent. (Notice society's insistence on stereotyping 'one-parent families' as failures – possibly because they can't cope with what it means when they aren't failures.) At all costs, the marriage breakdown, and the success at being on my own, had to be covered up as soon as possible – without much thought as to whether I was ready for another relationship, whether I wanted another relationship, and whether the person they had earmarked was remotely suitable! Even now, 16 years later, people are 'sorry' for me, and hope that one day someone 'nice' will come along for me to marry!

HEATHER

On one dreadful Sunday morning I was summoned to sit, after the service, at the front of the church, while three female church stewards 'consulted' me about how I would like people to be told about my marriage breakdown. This 'consultation' consisted of them arguing with one another over my head, as I sat and they stood, animatedly considering the problem. I did manage to remind them that it was me that they were discussing, but by this time I was beginning not to care what the church thought or did anyway.

One woman came to visit me and to share a meal, and arrived with a lovely bunch of flowers. She was concerned that I would be lonely living so far from the church. Then she prayed over me, in what actually became a 20-minute sermon over a captive audience; she told her God – and me – of her deep desire that I should go back to my husband.

Other friends came and went. I'm learning that even the best may need cultivating if you're newly single. Despite warnings, I was still amazed at which ones couldn't cope with odd numbers.

The relentless promotion of marriage is a marked characteristic of most manifestations of modern Christianity. To cite but one example, here is a *Church Times* editorial from 1990:

It can only be good news that there is to be a new charity to uphold marriage. The institution deserves all the support it can get. To cleave to one woman or one man throughout an adult life, seeking no physical satisfactions elsewhere, and with no traces of old partnerships to trouble the mind: anyone who has experienced it, or come near to it, knows that there is no happier state.[6]

This was in response to the launch of a new church body called Family Life and Marriage Education (FLAME). It seems that the *Church Times* editor would have been happier to replace the 'E' for Education with a 'P' for Promotion. But the editor would do well to recognize that eulogizing marriage as the pinnacle of relational achievement can have devastating consequences for those who experience marriage breakdown. If 'Christian marriage' is portrayed as a state of perfection, a priori, then the message communicated is that marriage relationships should not, and therefore do not, go wrong. Given that church people are actively discouraged from including the possibility of marriage breakdown in their world-view, is it any wonder that women like Sarah and Heather have faced insensitivity and crass mishandling?

There are few analytical options open to those who seek to make sense of marriage breakdown. The only model which the churches employ in their teaching is what we might call the 'failure model'. Those whose marriages end are portrayed as losers – albeit gallant ones. They didn't reach the pinnacle, or if they did they lacked the inner resources to stay there. In the Roman Catholic tradition a couple must seek an annulment to end a marriage, by which the partners agree that their relationship was never a marriage in the first place , but an illusion. What about the woman for whom divorce was a liberation from a violent and abusive husband: has she 'failed'? What about those couples who decide to end their marriage in order to bring about a positive change in the nature of their relationship? What about separation (temporary or permanent) as a mature and adult response to a particular set of circumstances? All the nuances and differences as to why divorces and separations happen are lost in the Church's monolithic description of marriage breakdown as 'failure'.

I am in no way seeking to minimize the pain involved when marriages end. Quite the opposite. It is at best questionable, pastorally speaking, that the only framework offered to those who would move on from such pain is to consider themselves failures. Recognition of what was positive in the marriage relationship, alongside a realistic recognition of what was negative, is rarely encouraged. Elizabeth Stuart's suggestion in her prayer book *Daring to Speak Love's Name*[7] that the end of a relationship deserves to be marked liturgically with a ceremony met with derision from many reviewers. Informal feedback to the author from her readers, however, suggests that many people have found her material to be extremely helpful. The situation as it is does nothing to help individuals understand and express themselves as relational beings. And this in turn prevents us becoming more literate as a community about what makes for good and bad relationships.

HEATHER

I still remember the agony of watching David Hare's *Racing Demon* as I prepared to leave my husband. I could have written many of the lines of both women: the one who was having an affair with the young priest until he denied their love and returned to the bosom of the Church; the other who'd been married to a clergyman for years and suffered great loneliness. Both these women are part of where I've been as a woman in relation to a minister. The tragedy was highlighted in the older woman's final line, as her husband tried to make contact. She went to her room saying 'I'm better on my own'.

We'd often filled our homes, our houses, our manses[8] with 'parish folk', my clergyman husband and I, at times like Christmas Eve and New Year's Eve. Our motives were both clear and hidden. We'd say we were 'inviting a few friends round'; we were also patronizingly deliberate in our inclusion of those 'needing friends': the poor souls of the parish. The motives and the irony were terrible. What we didn't know or admit was that we were, in later years, protecting ourselves at times when we would otherwise have been vulnerable to the obvious: that we were increasingly hiding our own despair and the silence between us. I was hiding my loneliness within familiar routines, and avoiding being alone with my husband at times when we might have noticed the yawning gap. The 'warm' welcome offered by our 'open house' was a sham.

On my last New Year's Eve there, I just couldn't summon the energy or the usual semblance of enthusiasm, only the terror of being alone with my husband or by myself as he prepared for the Watch Night service. My father had just died, an event even more momentous in its outcomes than ever I'd realized. At his funeral, his friend told us all how proud he'd been of his two children: of his son for his work and profession; of me for marrying a Methodist minister. God, the irony! What if my father had known what I was about to do? But then, he never could have known. I could only do it after he had died; I didn't even know I was going to do it before then.

My husband invited the guests this year; I had no instincts or concern about who might come. We were a mixed group of 'friends': the lonely, the old, the young, the happy, the distressed, the quarrelling. Our own children went out. I fed and watered the assembled company, and escaped for a cry. I played jazz with a lovely man in his sixties who can play the piano a bit and the drums a lot. We made drums out of tables and spoons and sticks, and I accompanied him on the piano as if I had to fill my head with sound.

At 11.30 everyone left for the Watch Night service at the church. I couldn't face it so didn't go. No one asked why. It was as if no one had noticed. I surveyed the clearing and washing-up that had to be done. It hadn't even been started.

Clergy marriages bear the additional burden of promoting the ideal of marital bliss to others, preferably by example. In the Church of England this is enshrined in the ordination service, at which would-be priests are asked: 'Will you strive to fashion your own life *and that of your household* according to the way of Christ?'[9] (my italics). In the past when priests simultaneously headed-up patriarchal families and church congregations it might have been possible to exert the necessary authority over one's wife and family to ensure that image prevailed over happiness. Now it would appear anachronistic. Yet the need for clergy to be exemplars of the Christian lifestyle is still the main argument employed against lesbian and gay ordination. It is thought impossible that a lesbian or gay household might set an example about how to live in right relation.

This is the case, of course, if by 'right relation' we envisage the kind of complementary gender roles described in Part One. The traditional model of the 'clergy family' depends upon the clergy-wife taking up a portable job such as teaching or social work, without expecting to advance much within it. Alternatively, she must be an ever-attendant 'lady of leisure' (which actually means that she works full time for the Church but is paid nothing, and forfeits any chance of financial independence). Neither option is one which would be expected to satisfy any man. Although it was never publicly expressed, this may well have been an important consideration lurking in the background in the debate about the ordination of women. If the Church were to ask as much of clergy-husbands as it has traditionally asked of clergy-wives, there would be a conflict between this and the promotion of clear gender roles which underlie its teaching on sexuality and marriage. For what kind of a 'real man' follows his wife around the country, sacrificing his career and income? The alternative, however, would be a total rethink of both models of ministry and models of family life and gender relationships. Neither option is a comfortable one for the establishment.

Women out of control

JACKIE

The Church is (in the main) run as a male club; men make the rules even where women form the majority of the local Christian community. This means that the male is seen as normal and women are seen only in relation to men. In my experience, if you are not attached to a particular man you are invisible to many people. Because women's sexuality is seen as dependent on men, a woman who is not part of a male/female couple is treated as having no sexuality.

The practical outworking of this is extremely undermining. I find that on a social level, unless there are a fair number of single people past their teens, I can forget social activities with my church. Social events are for couples, and single women are for babysitting. General attitudes vary from those who think that I am just longing to become part of their family so that I can mind their children in exchange for Sunday lunch (I'm a far better cook than childminder), to those who have never considered that I don't eat unless I cook; unless I have done the shopping and the washing-up.

There is a definite determination to pair off the single people, but it is clear that marriage is the aim. An ongoing relationship outside of courtship and marriage is unthinkable. At times it seems that burglary is a lesser crime than 'living in sin'! Some years ago a (male) colleague and I discussed the likelihood of our evangelical Christian employer finding a way to dismiss any unmarried employee who was found to be sleeping with her/his partner. Here there are (of course) double standards; time and time again I see that if a non-married heterosexual couple are found to be expecting a child it is the woman who comes in for the more severe condemnation. It seems that whenever women assert their sexuality they incur the disapproval (or worse) of the Christian community.

There is an approved interpretation of Christianity, which gives low status, if not invisibility, to women. Women are seen in the role of helpers (or servants) and this is 'justified from scripture'. Married women are seen as the servants of their husbands and children, and single women as the servants of all. Women in general are seen as dangerous temptresses, with single women being the greater danger as there is no man to control them. There appears to be a deep-seated suspicion and hatred of women's sexuality, which I experience as being born of fear. It shows itself in attitudes to women in authority, and in the conviction that women can never really represent Christ.

As a result, Christianity acts out its need to 'tame' women's sexuality through the approved sort of Christian Family Life, with its carefully designed roles. If this fails, increasing aggression is used, with stages of harassment and both verbally and physically expressed violence. I personally have not experienced physical violence, but I know women who have, and I have experienced verbal violence.

INGRID

I have lived a single lifestyle for the past eleven years since the death of my husband. I was 36 at the time. I would not have chosen to be single since I was very happily married. People in the church seem to assume that my sexuality died at the same time as my husband. This is a tacit assumption since the whole question seems to be so taboo that it has never actually been mentioned to me. I am still a human being with normal sexual desires and appetites. I do not want to be told to use up my energy 'doing good works' (not the same as saying that I do not want to help others who have had the experience of losing someone with whom they had a sexual relationship). If I claim I have struggled back to wholeness, then this must include my sexuality. It is part of me and not in cold storage or in ashes on the funeral pyre. I am not prepared to suppress this part of myself. I am glad to recognize it and express it. As long as we are told that sexuality can only be expressed within marriage we are continuing to wound deeply those who choose, or who have thrust upon them, differing lifestyles.

Returning to the *Church Times* editorial, it is interesting to note its title 'A problem about marriage is those who do without it'.[10] It is as though the validity of marriage depended upon its being embraced universally. Some Christians demonstrate a similar mentality when it comes to the relationship between Christianity and other faiths: Christianity is considered to be undermined by any suggestion that the other faiths may also embody cosmic truths. Each and every adherent of another faith is perceived, somehow, to undermine Christianity, just as every person who does not marry but insists on 'being sexual' in one of the myriad ways which are open to them, somehow undermines marriage.

I have already explored in Part One how the Church of England's bishops hint at coercion to ensure universal appreciation of the concept of complementarity. It is through the experiences of single women that we begin to perceive the dynamics of that coercion. Jackie speaks of verbal violence and worse. Here she has isolated one of many forms of male power which Adrienne Rich identifies as being important in the control of women and their sexuality:

> Some of the forms by which male power manifests itself are more easily recognizable than are others ... women have been convinced that marriage and sexual orientation toward men are inevitable, even if unsatisfying or oppressive components of their lives.[11]

Undermining the lives of women who choose to live alone is a clear example of the enforcement of heterosexuality, and this is borne out by the fact that such women are treated as subversive even when they are not intending to be so. Ingrid was apparently once told by a minister that she and the widows in his own congregation were worrisome to him because he found them threatening to the order of things. This comment was supposedly made in jest, which makes it all the more revealing.

Ingrid also told me about her attempts to reintegrate her sexuality into her life in new and creative ways. This has involved for her a development of her thinking away from sexuality as expressible only through genital sexual relationships and towards a concept of sexuality as something which is expressed throughout the whole network of her relationships. Her thinking in this regard has been met with incomprehension and sometimes even laughter in her circle of otherwise supportive friends, perhaps because any questioning of 'coupledom' is seen as threatening to those who have built a life around it. This illustrates the tyranny of what Mary Hunt calls 'the relational dyad'.[12] Hunt's own significant challenge to compulsory heterosexuality involves making friendship rather than marriage the central relational model. In explaining this she says: 'The point is not to make the world safe for dyads, but to shift the focus from "the two" to "the many".'[13] It is significant for our current discussion that she recognizes 'the hardest friend of all to name and celebrate, and perhaps the easiest to lose, is oneself'.[14]

MAUREEN

> I have given some thought to my own sexual orientation and remain heterosexual. However, I have always been attracted to gay men, and when, 18 months after our marriage, my husband came out as bisexual, Christianity and sexuality moved centre stage. It was in the early days of Higton and the witch-hunts, of Clause 28 and the reports in the Anglican and Methodist Churches on (homo)sexuality.

Marriage has been very positive for me. To be known and loved and understood and accepted is beautiful. I have learned something of what it means to love, in an open way which lets the other be. And I believe that the experience of loving and being loved has shown me something of God's love. My choice is not to have children. In some eyes this is still not an acceptable choice, and can in itself be marginalizing. I do object to the Church's and society's harping on about The Family. For me, marriage itself is a gift and quite sufficient.

So far, I am still within the Church, though I feel very much in a minority because of my feminism, my support for lesbians and gay men, and general liberal theology. I stay on my own terms, as a member of the Anglican and Methodist Churches, refusing to be pigeon-holed, and despite (or because of) having been described by one of my husband's former clerical colleagues as 'a handicap to his career'. I try to be my own person, refusing to conform to people's expectations.

RUTH

The most important factor in my life is my spirituality – I am a practising and active Methodist, a local preacher. My marriage of 22 years to a fellow Methodist (we met at the church youth club) has been through many strains and vicissitudes. I have a real affection for my husband, but we no longer have a sexual relationship. I express my sexuality in the relationship I have with my friend, Brian, who is also a Methodist local preacher. I think there are only one or two people in my local circuit who know and understand the circumstances of my life; there are many who don't want to know, accepting me, and my friend too of course, at our own evaluation. I am happy with this, I think. I don't want the intimate details of my life to be thought the property of all I work or worship with, within the church. I have always been ready to answer questions frankly and openly, but have never been faced with hostile questioning. Of course, I could be faced with disciplinary procedures if my relationship was brought completely into the open. But as I regard Brian as my intimate friend, and as we still all live together and people choose not to probe, things carry on and church responsibilities are given to me.

The one important effect of all this for many years, I think, was that within my relationship with Brian, the sexual element was stressed out of all proportion, and it took us a long time to sort it all out so that sexual expression took its natural place and was not given an undue significance. I do not think that the reason for this is down to the church's attitude alone, but it certainly was responsible in part. This thought interests me as I think it must be true too for those whose sexual lives are subject to more distortion than ours.

Maureen is living with the ambiguities of her marriage to a bisexual man. Her reward for supporting him is to be branded a 'handicap to his career' by his colleagues. Of course, they do not know any better because they remain unaware of the full story. But had they been aware of it, what are the chances that they would have dealt with it in a mature and constructive way? Ruth's experience leaves one pessimistic. She encountered a fixation with genital sexual activity which prevents any true appreciation of the nature of a relationship. This preoccupation, which I explored in Part One, seems to be particularly noticeable within the Christian community, and can take the most childish and absurd forms. Also evident is a very particular notion about appropriate boundaries between the 'public' and the 'private'. As other experiences in this book will demonstrate, those who adopt normative heterosexual lifestyles are afforded privacy (which borders on secrecy when marriages go wrong) while those who are lesbian, gay or single experience continuous public scrutiny, since the assumption is that they have nothing to be private about.

This unwillingness for open discussion in the wake of marriage breakdown can lead to ethical short cuts being taken in preference to any attempts to understand the complexities of people's relationships. Let me illustrate this point further by way of an example. I have put the following case-study (fictitious, but based on real experiences) before various workshop groups in the past:

SUSAN AND CAROLINE

Susan is an Anglican deacon. She is 35 and has two children, aged nine and seven. A year ago, she separated from her husband after several years of unhappy marriage. She found her husband, David, to be increasingly uncommunicative. He seemed incapable of telling her how he felt about their relationship, and they began to talk to each other less and less as time progressed. A year of being on her own has given Susan plenty of time to reflect on her past relationships. She has concluded that she finds closeness and intimacy with women much more fulfilling than with men, and that the most important people in her life have always been women. She is unsure about whether this makes her a 'lesbian', and she has done a lot of reading about women loving women. She has also been to a couple of conferences about sexuality. She feels that she is just beginning to discover herself, and some of the possibilities for relationships that are open to her.

At one of these conferences, she met Caroline. Caroline is also a deacon, in Durham. She is 28. They have begun a relationship. They both feel excited and happy about this. They love spending time together: offering each other support, making love, making each other laugh, exchanging ideas about work. The relationship feels good to them, although they are painfully aware of the rejection they face if they are public about it. They see each other alternate weekends . . .

Their time together is increasingly taken up with planning for the future. They both feel strongly called to the ministry, and neither wants to give that up. But they also feel deeply committed to each other. They resent the fact that the church institution seems to be encouraging them to lead lives that lack integrity. Either they pretend their relationship is less important than it is and retain their employment, or they sacrifice their vocation by publicly affirming that they are lovers. In addition, Susan would risk losing her children if she was open about the relationship. They feel that they are in a 'no win' situation, with very few people to talk to about it.[15]

Usually workshop participants approach this case with great sensitivity. On one occasion, however, a group concluded that their initial confusion about how best to make sense of this situation had given way to considerable relief and clarity when they realized that since Susan was technically still married to her husband, the matter could be dealt with as a straightforward case of 'adultery'. The fact that she was in a relationship with another woman was, they said, irrelevant. Their relief came from being able to apply a church-defined, pre-packaged 'solution' to the case which freed them from dealing with the troublesome specificities of the situation.

ALISON

After my college training, I became the minister of a Baptist church in West Yorkshire, and was there for two years prior to getting married last summer.

When I began the relationship, nearly a year into my ministry, he often came to stay the night at my house. I'm pretty certain that had my average church member realized this they would have held up their hands in horror. I considered myself lucky in the sense that my house was not right on top of the church, no one from the church lived in my road, the area was sufficiently impersonal for neighbours not to be particularly bothered about what others were up to, and cars had to be parked on the other side of the road, making it difficult to tell who had visitors! This may sound comical on one level, but I know of a male colleague in the ministry who was told he must not have his girlfriend to stay the night.

I felt for much of the time that I was leading a kind of 'double life'. On the one hand I was a sexually active woman, on the other hand I'm fairly certain that the vast majority of my church members saw me as being someone who wouldn't contemplate sex before marriage. The fact that I felt it necessary to keep the sexual side of this relationship so 'furtive' is an illustration for me of a church which is sadly lacking in its ability to talk about sex and sexuality, except in the context of marriage.

ABBY

I grew up in the Methodist Church from the age of five or six, and I can't remember feeling guilty about my sexuality until I started theological training for the ministry at the age of 25. I have been sexually active, heterosexually, since I was 15. In my mind and in my emotions, I couldn't find any reason at all why sexual activity in a monogamous, committed relationship, with all contraceptive precautions taken, could possibly be incompatible with Christianity, whether legally married or not.

I suppose I lived in a garden of Eden. My first brush with what life's really like in the big bad world of the Church and sex was when I was going through the ministerial selection process. All candidates have to see a Church-appointed doctor to go over the medical they have with their own GP. The doctor I saw (a woman, incidentally) asked me if I'd recently had a smear test, and before I could give my answer 'no' in all innocence, she'd added 'Of course not, you're not married'. I inwardly caught my breath, because I suddenly realized how close I'd come to revealing myself to have been sexually active outside of marriage – and that would never have done. She would never imagine I should have a smear test, whereas what I'd been about to tell her was 'No, I haven't, but I know I ought to have one'! I'd had a close shave. I didn't encounter any sexism during my selection process, but I'm sure I would have been out on my ear if my sexual history had become apparent. It was the beginning of the rotten time I've had during my training.

This summer I'm going to marry a man I'd been going out with for six months or so before I started at theological college. We'd been sleeping together regularly before I began my training and were very happy: when I started at college, it took several weeks for things to settle down because every night I stayed at his house, I felt guilty. It took several months before he even visited college, and longer before he stayed over. There's just something about the place that says Single Students Don't – even though they do! I have never before experienced the guilt I have felt about my sexual relationships since starting at college, though I've no idea where the sense of being judged I feel comes from. It certainly doesn't come from God. It seems odd that this is so in an environment that is supposed to be helping me to grow into being a more mature, loving Christian person. My sexual relationship is an act of defiance in a way it hasn't been before. It's a way of asserting my independence and individuality in an environment that often feels like it's trying to mould me and repress me.

This summer I begin full-time work in ministry. I don't think it's entirely a coincidence that we're also getting married. I know that most churches wouldn't entertain a single woman minister having a regular male visitor overnight. The social pressures on single ministers seem enormous: I know of at least one who turns the light on in his guest bedroom every night his girlfriend stays, then switches it off an hour or so later to give the impression that that's where she's sleeping in case anyone sees! I sometimes wonder whether if I were in any other line of work, this man and I might simply move in together.

JUDITH

What I find so painful and difficult is the double standard. Recently, I've faced that duality head on. Here at theological college it has raised no eyebrows when male students have had female companions to stay in their rooms – but imagine the consternation at a female having a man in her room! Yet worse that I refused to wear sackcloth and ashes and repent of my 'behaviour'. Now that I am married, of course, I'm acceptable again. After years of painful growth and recognition of my needs as a sexual being – and a woman – I was happy in expressing my sexuality, in my way. But that was not permissible, not for a woman anyway. What affronted them most, I guess, was my refusal to be ashamed. I am quite comfortable with my sexuality and don't feel I need to hide it.

Finally, 'coming out' to my parents last Christmas was a painful experience. For days my father literally skirted around the room, to avoid being 'close' to me. My mother could only cope with seeing my then fiancé, so long as she believed he didn't know that she was aware of our sleeping together. When I later explained the difficulties at college, my parents were both negative. If I could have 'restrained' myself – retained my virginity and hence my 'purity' – there wouldn't have been a problem.

It seems that young heterosexual women undergoing theological college training have a particularly acute appreciation of the oppressive nature of Christian attitudes to sexuality. This is worth exploring further.

I have heard many stories from middle-aged clergymen about life in theological colleges before the 1960s. In many ways these single-sex institutions seemed to have resembled life at a boys' boarding school. There were to be 'no girls after lights out' (and preferably no 'girls' at all, since they served only to distract the men from their studies); boys' pranks were indulged in with alacrity; and skill at football was the major currency of respect. More than three decades of rapid social change have intervened, but it seems that the models according to which these places function have remained pretty much the same.

There have been some concessions to modernity: students of both genders are now admitted, and 'married quarters' are available. On the whole, however, there remains little (if any) official recognition that students may be engaged in significant relationships (sexual or otherwise) with people to whom they are not married and may have no intention of marrying. The expectation at the core of theological college institutions is that those training for the Christian ministry will be either married, or heterosexual and celibate (with the exception, of course, of Roman Catholic seminaries which allow only the latter). This means that many (perhaps most) students choose relational options which do not officially exist.

My own experience of facilitating discussions about sexuality in these places has brought home to me just how powerful is the denial and fear engendered by such policies. The 'communities' are often sick with the hypocrisy upon which they are founded. Yet this is hardly surprising, for theological colleges play a key role in maintaining the ecclesiastical status quo. Their purpose is 'ministerial formation'. With regard to sexuality their trainees are apparently expected to perfect the habit of placing outward appearances and the image of the Church before the best interests of those who constitute it. For many ordinands the result is misery and disillusionment.

Confronting the power of institutions

FRANCES

I met my partner when we were still at school. We've always had a relationship which, as far as possible, has been based on equality. We wrote our own wedding service, and it was all about sharing. I remember vividly when he decided to go through selection to go into the Church. I was all in favour of supporting him through it – but I was absolutely terrified. I came from a religion that you could pick up and put down, so the prospect of being married to someone who would become a priest was really daunting. When he rang up to say he'd got through, I just sat on the stairs and cried. I was horrified.

Two days after getting married we were off to theological college – going to married 'pot luck' suppers. It was horrible. We seemed to have more in common with the single men. One had been sent off for counselling because he was gay. It transpired that gay students had all been told that it was 'OK' as long as they were celibate. There were frantic parties at college, men getting desperately drunk. After the 'corporate' services that we all had to go to, there was a high speed exit to the pub! It was bizarre. You were looking around at the potential priests of the land, and a lot of them were pretty screwed up. A lot of that was due to the system, and the way that it was containing them. We objected to the way that you were either a married student, or a single student – there was no in-between. People weren't recognized as being in relationships other than that. While we were there, the girlfriend of one of the students became pregnant. He was told that they'd let him get ordained as long as they were married. So it wasn't the quality of the relationship that was important – or its meaning, or anything – it was all image. They were effectively saying that whoever you are is OK as long as nobody knows about it. That really angered me and my partner, so we tried to stand up and say something about it. We wrote to our bishop.

There was a big showdown. We were invited to go and 'discuss' our letter with him. He was a 'liberal' bishop; on the surface very 'right on', but his basic priority was not to upset the applecart. He'd got too much to lose. There was more at stake than relationships and political attitudes – it extended to status and privilege – and at the end of the day my partner was told that his services were no longer required.

It was personally very hurtful for us. We were still very naive about the power of the Church and still developing our own relationship. By that time we'd been together for five years, married for one. To the bishop, therefore, we'd only been together for one year, so we'd still got L-plates on our backs. He was very manipulative. He started saying things to me like 'you're coming across as a very angry young woman' and 'have you tried to talk about your feelings?', a style which, at that stage in the conversation, was obviously calculated to break me down. By the end of it he said that he thought we had problems in our relationship and had we considered marriage guidance! We'd gone in really together. We felt prepared, very secure with each other. We trusted each other totally, and here was somebody saying 'you've got problems, you're not communicating with each other'. He was basically saying that my partner couldn't cope with going through college and training for the priesthood.

I came out blaming myself, looking back to the day I had sat on the stairs and cried, and thinking perhaps I didn't support him enough. Ironically though, at that time I was prepared to put myself second to the Church. I'd decided that I wanted to go into teaching, but I wasn't so ardently wanting to go into teaching that I wouldn't have dropped it. I needed an identity, but I could probably have managed that by sitting in a charity shop or something.

We moved on. We still had our mutual love and our shared faith, but we felt that didn't have any legitimacy. We couldn't walk into a church building and feel we could express it, because we felt that we were out of line with the Church of England, and even that the actual building – the physical structure of it – was symbolic of all that repression.

SARAH

I was married in the Catholic Church, and so we had a marriage preparation session with the priest. For the whole session the priest looked at and spoke to my fiancé, mostly about the service, and about his obligations of raising his children in the faith because he was marrying a Protestant. The only time he looked at me and spoke to me was to say 'and you my dear, must never refuse your husband'. I thought I had misheard or misunderstood, or that maybe he was joking. Before I could overcome my surprise, he had turned back to his conversation with my husband-to-be. I found out later that he wasn't joking, and not only that, but my husband completely subscribed to the same view. If I had known the law regarding rape within marriage, I would never have married anyone. But society doesn't tell you these things. Society tells you fairytale stories about couples getting married and living happily ever after. There is never any hint of the awful truth – that there may well be sex by coercion or even rape.

The problem with institutions is that the rules by which they are structured are never made explicit. One only discovers what they are by transgressing them. That is the nature of oppression. How were Frances and her partner to know that the golden rule of their theological college was not to verbalize reality? How was Sarah to know that the golden rule of marriage was that she ceased to maintain any control over her own body? Situations that feel perfectly satisfactory can suddenly degenerate when we take a course of action that takes us across an invisible line. That invisible line represents a rule in a game which is being played by those with power over us. Sometimes the injury of oppression is compounded by the insult of those who, having had just enough access to the rule-makers to maintain their own safety, blame the victims for their naivety.

There is an additional proviso here. The rules of any institutional game are designed to serve the interests of a particular kind of person. If you are the wrong kind of person, then you are at fault. What is more, the wrong kind of person can, by definition, never win. For even if she familiarizes herself with the rules, she is likely to find that they have an uncanny tendency to change just as she gets a hold of them. This will become more obvious when we come to the section on lesbian experiences. The institution of the church tends to put clerical interests before those of the laity, and men's interests before those of women. These are the habits of governance which imbue all areas of church life, but the stories which follow focus upon three in particular: economic arrangements; the concept of privacy; and the control of information.

HEATHER

Just before our separation, when I would have to move out of the Church's property, my husband went away on a three-week sabbatical. With some bitterness, as I quite enjoyed having the house to myself, I realized that, if it were not for the Church and my husband's work within it, and the 'tied cottage' situation, this could have been the permanent situation: him moving out and me staying. As it was, I would leave home and garden and friends and neighbours and streets – and the place where my children most wanted to be.

So the next three weeks were to be a bitter playing at 'what might have been', while in reality I prepared to leave it forever. It wasn't until more than a year later that I was really able to grieve at what I'd lost then, and begin to let it go.

Meanwhile I set about cleaning everything. Inside and out. I cleaned every drawer and cupboard, every nook and cranny, as if in some way this would erase my presence, as if I wanted to leave no trace of myself. The Church has never questioned the rightness of this. And how many would really think out the 'tied cottage' situation and its implications in a case like this? Then they might have to wonder how much hidden suffering there is in clergy marriages, where partners cannot always get out because they lack the financial resources I discovered I had – and certainly not without losing the children too.

I have a wonderful feminist lawyer. She had to warn me, gently but firmly, that even though my husband would be housed and cared for by the Church for the rest of his life if he needed it, and even though I had become technically homeless, he could at any time claim maintenance from me because I earn so much more actual money than he does. I doubt if he would, but it makes you think, doesn't it?

Unlike many clergy-wives (husbands?), I had the earning power to enable me to leave my marriage without losing my children. I feel so much anger and pain for those spouses – and I was nearly one of them – who are trapped into a marriage because they would inevitably be the one to have to leave the minister in his or her large and comfortable manse. The one who leaves a clergy marriage takes no share of property, no financial or emotional support: the 'stipend' will hardly support a partner who might leave with the children, and this may be after years of practical, emotional and financial support of their ex-spouse who will stay within the caring housing bosom of the Church. There is really very little choice for a wife who leaves a minister if she has no paid work: she stays in misery or leaves without the children. In the first situation the misery would have to be covered up, as mine was; in the second she would lose everything: house, children and her 'reputation' as she 'abandons' her children.

SARAH

Once, when I had gone to see the widower of a long-standing friend, I was taken aback when he suggested that long term we might think about marriage, or, if I wasn't interested in a sexual relationship, that we might just combine households for mutual support. I wasn't so naive that I didn't realize that the second would not work once the first suggestion had been made. On returning home, our minister enquired about the visit. We were in a large room with eight other people present, one of whom was a church member. I told him very quietly what had happened, not feeling very happy about the lack of privacy of the conversation. His response, in such a loud voice that everyone in the kitchen turned around to look and listen, was 'Well, if you're going to live with a man you will have to seriously consider your position as a lay preacher, and indeed as a church member'.

I have always felt that has summed up society's view that divorcees are irresponsible, desperate for sex at any cost, reckless, have no ability to reason and, above all, have no right to privacy in their lives, but their sexual activity is up for public judgement and scrutiny.

HEATHER

My husband was on sabbatical after I had moved out, and although now living in the manse again, he was not attending his church or working with any of the people there. He forbade me to talk to anyone at the church about what I had done, except to the chosen few who already knew or whom he had told. He wanted to be able to do it in his own way when his leave was ended. I shall always regret that I took any notice of this directive at all . . . . I lost all my opportunities to be creative in my farewells, or in possible new ways of relating to people and the Church. I'd assumed that the church was his, and the people that went with it. But he'd got everything else, why leave him the goodwill and friendship of all the people too? As it was, I ended up going to church during his sabbatical, suffering folks asking me questions about his state of health and happiness, and not feeling free to tell them that I was not even living with him any more. When he began to tell a few people, it got even worse, as I never knew who they were. Later, I left the Church altogether.

By now most of the members of the church could not cope with me, any more than I could with them. Once my husband had told them in his way, they would feel duped or embarrassed anyway, as they began to think back and remember some of those impossible conversations I'd had with them. My 'contracted' silence certainly hadn't helped me. Then their need to believe in the goodness of their pastor would cut me out, particularly as I had left the family home (their manse) and now the Church, too.

The flow of information is a boundary issue involving questions of appropriateness, professionalism, confidentiality, protection, avoidance, power, control, freedom – and many others. What I have come to look for in these situations is the reason for the control of access to information. When one is asked to keep secrets or say nothing or withhold information, one should always ask 'why?', 'for the protection of whom?' This seems obvious when written down on paper like this, but my experience has not testified to this, and I have been caught up in situations where I and others have been asked to 'say nothing' when it has not been clearly or honestly stated why and for whose sake.

When my ex-husband came to tell me about his new relationship with the woman who is now his wife, he asked me to keep it secret. There was a genuine fear that this information could challenge his security in the ministry. I believed him. I had known about this relationship for some months, and had not spoken openly of it, and was not likely to change my behaviour now. But I did make it clear that I would continue to remain silent for my sake and our children's sake, and not for the sake of the Church.

The Church's motives for wishing to know, or not to know, in these situations seem not to take account of those involved most painfully in the situation. It is a demand which seems to centre around reputation; the reputation of the institution and of the individuals who serve it, mainly the clergy. The protection of or care for the family involved would have led to some care for me and my children, too, about how we might react to the information being available or not. If someone had attempted to ask about our feelings or counselled us in our situation (particularly my children) I would have felt that the boundaries were both appropriate and caring. As it was, it seemed that we were buried within the institution somewhere, our needs not considered and our silence demanded and not appreciated. And all for what?

The victims are all of us, including the Church and the clergy, when this kind of 'cover-up' is involved. Instead of a careful and caring control of information, it becomes a secrecy and cover-up where men (and it is mainly men) who demand the secrecy are infantilized and the wife and children are victims. The Church can deny what it officially doesn't know, and can avoid the care which as a mature body it should give.

SUMMARY

Christian institutions are governed by strict rules about when to speak and when to keep silent. Careful control of information is the key to this institutional power. As the stories in this chapter have demonstrated, the inappropriate divulgence of information in some situations, combined with 'cover-ups' in others, ensures the protection of those with the power – who are, of course, rarely women. The overall aim is to ensure that outward appearances accord with the ideal which the Church chooses to preach. As we have seen in this chapter, and as we will see again, ecclesiastical institutions can be as ruthless (if not more so) as secular ones when it comes to casting out those who would tell the truth.

NOTES

1. Celia Kitzinger, Sue Wilkinson and Rachel Perkins, 'Theorising heterosexuality' (Editorial introduction), *Feminism and Psychology Journal* special issue on heterosexuality, vol. 2, no. 3, October 1992. Sage Publications, London, p. 293.
2. Adrienne Rich, *Compulsory Heterosexuality and Lesbian Existence*. Onlywomen Press, London, 1981, p. 9.
3. *Presbyterians and Human Sexuality*. Office of the General Assembly, Presbyterian Church, USA, Louisville, KY, 1991, p. 2.
4. Sheila Jeffreys, 'Heterosexuality: a feminism and psychology reader', *Feminism and Psychology*, Vol. 4, no. 2, May 1994. Sage Publications, London, p. 307.
5. Adrian Thatcher, *Liberating Sex: A Christian Sexual Theology*. SPCK, London, 1993.
6. 'A problem about marriage is those who do without it', Editorial, *Church Times*, London, 5 January 1990, p. 8.
7. Elizabeth Stuart, *Daring to Speak Love's Name: A Gay and Lesbian Prayer Book*. Hamish Hamilton, London, 1992, see especially ch. 4: 'Partings', pp. 95ff.
8. 'Manse' is the Methodist equivalent of a vicarage, i.e. the church-owned home of the minister.
9. 'Ordination of Priests', in *Alternative Service Book of the Church of England*. Oxford University Press, Oxford, 1984, section 14, p. 358.
10. *Church Times*. London, 5 January 1990.
11. Rich, *Compulsory Heterosexuality*, p. 12.
12. Mary E. Hunt, *Fierce Tenderness: A Feminist Theology of Friendship*. Crossroad, New York, 1991, p. 119.
13. *Ibid.*
14. *Ibid.*
15. Alison R. Webster, *Discussing Sexuality: Workshop Resources for Christian Groups*. Institute for the Study of Christianity and Sexuality, London, 1994, p. 53.

5 sexual exploitation and violence

I recognize the potential for confusion which lies in my inclusion of a chapter on sexual abuse/violence in a book about sexuality. I am aware of the discussions about whether sexual violence is primarily an issue of sexuality or of violence. In my discussions in Part One about the age of consent and the construction of male sexuality as uncontrollable, I stressed the urgent necessity for people within the Christian community to establish clarity about sexual violence and distinguish it from 'sexual activity'. This chapter is included with that aim in mind. I have found the trenchant analysis of Marie Fortune to be invaluable in this area, not least because it is drawn from her extensive experience of working with both survivors and perpetrators of sexual violence:

> If I were to approach a good friend and reach out with my hand to touch gently that person's face, that gesture would be interpreted by the person as an act of affection and friendship. If, on the other hand, I approached that person with my hand in a fist and struck him/her on the side of the face, the gesture would be interpreted as an act of hostility and violence . . . .Likewise, in sexual activity, a man uses his penis or any other part of his body as a means of giving and receiving pleasure and affection. But in sexual violence he uses the same part of his body as a weapon to violate and assault another person. Just because he is using sexual organs in the process does not mean that his primary motivation is sexual.[1]

This has been put in a rather more direct way: 'If you hit someone over the head with a frying pan, you wouldn't call it cooking.'[2]

Nevertheless, as Marie Fortune is keen to point out: 'The sexual aspect of sexual violence is relevant. The nature of the assault makes clear the totality of the violation of the person.'[3] There are aspects of sexual violence which distinguish it from other forms of violence, and these are very much tied in with our anxieties and confusions about sex and sexuality – particularly within a religious context. Firstly, there is a taboo against talking about all things sexual. As Carol Adams points out:

> The lack of comfort in discussing a woman's physical body compounds the problem of naming [sexual violence]. We must be able to name female body parts – breast, clitoris, vagina – and to hear them named without feeling squeamish, if we are to name what has happened or hear it named.[4]

Secondly, there is a strong resistance to believing that sexual violence can happen at all within religious communities. It is a well-documented fact that sexual violence is perpetrated by people (usually men) of every religion, race, ethnicity, age, socio-economic situation and educational level. Instead of recognizing that sexual violence is endemic within the Christian community as it is elsewhere, and tackling its systemic roots, churches tend to treat sexual abuse cases as 'isolated incidents' best dealt with in secret. The belief persists within churches that being 'a good Christian' makes a man accused of sexual abuse less likely to be guilty. This was graphically illustrated recently when a psychiatrist, Dr Gordon Maden of Rawtenstall, Lancashire, was convicted of abusing many of the young men he was treating for drug dependency. According to reports in the *Guardian*, his local vicar, Revd Sam Read, was in no doubt as to his innocence. He described Dr Maden as 'a devout Christian man who couldn't possibly have done what he was accused of doing'. This abuser's Christian commitment was, for his vicar, apparently enough to outweigh the evidence of numerous young men who testified against him. And the abuser in this case is just a lay man. Imagine the force of the word of a clergyman against one young person – especially if that young person is also female.

The extent and nature of the silence which surrounds sexual violence within the Christian community can be illustrated by a couple of other examples. Some years ago a leading British opponent of the ordination of women was giving his reactions to the enthronement of Bishop Barbara Harris in the USA in an interview on the radio. He summed up her ordination as a 'rape of the church'. I recount this story not as an example of a shameful misogynistic misappropriation of the term 'rape' (although it is that); I mention it because of what happened afterwards. As a result of his interview, the priest concerned received a number of letters from women who had been raped and had met a wall of silence from the Church. To hear the words 'rape' and 'church' in the same sentence was so rare that they wrote to the only person whom they had ever heard utter them. The irony of the situation is deeply shocking.

The second example occurred in October 1993 when a service was held in Manchester Cathedral entitled 'Out of the Shadows: Women Overcoming Violence'. This was a consciously inclusive service, with no sexist language, containing prayers and readings which drew upon masculine and feminine imagery for God. A wall-hanging by Christian survivors of sexual abuse was displayed, together with a collage of 'Christa' (an image of Christ as female) which had been designed by a woman artist in remembrance of women raped by soldiers in Bosnia. Some weeks after the event a small group of Anglicans in the Manchester diocese (who were not present at the service) protested to the bishop that the event should have been banned, and that such a service should never again be allowed to happen in 'their' cathedral. There was considerable debate in the local press, which focused on the predictable issues: accusations that those who planned the service think that God is a woman; that they wish Jesus was one too; and that the event was little short of an attempted coup by militant feminists to take over the Church of England. Most interesting of all, however, was that in all but one of the press cuttings (which covered both local and national press), the *theme* of the service (overcoming violence against women – remember?) was not mentioned. For me this incident represents a typical example of the way in which attempts to name violence against women are erased from public record.

In their book *Christianity and Incest*,[5] Annie Imbens and Ineke Jonker interview women who have experienced sexual abuse perpetrated by male members of their families. Their aim is to discover what difference is made by the fact that the abuse happened within a Christian context. One of their most important conclusions is that in considering the effects of Christianity, it is the *women's experience of it* that matters, rather than any *theoretical propositions* about what Christianity is supposed to stand for. The authors also discovered that religious professionals find it extremely difficult to comprehend this apparently simple finding. Again and again, priests and pastors who read the stories of abuse responded to the women's reflections upon their experiences with comments such as: 'that's not the right way to look at forgiveness . . . ' and 'it's funny she should think of God like that . . . ' The implication of such comments is that survivors of sexual violence are wrong in their understanding of Christianity, and if they could only correct that, they would not see it as the oppressive force that many of them experience it to be.

It is a central assumption of this book that what matters in assessing the impact of Christianity upon women's lives is how they have experienced Christianity. The effect that it *could* have had in different circumstances – given, say, lots more luck, a better Sunday school teacher, parents with a sounder grasp of theology – is not important. For the impact of Christianity is felt not in the realm of the abstract and theoretical, but in concrete reality. I begin with three stories which reflect that reality.

PAULA

I have gone right back to early childhood in these last few weeks, and it has been an agony I didn't believe possible. I am here and I have survived, so there's cause for celebration. But I have one strange memory, and I have had the image for a long time but not realized. When I am especially afraid I have an image of Jesus lying with his back turned to me and weeping. At least I always thought it was Jesus. Then I realized that it was my mother. And when I knew that it was my mother I knew that at the age of two I made the momentous decision to live, to bear the suffering of the woman I most loved in the world. So bear it I did for 25 years, with a passion and a pain which tore and wrenched and writhed but would not let go.

And then suddenly at Christmas something happened which made me realize that if I was to live, not only fully, but to live at all, I must leave this pain, take no more responsibility for it. That it must cease to be mine. And, as desperate a bid for freedom as it has been, it has come about; what it has enabled me to do is to face the pain, not of the abuse of another but my own. It was terrible but ultimately the truth I had to bear.

And it was then that I understood what a powerful and dangerous force the Church and Christianity had been in my life. I left the Church on earth two years ago. I left Christianity (though not Christ) this Easter. I don't think it's coincidence. For 2,000 years we have been told to take up the cross, to bow our heads and bodies as women and take pain. Christianity is overturned with the realization that the crucified body, be it that of my mother or that of Jesus, did not need to be borne. It did not have to be. We did not have to nail our hatred through another's limbs. We could have chosen to listen, to let live. We did not. When that becomes clear the weight of the body of Christianity is heaved away. And in its place there is the fragile but immensely sure, brave knowledge that there is another way, another possibility – that we have the choice to go on hearing, delighting in and acknowledging the life of any other person's miracles, parables and wisdom, and that the end of the story is not endless pain but honesty and hope.

REBECCA

In my childhood it was made clear who the goodies and baddies were. My father was a rather high Anglican country priest, eventually a rural dean. Looking at my Christian children's picture books of the 1950s, I recall a complicated cosmos bristling with saints and angels and devils. Mary ('Our Lady') was ever-present but not particularly friendly; in prayer she had a way of acting as an over-protective receptionist who had to be dealt with first, before she decided to let you through to God, which fitted the austere, humourless expression on her statues. Satan was slate-grey with tangled hair, horns, and a striped snake's tail. Every moment of church liturgy was controlled by rules, as if the spell would unravel if the words and movements were wrong. For instance, when the first sanctuary bell was rung during Communion, I was warned that everyone covered their eyes because Jesus was there, and something terrible would happen to a little girl who peeped (I did, of course, and it didn't). All this slides into my sense of the 1950s as a time when there were rules for everything, and life was very difficult to get right. I described this somewhere else as 'tightrope-walking over the abyss'.

Somehow the old-fashioned nervous undergirding, the kind of Christianity you hold on to for fear, absolutely literally, of the Devil, attached itself to the back of my mind, so that years later, even when I thought I had splendid, rational, liberal reasons for staying in the Church, they had a superstitious, not-stepping-on-the-cracks quality. Only very recently have I realized this, and realized it not from what I consciously believe, but from dreams and sudden panics.

At some time in my early childhood (I still haven't quite remembered when) I acquired twin foster brothers who sexually abused me, and the abuse became more serious in a single incident, involving one of them, when I was eight. I was left with an almost overwhelming sense of being evil, defiled and defiling, beyond rescue. And although I can't remember a hell-fire sermon being preached to me in so many words, I knew that eternal darkness was terribly close, and had to do with the demons I saw creeping out of the shadows and whispering in my ear. Outside certain evangelical quarters, Christians don't, fortunately, invade children's brains with these particular nightmares as they used to. The feeling was compounded as I approached my teens (with a passionate desire, though by then I'd forgotten where it came from, to avoid being a teenager if at all possible). I found myself compulsively reading horror stories and books about medieval witchcraft – suggested for a school project, for some reason. In Margaret Murray (*The Witch Cult in Western Europe*) I homed in on the sections of 'confession' narratives which described sex with the Devil, convinced that whatever her theories about them, I knew them to be literally true. All that was left for me to work out was whether I had sold my soul already, in some dream around the corner of my memory, or whether I still had a chance to outsmart Satan.

I can't pick out from all this how much was the intensity that always goes with being 13, how much was the product of abuse, and how much was Anglo-Catholicism's 'fault', but clearly the Church hadn't helped. Once I grew a bit older I forgot that I had panicked about evil in this way, but the panic just bubbled down inside me.

LINDA

In 1983 Linda was sexually assaulted at her place of work. Four years later, she wrote this poem.

Four Years On – What's Left?

Filthy invasion,
Into my secret place,
Pain wrecks me, even now
At the memory.
Violence
Naked in your eyes;
Sex
The instrument at your hands.

Oh God, why have you forsaken me?
At this moment where are you?
Did Christ know this pain?
This ultimate degradation?
How could he, a man,
Feel this?

Hate burns in me
Against the aggressor.
I see his hands in my sleep;
I feel the burning sense of shame
At each memory, each recall.

'Only a minor assault'

Yeah, sure,
A bit of an upset to a manager's day.
It's taken *four* years!
Four years to come this far,
To be this much 'better';
Four years of fear,
Scared of letting down the barriers that lead to the real me
The me in pain,
The child woman, crying for my mother
Wishing to be whole,
Clean,
Free.

He didn't reserve the fear to the night,
No
Broad daylight – the time;
Familiar ground – the venue,
Beer the excuse.
Excuse! Hell
I want reasons
Reasons for spending months trying to prove I'm not frigid.
I want reasons for the hate building up,
The bitterness, eating my insides out.
I want to know if I can really love a man,
Give myself
To the love 'of my life'.
Night heightens fear
Yet, I look over my shoulder day and night;
Watching alleys and gates
Turning shadows into rapists
And the sound of the wind into howls.
Confidence ran from me.
I am aware that I'm no longer in control.

My body is my own,
Yet, what respect can others give it
Now that he has corrupted it?
To the extent that I have little respect for it also.
My place in Creation
Is as vital as that of each being,
Yet, I feel lower than the worm,

Worms can't be assaulted
Unless,
It's by being cut.
I've been cut
Into tiny pieces
Put together with one missing.

On the outside
It's okay, my life
Getting on well
Popular
Yet, men don't stay long.
Is it because
I'm bright and capable?
Or
Is it that I bite?
Or
Is it, perhaps
That I've so many walls around me
That somewhere behind them all
The real me
Got up and went away,
Just leaving the walls,
Just leaving the smiles;
Polite hellos,
Tearful goodbyes
And ice-cold showers of fear?
The real me
Got up, went away
And sits
Watching and crying,
Waiting for the walls to fall down,
And the truth to be revealed –
That there's no one there anymore.

What I remember distinctly about the time of the assault was feeling unable to tell anyone at church. The minister, the youth leader, the Junior Church Leader (the obvious people to go to perhaps) were all men. I doubt I would have gone to them even had they been women. Somehow the guilt associated with what had happened and the embarrassment of telling the story was not something I could get through. I remember compartmentalizing my life.

Church was one part, work another and family life yet another. I did not tell my family about what had happened for six months, and even then it came out in an argument (not a constructive approach). Inside I was a total mess and on the days when I let myself think about anything more than surviving the next 24 hours, I found myself resenting the church more and more.

Someone once said to me, very piously, that Jesus had experienced every possible form of suffering so that Christians did not have to suffer alone. This was to me clearly untrue. This, combined with constant reminders that the Christian thing to do is to forgive, left me feeling that I was losing my faith as well as my identity (and even sanity). Forgiveness is something which can come across as a magic wand waved and everything will be all right. This denies the incredible cost and struggle involved in forgiving someone who has invaded our lives in a way that is never 100 per cent resolved. Over the intervening years I have achieved some sort of ability to forgive the man, but it has been harder to forgive the church.

It cannot be proved that it was because of Christianity's teaching about the value of vicarious suffering that Paula dealt with her childhood abuse in the way that she did. But such messages had a significant impact, as she readily identifies. After all, Jesus Christ took on the pain of the world through his crucifixion, and Christians are taught to follow his example in order to gain salvation. Theologians Joanne Carlson Brown and Rebecca Parker point out the potentially damaging implications of Christian theology in their essay 'For God so loved the world':

> The central image of Christ on the cross as the savior of the world communicates the message that suffering is redemptive. If the best person who ever lived gave his life for others, then, to be of value we should likewise sacrifice ourselves ... Our suffering for others will save the world. The message is complicated further by the theology that says Christ suffered in obedience to his Father's will. Divine child abuse is paraded as salvific and the child who suffers 'without even a word' is lauded as the hope of the world.[6]

This is not to say that no woman who has suffered sexual violence has ever found Christianity to be helpful. That is clearly not the case, for some women do find the Jesus story to be liberating. But the experiences of women who find that their abuse is compounded by aspects of Christian doctrine raise important questions about both the theology and practice of Christianity. The emphasis in the Christian tradition upon finding meaning in suffering encourages us to search for a divine purpose in what is actually human criminal activity. This in turn switches the interrogative focus away from the perpetrator to those who have been violated, for whom the abuse can appear as some kind of divine punishment for past sins. It is not unknown, incidentally, for priests to direct survivors of abuse to confession for their 'sin', while granting the abuser instant forgiveness.

Paula is liberated from some of the pain of her abuse when she is liberated from Christianity. Her story provides a powerful challenge to the seldom-questioned self-abnegation which Christianity recommends. Her experience also reveals the gender-specific nature of certain Christian teachings. Why is it that women are encouraged to embrace the drudgery of the menial tasks which keep churches afloat, while men aspire to the privilege and finery of the bishop or the cardinal? In Part One we observed Jeanette Howard's call to women to locate and embrace their 'gentle and quiet spirit',[7] while allowing men to take up all the leadership roles. It seems that it is not so much that the content of the message is different for men and women, but rather that the same teaching has very different gender-specific implications.

A possible explanation for this has been proffered by feminist theologians as part of their exploration of the origins of certain Christian teachings. In short, they have identified that theology was devised by men to overcome men's problems. Since men are more likely to think too much of themselves than too little, the theological emphasis has been on overcoming pride and self-importance. Self-abnegation and self-sacrifice taught in this context is somewhat different from its existential enactment in the lives of women survivors of violence. Daphne Hampson has outlined this point as part of her assessment of the Christian ethicist Reinhold Niebuhr:

> For Niebuhr ... conversion consists in the breaking of an egotistical self. Quoting Paul he writes: 'the sinful self, the self which is centred in itself must be "crucified" ... shattered at the very centre of its being.' ... The question is whether such an analysis is appropriate to women's situation. If women have not on the whole suffered from an egotistical self, if they have not been in a position to dominate others, then such a prescription is beside the point. Rather than breaking the self, women, it may be suggested, need to come to themselves.[8]

This observation is borne out by Imbens and Jonker, who discovered that not one of the women interviewed for *Christianity and Incest* had applied to their own situation the second half of the commandment to 'love your neighbour' – that, is, 'as yourself'. What they had understood was more akin to 'love your neighbour, not yourself'.

Forgiveness

REBECCA

> History intervened in my life again, by throwing me into grief. My lover was killed, and killed violently. She was not in fact part of my life for that long – a few months, and the relationship wouldn't have lasted many months more – but the waste of her, aged 27, the suddenness of her death, and the fact that I knew her killer, all flung me completely into what felt like a kind of madness. It took years to pick through the effects of this and to put my life back together, as it does with grief, but one of the urgent themes for me was forgiveness. I struggled with feelings for the man responsible, knowing that Christian friends expected me, through some miracle of prayer, to do something called forgiving him. I also knew that I had to let go of hating him for my own sake, but that was a different process; I wanted him out of my way, but real forgiveness, giving him something, was ridiculous then, beyond me, and beyond any relationship with 'God' that seemed to make sense. Some part of me decided (again) that I was beyond the pale, cut off from my own spirituality by this conundrum.

Very much tied in with the Christian ideal of self-abnegation and self-sacrifice is the concept of forgiveness. In my experience this is one of the most important issues for women recovering from violence. Linda speaks of the pressure she felt to forgive, and the impression that what was being asked was inappropriate, if not impossible. There are important institutional issues involved here. As Marie Fortune puts it, the phrase 'forgive and forget' often really means 'you must forgive so that we can forget'.[9] This is rarely the explicit agenda; other rationalizations are usually in evidence. For instance, women are often treated to lectures on how they should forgive 'for their own good'.

As Rebecca's story illustrates, women, of all people, are aware that prolonged anger, bitterness and hatred may not be the best use of their energy. The problem is that the construction of Christian femininity rules out any expression of anger by women. At best, women are allowed to be angry for a finite and externally defined period. Once that period is over, if women continue to show their anger, they are deemed to be insane, unchristian/unforgiving (the two are often equivalent in this context) or deliberately obtuse. What is needed is an affirmation that women's rage is legitimate, and a vision as to how it can be constructive. The work of Mary Daly is instructive here. Under a heading 'The Virtue of Rage', she says:

> It became clear to me that Woman-identified Rage is not simply a feeling, and it is not negative. This Rage on behalf of women is not mere anger. It is a Passion and a Wicked Virtue which, when unleashed, enables Furies to sever our Selves from the State of Severance, breathe Fire, and fly into freedom. As I wrote in *Pure Lust*:
>
>> Rage is not 'a stage'. It is not something to be gotten over. It is a transformative, focusing Force.[10]

Of course, the transformative Rage which Daly describes, once unleashed, would demolish the political systems which have institutionalized male violence. It is hardly surprising, then, that the churches would prefer women to turn our anger inwards, thus destroying ourselves.

Rebecca's story also shows how the call to forgive can have the devastating effect of cutting women off from their spirituality and religious community. Through the imposition of a demand which women feel unable to meet, the community that promised unconditional support ultimately colludes with the abuser. This is done whenever forgiveness is portrayed as something which an individual must 'do', or grant, irrespective of the attitude of the offender and any action by the community to elicit restitution.[11]

Pulpit power

HELEN

> Peter was my minister, and I developed a friendship with him over the years he was working here. Time and time again during this relationship we decided to finish it, usually at my instigation. It started at his instigation – mutual instigation, I suppose – but he was the one who declared how much he loved me first. I was still married throughout those eight years – I'm still married now, though my husband and I have been separated for the last two years.
>
> When Peter moved to Liverpool, which was three years ago, it was going to be all over. All along, during this time, he had maintained that he wasn't going to break up his family. But he came back. He moved in August, but by the October he was back again.
>
> I don't know how my husband never noticed before, but in the summer when Peter told me he was going to Liverpool I was so distraught that he couldn't help but notice. I told him what had happened and he said that if I

couldn't say that I loved him more than I loved Peter, he didn't want the marriage to continue. I couldn't say that. I'm not sure that I could say that now because although we have a reasonably amicable relationship, I don't love him like I loved Peter. So my husband and I separated in October, just before Peter came back.

Soon Peter was coming every day to visit. I was in hospital and he came every day – we spent hours on the phone. I don't know how we got away with it, to be honest, or when he did his work. Soon he decided that he couldn't carry on this double life any longer and was going to leave his wife and possibly leave the Church, and move in with us. And we were working towards that.

He went to marriage guidance, not to rebuild his marriage, but as a way of telling his wife that he was leaving her. The idea was that the marriage guidance would reveal that the marriage was over and there was nothing left. Then he could say that it was her decision. He wanted her to say that they had nothing left. He wasn't going to tell her.

He said, though, that he wanted to sort out Christmas, and he couldn't leave his job before then because he had all these things to sort out and he couldn't just walk out and leave people in a mess. In the intervening time he was going to go through a proper separation process with Jo, his wife. We had dreadful fights because I could see that he wasn't doing that separating. I used to say to him 'Look, I can see that you're not doing what you said you were going to do'. And he'd say that I just didn't trust him and that I was being manipulative.

Christmas came and Christmas went. In March he went off on retreat. He came back and said 'I just can't do it'. He said he didn't have the courage to make the break and he didn't feel he could face losing his career and his family. And I can understand all that in my head – but it seemed to me to delete all that had gone before, because I felt used. He'd found his sexuality (his marriage had never been consummated, and he'd only learned to ejaculate in the last two years, with me). He'd found wholeness himself – and I was left to fend for myself.

It was therefore supposedly all over again. But then, on my birthday (in August) I was sent anonymous flowers and it all started up again. Not the same intensity – but the letter writing and the communication – we were back in touch. He said he couldn't come to see me because if he did he'd be 'weakened' – and anyway, his wife wouldn't let him.

So it was reduced to letter writing. Then at Christmas – a really awful Christmas for our family – it came to my attention that Jo had sent out letters saying how wonderful things were in Liverpool, and how happy they were together. I just flipped. I picked up the phone on Christmas Eve, and I gave him what for. I'm not ashamed of what I did. I said 'I and my family are living in sheer hell, and you're sending out letters about how happy you are – and you've done this to us'. I harangued him. And I phoned him again the next day and harangued him again, because it was just awful. I still think I was perfectly justified, but the retired chairman[12] who was supposed to be helping us find a solution to all this, came down on me like a ton of bricks. 'How dare you?', he said. 'How dare you interfere with this man's Christmas? What are you doing? The man's told you he doesn't want anything more to do with you ...' But when? When had he said that?

I'm actually managing to talk about it now without totally breaking down, but it's still painful. He still intrudes in my life. Recently, I went to a conference and had a brilliant time. I thought to myself that this was somewhere that I could enjoy being with like-minded people. Then they announced the theme of next year's conference, and I immediately realized that because Peter has expertise in that theme, he will be there – so I won't be able to go. The retired chairman I mentioned earlier said to me 'I've told Peter that he's not to look over his shoulder, he's to go about his ministry as though this door is now closed and I'm telling you the same. You've got to pretend this chapter of your life has never existed.' But how can I do that? You think you've found a safe space but then it's usurped. There isn't a safe space, particularly in Methodism, which is so small, and it means I now have to deny the things which brought us together: my interest in interfaith issues; liberation theology; radical theology, etc.

A lot of the pain was that he went off to Liverpool and he's left me to deal with everything here. A few people now know about our relationship, but at the time only one person knew. That's been an enormous burden to carry for the last eight years, and I'm still left to carry it now. He was a well-loved and well-respected man. There are one or two people I've talked to in the church; one woman kept bringing up his name so I felt I had to tell her. She was devastated because she felt he was a very fine chap.

I'm left with all the old associations, trying to rebuild my life. He used to get very angry when he found out that I'd told people, but I had to tell people because I was on my own. At least he had some kind of marriage for mutual support. He used to say things like 'Well, if you tell people it will backfire on you'. There's an element of truth in that, of course, because he has got the power, the authority, the credibility; people will look at me and say it was my fault.

Throughout the relationship Peter was someone I trusted implicitly and believed in, and respected as a minister. So what he said was right. I can see now that I was denying all that I was feeling and believing, because every time I challenged him he would put me down. I wasn't confident enough in what I was saying to know that I was being put down – so he was still in a powerful position and he rubbished me. When we were in our letter-writing stage I was writing him what I now consider to be brilliant pastoral letters, but he would say that I was talking a load of rubbish. I can see now that I was the only one facing up to the reality of the situation. I do still wonder how on earth he lives with himself, what sort of marriage he's created. And I think of him going about, pretending everything is all right, getting up in the pulpit and preaching his gospel of love, when all the time there's a decimated family back here.

In making sense of Helen's story I would like to refer to an article which appeared in the *Church Times* in 1990.[13] Apparently, a woman known as 'N' had written a letter to that paper asking the following question: 'What should a clergyman's wife do when she realizes that her husband is a persistent adulterer?' As the article points out, the usual sources of help in distress are barred to the wife in such a case, because 'those sources are her husband's bosses'. 'N' is left asking herself whether she should leave him: '"I've offered to leave", she says, "but he asks me to stay, and anyway, where would I go?" There are children. She still loves her husband. He wants to continue in his ministry.'

What is interesting about this article is, firstly, that those with whom the clergyman is said to have 'adulterous relationships' receive little attention except to be written off by comments like this one: ' "the Church attracts lonely, unhappy women who easily confuse their love of God with their love for their vicar".' At the same time, 'N' remains the focus of speculation throughout, rather than her husband. ' "We don't actually know", says one commentator, Mrs Baughen, "whether all this has become exaggerated in her mind." ' And a bishop, reflecting on the case, apparently pointed out that: 'there could be no hard evidence of adultery without the man's own confession or the accusations of the women with whom he had been misbehaving. "All we know is that he goes sweet on some silly women, but the extent of the misconduct . . . that might be in her own mind." '

Helen's suspicions about what would have happened to her had she 'told all' would seem to be more than borne out by this article. The implication is that those with whom priests 'commit adultery' are members of their churches. That's why I have, throughout, used inverted commas around the phrase. What such a priest has really committed is an act of gross professional misconduct akin to a doctor sleeping with a patient or a counsellor sleeping with a client. The difference, of course, is that churches have no clear guidelines which stipulate that such behaviour *is* misconduct. In presenting this behaviour as adultery, the focus is shifted from professional standards to the moral standards of the individual priest. This is a clever way of absolving the church as an institution from the responsibility which it should be shouldering, while at the same time forcing a priest's wife (if he has one) to take responsibility which is in no way hers. If sleeping with a parishioner is an act of professional abuse, then whether or not the priest is married is beside the point when it comes to assessing his behaviour *as a professional.* I am not saying, of course, that his unethical behaviour towards his wife should be overlooked, or that she herself is unimportant – just that in terms of his professional future his abuse of a parishioner should be the focus. Indeed. proper pastoral care for the offending priest's wife is only possible if it is clear that she is in no way to blame for his behaviour – an awareness that is sadly lacking if the *Church Times* article is anything to go by.

It would seem that such professional misconduct is by no means uncommon. A survey conducted in 1984 of ministers in the USA[14] found that 38.6 per cent had had sexual contact with a church member; 12.7 per cent had had sexual intercourse with a church member; and 76.5 per cent knew of a minister who had had sexual intercourse with a church member. The middle figure should be compared with a similar survey of therapists, 5.5 per cent of whom had had sexual intercourse with a client.[15]

Some clergy have a lot of trouble with the use of the term 'abuse' to describe what they would prefer to call relationships with members of their congregations. Often this is because they do not fully grasp the power which they wield within the Christian community. If it is true that, as 'N' puts it, 'women . . . confuse their love of God with love for their vicar', then this is hardly surprising given that the church bases its whole theology of ministry on just such a confusion. The ordination of women debate within the Church of England was in large part a discussion of whether women were capable of 'representing Christ to the people' in their work and in their celebration of the Eucharist. Clergy often want to have it both ways. They want to 'represent God', but they also (sometimes) want to be everybody's friend. The most radical want to 'share their power' and conduct egalitarian ministries – which is all well and good as long as they realize that at the end of the day they are paid and housed by the church institution, and their congregants are not. They are paid to do a job, and with that job goes authority, power and the responsibility for maintaining appropriate boundaries between themselves and those in their care. If they want to give such power away, the only way they can really do so is to give up their jobs. But as the *Church Times* article shows, that's not usually what abusive clergy have in mind.

There will be those who consider that Helen entered into the 'relationship' with Peter of her own free will as 'a consenting adult'. In her consideration of abuse by ministers, Marie Fortune offers a powerful counter to such an argument through her development of the concept of 'meaningful consent':

> Meaningful consent to sexual activity requires a context not merely of choice, but of equality; hence meaningful consent requires the absence of any constraint or even the most subtle coercion. When there is an imbalance of power between two persons arising out of role differences, there is no real equality. There is always some imbalance of power and thus inequality between a minister and those whom he/she serves or supervises. Even in the relationship between two persons who see themselves as 'consenting adults', the difference in role (and usually other factors as well) precludes the possibility of meaningful consent.[16]

In Chapter Four I suggested that the rules which govern institutions are discovered only in retrospect, after one has transgressed them. Similarly, it was Helen's experience that the power available to a clergyman is often not obvious until it is being used against you. Only then does one discover that he has the power as a 'man of God' to define the situation, together with the likely support of male colleagues and superiors who may well feel, 'there but for the grace of God . . .'.

Sexual harassment of female clergy

Interesting questions arise when we consider the case of female ministers. Where are they to be located in the hierarchical scheme of things?

LIZ

> Over the years, I came to respect one of our church members greatly. He seemed to be pastorally sensitive and supportive. He often noticed things others didn't. But once or twice, I felt uncomfortable about comments, his body language or gesture, but put it down to accident, or him not meaning it to have the interpretation that came over. Then came the bombshell. One day he left messages to say he needed to see me urgently. When I met with

him he fired a barrage of very personal questions at me, and then made a series of very fanciful and fantasized intimate observations about me. He then went on to suggest that he could solve my imagined intimate problems and would 'put some physical loving back in my life'. He proposed we meet somewhere!

I was so taken by surprise by this terrible turn of events. He had been someone, I thought, to whom I could reveal some of the pain of ministry. Instead, he had suddenly abused this trust and admittance of vulnerability to get his foot in the 'sexual door', so to speak. I felt betrayed, exploited, and used. I felt angry with myself for misreading the man and his intentions, and for ever having trusted him to start with. I was also seized with immediate panic. Having rejected his overtures, how would he respond? Would he make trouble? What if his wife found out what he had suggested? Who should I tell? Would anyone believe me?

In the event, I shared what had happened with my immediate colleagues. Steps were taken to make sure I wasn't ever left in a position where I would be alone with this man. It turned out this was not the first time this person's behaviour had been questioned. He responded by publicly belittling anything I said after the event.

The questions with which Non-conformist women ministers have struggled for decades will perhaps gain a higher profile now that the Church of England has begun to ordain women too. For instance, is it safe for a woman minister to see male parishioners in her home, alone? Or for her phone number to be permanently displayed on the church notice board? What level of harassment will she have to put up with from her male colleagues? How can she complain about such colleagues when her bosses are all male and may have accepted her only under sufferance in the first place? What if sexual harassment by her colleagues, superiors or church members impairs her ministry? To whom can she go? Outside help is impossible, for the Church is exempt from equal opportunities legislation. Remember that the Church of England is a denomination where declaring that women priests are 'bitches' who should be burned earns you nothing worse than the opportunity to be 'famous for 15 minutes' via an interview on Radio 4.

In this context the importance of the sexuality aspect of sexual violence is particularly striking. The problems which men have in encountering women's sexuality played an important role in Anglican opposition to women priests. All the more important, in fact, because it was rarely expressed openly. There were mumblings about the horror of pregnant or menstruating women celebrating the Eucharist (thereby defiling its asexual disembodied purity with evidence of their own bodiliness and sexual activity). There was also the celebrated occasion when Graham Leonard (then Anglican Bishop of London, now a Roman Catholic priest) admitted that an element of his own resistance to women priests involved his expectation that if a woman were with him in the sanctuary, he would be tempted to 'take her in his arms'. Carol Adams offers an analysis which is particularly pertinent to the sexual harassment of female clergy:

> We see a trend in pastoral care these days to focus on sexual harassment and sexual abuse as 'the abuse of power'. MacKinnon's explanation of the problem with this renaming and refocusing is extremely helpful:
> 'The way the analysis of sexual harassment is sometimes expressed now (and it bothers me) is that it is an abuse of power, not sexuality. This does not allow us to pursue whether sexuality, as socially constructed in our society through gender roles, is *itself* a power structure . . . . It seems to me that we haven't talked very much about gender as a hierarchy, as a division of power, in the way that's expressed and acted out, primarily I think sexually. And therefore we haven't expanded the definition according to women's experience of sexuality, including our own sexual intimidation, of what things are sexual in this world.'[17]

In other words, as I tried to say at the beginning of this chapter, we misunderstand sexual violence and harassment if we construe it as primarily an abuse of power and downplay the difference which sexuality makes. What the sexual harassment of women clergy highlights about sexual violence against women in general is that sexuality cannot be isolated and removed from the equation. Sexuality is inextricably linked with power. Women have been constructed in the Christian tradition as the embodiment of all that is earthy and sexual (and therefore evil); this is the rationale for our subjugation by men, and violence against us is a symptom of our subjugation.

The overarching question that remains for women clergy is whether, in an atmosphere of potential hostility, women will be allowed to articulate what is specific about their work situations in contrast to those of their male colleagues. Will this be possible, or will 'equality' in this case (as in the secular workplace) mean playing by the rules of male normativity? Will the specific needs of women for protection from male violence be treated as 'special privileges' or a sign of weakness, to be blamed on the women themselves, rather than upon the men who make work an unsafe place? We watch and wait, working for the safety of women in the meantime.

NOTES

1. Marie Marshall Fortune, *Sexual Violence, the Unmentionable Sin: An Ethical and Pastoral Perspective*. The Pilgrim Press, Cleveland, OH, 1983, pp. 16–17.
2. Carol J. Adams, 'Naming, denial and sexual violence', *Miriam's Song* V (newsletter of Priests for Equality, USA). Priests for Equality, USA, West Hyattsville, MD, p. 21.
3. Fortune, *Sexual Violence*, p. 6.
4. Adams, 'Naming, denial and sexual violence', p. 19.
5. Annie Imbens and Ineke Jonker, *Christianity and Incest*. Burns and Oates, London, 1992.
6. Joanne Carlson Brown and Rebecca Parker, 'For God so loved the world', in Joanne Carlson Brown and Carole R. Bohn (eds) *Christianity, Patriarchy and Abuse*. The Pilgrim Press, Cleveland, OH, 1989, p. 2.
7. Jeanette Howard, *Out of Egypt: Leaving Lesbianism Behind*. Monarch Publications, Eastbourne, 1991, p. 191.
8. Daphne Hampson, *Theology and Feminism*. Basil Blackwell, Oxford, 1990, p. 127.
9. Marie Fortune, workshop on 'Forgiveness, the last step', at 'Called to Make Justice', bi-national meeting of workers to prevent sexual and domestic violence, Chicago, 2–5 May 1993.
10. Mary Daly, *Outercourse: The Be-Dazzling Voyage*. The Women's Press, London, 1993, pp. 196–7.
11. For a full exploration of the issues of forgiveness, see Marie Marshall Fortune, 'Forgiveness, the last step', in *Violence in the Family: A Workshop Curriculum for Clergy and Other Helpers*. The Pilgrim Press, Cleveland, OH, 1991, pp. 173ff.
12. In Methodism, a Chairman of a District is an approximate equivalent of an Anglican diocesan bishop.
13. *Church Times*, London, 19 January 1990.
14. Richard Allen Blackmon, 'The hazards of the ministry', unpublished PhD dissertation, 1984, Fuller Theological Seminary, quoted in *Clergy Misconduct: Sexual Abuse in the Ministerial Relationship*. Center for the Prevention of Sexual and Domestic Violence, Seattle, USA, 1992, Overhead 1-G.
15. Holroyd and Brodsky, 1977, cited by Blackmon, 'Hazards of the ministry'.

16. Fortune, *Sexual Violence*, p. 48.
17. Carol J. Adams, quoting Catharine MacKinnon in 'Towards a feminist theology of religion and the state', *Theology and Sexuality Journal*, edition 2, Sheffield Academic Press, March 1995.

6 experiences of being lesbian

Introduction

Lesbians are all but invisible in the Christian community. As in secular law, lesbians are included in Church pronouncements about 'homosexuality' (i.e. pronouncements about gay men), but by implication only. Explicit mention of our lives or our experience is rare. This poses a dilemma. Is it advisable for lesbians to protest about this denial of our ontological status, or is it better to leave well alone? The likely outcome of the former is that the religious authorities would respond by affirming that lesbian sexuality is as disgusting as any other form of 'homosexuality' – they'd just forgotten to say so. Might it not, therefore, be better for lesbians to embrace the 'freedom' that such invisibility creates and be satisfied?

The assumption that invisibility creates freedom requires further exploration. In undertaking this, let us begin with one of the rare occasions when the specificities of lesbian experience have been recognized by a denominational body. In the late 1980s a small group chaired by Revd June Osborne was given the task of drawing up a report on human sexuality for that church's House of Bishops. This report was never published (perhaps because it was too liberal, although the bishops maintain it was never meant to be a public document). Its leakage to the press earned it significant public attention, and it became known as the Osborne Report. It said this:

> One of the powerful forces in the background of homosexual lifestyles
> concerns the experiences people have of male/female power relationships in
> society. This is particularly evident in the background of lesbianism in our
> society. The poor experience some women have had in relation to the way

men exercise power in society and its institutions, including marriage, has been a contributory factor in the way the women's movement has developed in our own time. Many women look to community with other women as a way of preserving a sense of dignity and developing an alternative identity in the face of the way society functions on the basis of male power and perceptions. For some this leads to the rejection of community with men and an affirmation of sexual relationships with other women. In other words an inability in society to strike a co-operative and mutually affirmative culture between women and men in the way it is organized renders some women unable to experience a sense of mutuality and interdependence in personal relationships. The Church ought not to consider the questions raised by lesbian experience in isolation from the wider social issues. Neither ought it to consider how to respond to lesbian lifestyles and choices in the Church without considering its own social culture of male/female power relationships in the Church.[1]

One might almost congratulate the authors of this report for their recognition that some women enter lesbian relationships as a feminist reaction to the in-built power differences between men and women in our society. Their suggestion that such injustices are replicated in the church is also to be welcomed. What comes next in the report, however, demonstrates the partial nature of their understanding: 'There are connecting themes here with male homosexuality. A poor social experience of women at crucial developmental stages of growth can contribute to men moving into lifestyles which involve a positive rejection of women.'[2] This is, of course, a highly questionable psychological theory of the roots of male homosexuality which hints that the mothers of gay men are ultimately 'to blame' for their sexuality. Might it not be equally likely that bad experiences of women in childhood attract men to heterosexual relationships through which they can then punish women with little interference from the rest of society? The real point to be made here, however, is that a false equivalence is drawn between the psychological problems of *individual men* and the structural social and political inequality experienced by *women as a class*. This confirms my suspicion that the authors of the report have, at best, only a partial understanding of lesbianism as a tool for subverting hetero-patriarchy.

Hints of its limitations are evident in the first paragraph quoted, when lesbians are presented as women who are *unable* to experience mutuality and interdependence in heterosexual relationships, rather than as women who are *unwilling* to devote a vast amount of emotional energy to this task while unjust social structures ensure that they are attempting the impossible. The tenor of the Osborne Report is that lesbianism is a cosy refuge for the damaged, neurotic and unfortunate victims of patriarchy – a negative avoidance tactic for those who cannot cope with the world as it is.

If this sounds like rather a harsh assessment, the reader should be aware that the report gives no significant attention to themes which one might expect them to focus upon had they truly appreciated the lesbian feminist critique of structural sexism. There is no discussion, for instance, of the construction of heterosexist masculinity and of Christianity's significant contribution towards it. There is no attempt to explain how it is that nine out of ten women do not embrace lesbianism as one might expect in the light of their theory of its origin. Anyway, their attempt to get to grips with the complex nature of lesbian sexuality turns out to be a one-off, for the report immediately reverts to gender-neutral language in its treatment of gay and lesbian sexuality. Under the heading 'Homosexual people' we find the following: 'So often the choices seem to be between loneliness and the risks of casual clandestine relief and living in what the Church sees as sin but is experienced as companionship and love.'[3]

The report demonstrates, as it happens, something of a preoccupation with the concept of 'casual clandestine relief'. Leaving aside the question of to what extent lesbian women adopt casual and anonymous sexual encounters as part of their lifestyle, there is a perception among churchmen that gay men do nothing else (and a fascination with what that might be like). We can safely assume, therefore, that lesbian experience is not at the forefront of their minds when they pursue such discussions.

This brief foray into lesbianism by the Anglican working group helps us to appreciate just some of the misconceptions which are at work in what we usually experience as silence. This mixture of the misapplication of gay male experience, half-baked psychologizing and partial appreciation of the links between sexuality and gender forms the context within which lesbians experience Christianity. Its effects upon women's lives will be demonstrated later.

Another ecclesiastical example will help us to explore further what lies behind the church's silence about lesbians. In January 1994 the Central Committee of the World Council of Churches (WCC) met in Johannesburg, South Africa. Because the WCC had worked unstintingly to combat apartheid, this meeting was something of a celebration since it met in the run-up to the first post-apartheid elections there. The WCC is, in fact, renowned for its justice-making work on many fronts. Readers will gain some idea of its ethos if I say that the Archdeacon of York, George Austin (the media-recognized source of 'the conservative Christian viewpoint'), seems to take exception to most of its pronouncements. What happened at this particular meeting of the WCC is therefore all the more interesting. The following snippets from the daily press releases tell the story:

> 22 January 1994.
>
> Churches should own up to the violence against women committed by those within their own organizations, Melvin Talbot of San Francisco, a bishop of the United Methodist Church, told the World Council of Churches today.
>
> His call for churches to own up to the problem [of violence against women] was greeted with loud applause by many members of the Central Committee . . .
>
> Paul Sherry, a minister in the United Church of Christ in Cleveland, USA, said that he hoped the Central Committee would take up the issue of violence against lesbian women, which was occurring around the world.[4]

So far so good.

> 28 January 1994.
>
> Following a lengthy discussion the WCC Central Committee approved a recommendation . . . to establish a WCC 'Programme to overcome violence'
> . . .
>
> The recommendation . . . broadens the scope of decisions taken by the Central Committee at its previous meeting (August 1992), when it affirmed 'active non-violent action' as a clear emphasis for the WCC and asked for study and reflection on the extent to which fellowship in the WCC, 'is called into question when churches fail to categorically condemn any systematic violation of human rights' in their country.[5]

Later in the press release of the same day we find the following:

> A heated debate was sparked by one sentence in the latter section of [a report]. It said, 'Issues of violence against lesbian women and differently abled women should be of special focus' in the WCC's work on violence against women – one of the priorities of the Ecumenical Decade of Churches in Solidarity with Women. A proposal by Georges Tsetsis (Ecumenical Patriarchate) to delete the sentence was narrowly defeated (43–44, with 4 abstaining).

But several subsequent speakers expressed concern that the specific mention of lesbian women implied – or might be interpreted as – approval of their sexual practice, despite the insistence by Unit III committee moderator ... and several others that what was being addressed was only the need to protect these women from violence and to heal those who have been its victims. Moreover ... the text before the Central Committee was only a report of the discussion in the Unit III committee which did not call for action or endorsement.[6]

In a final 'round-up' press release, also dated 28 January, the issue arises again:

Alluding to the Committee's intense debate of a call in the Unit III committee report for special focus on 'violence against lesbian women' Raiser [General Secretary of the WCC] spoke of 'deep divisions within this Central Committee and among member churches about the theological and ethical issues of human sexuality and sexual orientation'. Since he sees it as his responsibility to make 'every effort to maintain our fellowship in the face of sharp differences of conviction and to manifest pastoral sensitivity', he asked all 'to refrain from urging the WCC to take positions on this issue, for which we are not responsibly prepared'.[7]

This account of the WCC's discussions reveals it to be a body which boasts advocacy of non-violent active resistance against economic and political oppression and at least a residual awareness of gender violence. Unless the 'loud applause' which met the call to combat the latter was for nothing, was it not disingenuous for Raiser to claim that the WCC is 'not responsibly prepared' to resist violence against lesbian women? Or are we to conclude that such violence does not fall under the category of a human rights violation; or, alternatively, that lesbians are not human? Or perhaps we have forfeited our human rights by adopting lifestyles which some Christians cannot understand or affirm.

To give Raiser the benefit of the doubt, he may have meant that members of the WCC should refrain from urging the Council to take a clear position in the future on *lesbian and gay sexuality itself*. This would be in line with the 'liberal' Christian position that social attitudes towards lesbian and gay people are benign and that taking any action against institutionalized heterosexism in churches and secular institutions is unnecessary – or at least not a priority. Whatever Raiser meant, it should be noted that church unity is, in this case, considered to be more important than the human rights of lesbian and gay people, and the action proposed to maintain that 'unity' is to stop talking about sexuality: to quell debate. Yet again, we return to the issue of silence.

The big mistake which Raiser and others make is to equate lack of debate with lack of conflict. There is a parallel here with the ordination of women in the Church of England. Those who raised the issue and forced the debate were blamed with 'causing' the ensuing conflict and supposed 'schism'. All that had happened, in fact, was that those who had been forced to keep silent because their oppression had remained unnamed were given a voice, and the conflict, which had always been present, came out into the open. Likewise, lesbian and gay people experience *now* the social and religious conflict which surrounds our sexuality. As long as silence is experienced by us as a denial of that ever-present conflict, it is in no way preferable to open discussion and debate.

Through its debate about the vices (or virtues) of violence against lesbian women, the WCC was forced to break its silence about our existence. That it proved to be well-nigh impossible for a group of socially and politically aware Christians to condemn such violence teaches us much. It shows that although we are not technically included in church pronouncements on 'homosexuality', this makes little difference to the level of tolerance we may expect for our lifestyles. Our conclusion must be that silence about lesbian existence is not a sign of benevolence or of indifference, much less of tacit approval. Far from it. Rather it could be seen as an active force whereby even the possibility of being lesbian is obliterated from the world-view of women within the Christian community.

Any suspicion that lesbian invisibility indicates anything more positive in the secular sphere is erased by incidences such as the recent hysteria over lesbian mothers. Public reactions to the idea of two women who love each other bringing up children have brought to light all sorts of dynamics which, again, have hitherto only been known by lesbians. The first unexplored assumption is that while heterosexual women have children for altruistic reasons, lesbians have them for purely selfish ones. This could be, in part, an unfortunate spin-off from the media's flirtation with 'lesbian chic': the logical extension of which is that, as with the 'yuppies' of the 1980s, 'lipstick lesbians' are accused of having babies merely as a fashion accessory. If there was an element of truth in this, then these professional middle-class heterosexuals certainly didn't come in for the same condemnation.

In addition, rather than being allowed to state the obvious advantage of a lesbian household – that children will grow up in homes where the threat of male violence is significantly reduced – lesbian mothers have been forced to parade their man-loving credentials. They have been called upon to declare that no, they don't hate men and no, their child will not be deprived of the normal lessons instilled in all children, that manhood is to be worshipped and womanhood despised. Under these conditions they may stand a chance of being tolerated. In turn, the child is encouraged and expected to recognize that if her/his primary carers are two women who happen to love women and devote their primary emotional attention towards women, then they are abnormal parents and it is appropriate to be ashamed of them.

Silence and the lives of women

JUDITH

I am now 65 years of age. I find it difficult or even impossible to unravel the various influences and causes which have brought me to my present position regarding the Church, theology, the spiritual, and personal relationships, including sexual.

I was brought up in a very religious family, Anglo-Catholic (my mother's family; I know little about my father's). One of my earliest memories is of being taught the 'Hail Mary' by my mother. I was taken to the Sung Eucharist (a High Mass one in the earlier years) from the age of three every week. I remember being frightened by some of the language of the liturgy, especially 'if any man sin, we have an Advocate with the Father, Jesus Christ the righteous: and he is the *propitiation* for our sins'.

Church-going and saying one's prayers were duties – extremely important ones which it was sinful to omit. When I enquired of my mother a few years later 'What does *loving* God mean?', I was told that love of God was not an emotional thing – it didn't depend on feelings – it was shown by doing one's duty to God and keeping the commandments.

I was confirmed when I was eleven and from then on went to confession five times a year. We were given a manual to use for preparing for confession, and I remember having to ask what some of the sins listed in it were! I also felt that I had to invent some every time, as I had been told that there should be about twelve sins on my list.

I went to a Church of England girls' school for my secondary years, where many of the teachers were of High Church persuasion. Most of the other girls, however, were there because it was the best school in the town, and not for religious reasons – and I was terrified that they might find out that I went to confession, and belonged to a young people's group called 'The Rock'.

I fell in love with two of the girls in my own form, and with two of the teachers. There was excitement in this and some pleasure, but I also felt ashamed and embarrassed. I viewed them as schoolgirl crushes, which were common, of course, in those days. 'Scripture' was one of my best subjects, and school experience of this (including my feeling for my divinity mistress) had much to do with my interest in theology later.

It was while I was an active member of the Student Christian Movement[8] that I began to have doubts about my beliefs and spirituality. These doubts continued and grew with the years, but I always blamed myself for them – 'doubt is sin' – and felt so guilty that it wasn't until my early fifties that I was able to accept my position and give up the Church – and even then continued to feel apologetic about it.

My first two teaching posts were in Church of England girls' schools – High Church again. In both, I did some 'scripture' teaching, though it was not my main subject. In the first one, I had my first experience of a lesbian relationship. One of the teachers, seven years older than me, fell for me. When I realized it I didn't like it, and was scared, but she managed to seduce me into a relationship which became exciting, very absorbing but also very frustrating and painful. It had to be kept secret (though it was obvious to many others). We engaged in some fondling, fully clad, and never went to bed together. I handed her all the power in this relationship, never said what I wanted, and in the end was jilted for a new arrival on the staff. I felt bitter for many years.

I have been attracted by some other women since but have had only one real lesbian relationship. That one has been a partnership between the two of us for many years, living together for over twenty years in a shared home of our own, having been very close for ten years before that. For nearly twenty years of that relationship, though recognizing and expressing its physical, sexual aspect, we kept it secret. We appeared to be good friends who found it convenient to share a home. We had no idea if there were others like us, and we had no one to model ourselves on, except for heterosexual couples. I particularly felt much guilt about the sexual aspect, due, I am sure, largely to my religious upbringing, though of course to social outlooks also. As teachers we didn't dare let it be known.

Some while after first hearing about the Gay Christian Movement, we 'came out' as far as other lesbians were concerned, and have since made some good friends amongst lesbians. But we are still not fully 'out', never speaking of it to relatives and to friends of earlier days.

Though I still, at present, want to maintain my contacts with Christianity, I am, vis-à-vis the Christian Church, out in the wilderness. I have put myself there because I no longer believe the traditional theology, so cannot say the words or sing the songs of Christian worship.

DEBORAH

I've felt invisible, absent for much of my life. Other people matter, I don't. Other people have emotions and relationships, I don't. The best kind of love is the spiritual kind. It's more constant, enduring and politically useful. Emotions don't help in the cause of justice and peace. I have ended up feeling like a walking reflection of other people's images and expectations of me, with which I have complied.

I 'went out with' the occasional boyfriend at school and as an undergraduate. It never went further than kissing, as even that did nothing for me. There was no connecting. Simultaneously, I had crushes on other girls, other young women. These became increasingly powerful, though very ill-defined, and I don't remember thinking about what it all meant. Either I blanked out, or I was in un-thought-through inner turmoil. Initially, I admired from afar, fantasizing (non-sexual) encounters. Then I began trying to make contact with the objects of my unfocused desires, but that was usually excruciating and sometimes embarrassing. I simply had no idea what feelings were about, let alone feelings for other women. From late teenage onwards, I think I've had a non-stop string of crushes on women. As soon as one faded, another one would take its place. And not until I was in my mid to late twenties did I hear the word 'lesbian' in a positive context, or one that could remotely have anything to do with me.

I don't think it's a coincidence that by the time I became aware — intellectually — of my sexuality, I'd already drifted away from organized Christianity. The year in which I did a one-year postgraduate course entitled 'Women and Religion' was truly a time of reckoning. By the end of it I'd rejected Christianity as misogynist and homophobic and fallen in lust with one of my women tutors (this time the fantasized encounters were definitely sexual!).

Intimate relationships are difficult enough in our crazy, impersonal, insecure society. They're even more difficult, surely, when you've always considered a kind of spiritualized love to be more valuable than messy real relationships, and when you're a woman who loves other women in a heterosexist and misogynist environment. Both those situations characterized my upbringing and church-based involvement.

I feel a lot of anger and pain and also loss when I think about the years during which I've been, alternately, locked inside my body or floating somewhere outside it. I also have many questions and half-developed theories. Is Christianity about control? If all of us are supposed to be the Good Samaritan, who is there left to be our stage prop, the mugged traveller? In whose interests has sex and sexuality been labelled 'unclean' by the Church? Why does the 'as thyself' get so often left off from the commandment, 'thou shalt love thy neighbour'? Why does self-love have to be equated with selfishness? Why do passion and playfulness have to be frowned upon? Does belief in God or worship of Christ necessarily involve sublimation of sexual passions and desires, and of positive feelings about ourselves?

In a sense, though, I'm simply not interested any more. For 28 years a Christian spirituality and consciousness formed a fundamental part of my self-image. And I was desperately depressed, looking back: all that energy spent on holding my emotions at bay, philosophizing and dreaming about peace and justice on earth, being unaware of the significance of myself as some-body: a woman with a body that wants to be held and loved and wants to give warmth and love in return. That, I realize as I write, is the painful nub of the issue. Loving spiritually (in its old conventional sense) involved keeping others at arm's length so I could be in control enough to give, to offer comfort, to care.

As a lesbian (presumably even more so than if I'd been heterosexual) the worst legacy of my spiritualized existence has been not connecting with myself, being kept apart from myself and therefore from others too. And this in two senses: ignoring my body-self, living in and out of my head, and being unaware of the reality and beauty of lesbian love and community.

ANN

I used to go to church. I went from the age of eleven until I was 24. I went three times a week and was very involved: Parochial Church Council, choir, youth club, Bible study, and house prayer groups. Church was central to my life at that time and was a great help to me through my difficult teenage years.

As I grew older, though, and became more exposed to 'feminist' ideas through my work, I began to feel more and more resentful of what went on at church: men held all the positions of authority. For me, church was an escape from a bullying, mean-spirited father. Increasingly, it began to look to me as though my church 'family' was headed by just such an oppressive 'father': his word was final, his wife was a drudge, the women who went to church were used by him, and manipulated into doing his bidding. That sometimes meant sleeping with him. I know because I was one of those 'chosen' to sleep with him.

That was 16 years ago. These days, at the age of 40, I can at last celebrate my sexuality. I am so happy to be 'out' as a lesbian. What used to be my Guilty Secret is now a source of joy and pride to me. I have a very happy and loving relationship with my partner, who is also proud to be a lesbian and refuses to be hidden. We wasted a lot of years denying our sexuality, refusing to accept it, pretending to be heterosexual.

I still can't believe how good sex is with another woman, how good is the totality of our relationship. There is so much tenderness, sharing, talking, giving, receiving. I see it as a process of healing for myself, and because I'm regaining a sense of personal worth, I'm better able to reach out to others.

NAOMI

Waking up to the oppressive structures imposed by Pope John Paul II (the godfather) and the Vatican hit-men (the cardinals), was both a frightening and exciting experience for me. Frightening, for as a member of a religious order I had previously said yes to the 'smells and bells', believing that I could somehow change things from within; exciting because, for the first time in my life, I was truly opening to that which gives life – God. I was finding energy to claim power that was rightfully mine as a woman free from the imposed guilt of Eve.

It is extremely difficult to break out of the process of being moulded, and most of us are, not in the image and likeness of God, but into subservient roles fashioned by those in positions of authority. That plastic mould, indeed, this plastic church, is man-made. I must admit to having experienced a deep sense of 'aloneness'. The church of my birth has now gone from me, or I have outgrown it. Either way the umbilical cord has been cut, and I have a tremendous feeling of isolation.

It was at 37 that I managed to come out of the 'homosexual closet' in which I had locked myself, with the help of church and society. Reflecting back on my early school memories, I can remember being taught that if you were not heterosexual you simply were not sexual. In other words, as stated in Genesis, God only created one type of human love, that between a woman and a man. Anything else simply did not exist.

One of the most important effects of lesbian invisibility which is evidenced in all of the above stories is that it keeps women apart from each other. It is interesting to me that although Judith, Deborah, Heather and Naomi cover an age range from late twenties to mid-sixties, they have all experienced, at some point, feelings of isolation. As women discovering their lesbian identity they have felt the need to think through issues of sexuality alone, and often in ignorance of the existence and possibility of lesbian community. In *Outercourse*, her philosophical autobiography, Mary Daly describes her own experience of feeling alone as she developed her Radical Feminism:

> I was, in my immediate environment, a cognitive minority of one. There were, of course, Other women with comparable cognition, each of whom experienced her life as that of a cognitive minority of one. Virtually none of us had a Name for our identity, however, and virtually none of us knew each other.[9]

This analysis would seem to be applicable to women naming their lesbian identity. It is also significant that there is often a link, as in the stories above, between questioning the role prescribed for us as women and becoming lesbian. Feminism is often of crucial importance to lesbians of Christian heritage, and this can mark an important difference between them and gay Christian men. While for gay men the primary root of alienation from the church is likely to be its attitude to their sexuality, for women the roots of such alienation will be manifold – but the crucial factor is generally the church's attitude towards them as women (although for Black women the church's racism may be the most significant alienating factor).

To the extent that lesbians prioritize other women in our personal lives and political activity, we are unlikely to be happy with churches that make women invisible, in both institutional and theological terms. At a recent gathering of lesbian and gay Christians, one woman spoke of not wanting to conceive of God as male any longer, a comment which apparently met with audible disapproval from male members of the audience. While the grounds for gay male disaffection from the Christian community are potentially (though not necessarily) narrow, the grounds for lesbian disaffection are potentially as all-embracing as her spirituality. Lesbian women often face a choice between involvement in the 'lesbian and gay' Christian scene, in which they may feel inhibited about questioning traditional theology, and involvement in the Christian feminist scene, where they may feel unsafe about being openly lesbian. For Black lesbian women this choice may be no choice at all, since both movements are predominantly white and the need to challenge racism is ever-present.

LESLEY

For me, religion and sexuality have been intertwined from childhood, although neither of those words or concepts appeared until later. The two came together in a basic sort of way when my non-churchgoing parents sent me to a Congregational Sunday school when I was about eight years old, and I fell in love with the Sunday school teacher. As I grew older I became more passionate about the next Sunday school teacher.

I was next sent to a Church of England secondary school and became increasingly 'religious' if not pious, and increasingly passionate about prefects and teachers, which was quite ordinary and acceptable. The religious aspect of all this led me to study theology at college and become a Religious Education teacher; the sexual aspect led me into a lesbian partnership for 25 years which is still a very close friendship.

When this partnership started I knew nothing about sex of any kind, and I had certainly not heard of homosexuality. However, I instinctively knew that such a relationship was deemed 'wrong', and therefore never spoke of it. In a way there was a naivety about both of us which stood us in good stead. We were two 'respectable' RE teachers, regular church-goers, on the PCC [Parochial Church Council], running the Christian Aid Committee, and welcoming Lent groups into our home. But as we became more aware, and homosexuality began to be more openly condemned by the Church, it all became more complex and difficult and obviously hidden. In my mid-twenties I had 'worked my way round the world' for a year and a half – partly to try to find some answer to it all I think, but none came. I learned many things, mixed with all types of people, but remained a devoted church-goer and still committed to that one relationship. I returned home and we bought our first house. Major change for me did not take place until the late 1970s when we both joined a co-counselling group as a couple and actually talked about it all. Up until then we had only each spoken to one other person about it.

By then I was in a very responsible middle-management job and feeling I had to present myself as asexual to avoid detection. I felt I was denying a vital aspect of myself. Up until this point I had remained a church-goer, and played quite a lead role in modern Religious Education. Although I had visited the charismatic movement en route, I had steadily explored liberal Christianity from my time in the Student Christian Movement in the late 1950s and early 1960s. The *Honest to God*[10] debate meant a great deal to me, and the founding of the Gay Christian Movement (now LGCM) was an eye-opener. At the time I was in an advisory post and the GCM journal passed across my desk. No staff member read it more avidly than I!

In the early 1980s I became aware of feminism, as well as the sexist language and the homophobia of the Church of England. The church which had nurtured me up till then, and whom I had served wholeheartedly, became increasingly irrelevant and a cause of pain to me. I found that I had long ago given it up as an authority or parent figure and had turned to finding my authority from within with the help of individuals I respected and trusted. I ceased going to church and began to operate as a religious person through religious feminist groups. These seemed to create much more worthwhile acts of worship which were linked to my experience and seemed a much deeper expression of spirituality. This phase came when I was looking after my elderly mother prior to her death and holding down a very respectable full-time job. The church had nothing to give.

I miss the community of the church, or the ideal of it. But when I go with a friend, or for a friend (for an ordination, say), I am often appalled at what I hear. The maleness of the whole show is amazing. Will women priests and ministers improve this? I hope so.

I no longer accept the brand of Christianity that the early Fathers of the Church decided to be dogmatic about. I am very suspicious of dogmatism of any kind. Such doctrines as the divinity of Christ, the uniqueness of Jesus, the atonement, the Trinity, Original Sin, Revelation and even theism itself have been and are being, I suppose will always be, reworked by me. Some are discarded as useless and dangerous heresy; others have been reborn by my life's experiences. The importance of prayer, meditation and the community remain for me.

My understanding of sexuality has also broadened out, although at times I still feel totally ignorant. It seems to me that I have been able to set off on a rather independent search spiritually; because I have had to establish a sexual identity without any guidelines. There were no norms to follow, no parents to talk to, no community to bless us, only a morality to defy. The stereotyped heterosexual couple was the only pattern, and that pattern was a hindrance not a help. In the first 20 years of life when I was sexual, I did not read of anyone sexual like myself, or see any film or documentary on television. So having had to create a 'do it yourself' sexual lifestyle, I suppose I was prepared for a 'do it yourself' spiritual lifestyle. I see sexuality as a way of union and creativity, and I suppose I think spirituality is something to do with those two things as well. Both states can only be entered into by daring to approach separateness.

SALLY

I was brought up as a Roman Catholic in a family where religion was never a duty, just an important part of life. Catholic practice was very deeply ingrained in me – mass every Sunday (the more difficult it was to get to church, the more heroic one felt!) and on all holy days of obligation, confession every month. Through the Catholic schools I attended (state primary, convent grammar, co-ed sixth-form college) I was enabled to develop my own personal faith and grew away from what I perceived to be my parents' rather desperate clinging to the rules of a joyless religious practice. As a teenager I hated attending the main Sunday morning mass with them in the local parish church: everyone dressed up and celebrating their prosperity while the Sunday joint cooked at home. I preferred to walk to the early morning or evening mass by myself. I loved school masses, especially the singing. In the sixth form I became involved in the Catholic Charismatic Renewal, took part in prayer groups, walks of witness, retreats. I took it all very seriously but felt strongly that belief in God should not call for the suspension of reason and any other gifts I happened to have. I have never been popular with RE teachers.

In my second term at university I discovered that I was lesbian – something that was difficult for me to name if only because I had never encountered the possibility that homosexual women existed! When I fell in love I did not cease to be the person I had known myself to be before, and the very silence surrounding lesbianism as I was growing up made it somehow easier for me to accept that lesbian relationships were just different, not something to shrink from or condemned by God.

I am now 29. Am I 'religious' or 'spiritual'? The former term conjures up many of the worst elements of Christianity – fanaticism, sectarianism, self-hatred – and yet I do still attend Sunday mass regularly, so to an extent I am religious, though I do not like that self-image particularly. 'Spiritual' evokes a whole list of more positive qualities and preoccupations that just are not me: living on a higher plane, meditating, detachment, engaged in music and painting, reading theological works. Thinking about it, I wonder whether I am equating 'religious' with working-class experience and 'spiritual' with middle-class experience. After an Oxbridge education I am irredeemably middle-class but cut off from much of the certainty and vigour of working-class Catholicism which nourished me as I was growing up. I know that 'spirituality' can embrace much more than this definition and can be tough and engaged with life.

I think that I would prefer to describe myself as a person of faith, as I have a stubborn and instinctive faith in God that, sometimes very inconveniently, just will not leave me. I believe prayers are answered. I believe that God is in the mess of people's lives, not in absolutes like Truth or Beauty or Holiness. The only bad reaction to my being lesbian came from my parents, whose understanding of Catholicism did not leave them with the option of accepting their own daughter as she was. When they looked to the church for support and advice they did not seem to be contradicted in this view (though perhaps they did not hear opposite opinions). As a result, I am now very suspicious of appeals to absolutes, particularly in matters of religion, since these can be used to justify the crushing of humanity and exerting power over others. Where theory clashes with my experience or instincts about what is right I tend to disregard it entirely. I know that this leaves me open to the charge of being completely subjective and amoral, but I do not live in a tidy world where Right and Wrong are clearly labelled. In making decisions I suppose I would say that I try and follow my conscience. My aim would be to put respect for other human beings before anything else, though in practice I find this is as difficult as any other precept to apply.

I am very committed to challenging Catholic teaching and general attitudes to homosexuality, feeling strongly that the difficulties I ran into with my parents were due to ignorance and prejudice, and that increasingly the visibility of lesbian and gay Catholics is an essential first step to making life easier for others in the same position. I do not see Catholic teaching on homosexuality as vitiating the whole of Catholicism. This is probably because Catholicism is part of my cultural identity, rather than a theological system to which I have consciously assented. That said, I am much less committed to the institutional church than I once was.

PAULINE

I became an undergraduate in 1968, a time of ferment and upheaval. I got involved with the college chapel, both because it provided a ready-made social group in what was otherwise a rather bewildering mass of people, and because the 'big questions' fascinated me. However, the Christian Union tried to co-opt me and tell me the 'right answers', so I fled and found the Student Christian Movement, a much more congenial 'home' in a very political phase of its existence. One of our more liberated/liberating actions was to picket a Billy Graham crusade at the university!

I engaged in remarkably little sexual experimentation during my student days, and didn't 'lose my virginity' until I was twenty-three – at that point deliberately and premeditatedly, as I felt it was becoming an embarrassment. I think I was quite frightened of intimacy – emotional or physical – with men, because they seemed such strange creatures, a different species, not quite human. But I did not carry within me lots of religious prohibitions about sex, and I remember being amazed when a close friend explained how her High Church upbringing had taught her that the body was the temple of the Holy Spirit, and that therefore sexual sin was a sin against the Holy Spirit, which was the one sin that could not be forgiven. What was this gobbledygook? It seemed quite bizarre to me.

All my closest affective bonds have been with women, but it never crossed my mind in my twenties (the early 1970s) that sex meant anything other than sex with men. I had a series of unsatisfying (emotionally and physically) relationships with men, retained my friendships with women as the anchor of my life, started out in the teaching profession, and lived alone, as it had never crossed my mind to do otherwise.

My closest friend from university days married and had a baby very soon after graduating, and I was very close to that process and became very involved with that child and her later children. At some point in my late twenties I found myself feeling sexually very drawn to her, and told her about it. We discussed it, without either of us ever contemplating 'doing anything about it'. Being sexually attracted to another woman didn't feel like a great problem; being sexually attracted to my best friend, who was married with small children, did. So somehow that all got buried, and it was ten years before I found myself being sexually drawn to women again.

It transpired that I had to have a hysterectomy in my late thirties. The loss of the choice about whether to have children was a real loss. I discovered that, quite unconsciously, I had been holding part of myself back from living; waiting, somehow, 'in case' I should have a child. With this realization came an enormous sense of relief. If I could no longer have children then I didn't have to make the effort to relate to men ever again. I had not realized that this had been my motivation; certainly it had not been conscious. But now it was so clear – I was free to love women, all the bits of me were suddenly in the same place and it was such a relief. There was no angst, doubt or trauma about it. It was just, quite simply, how things were, and I was quite pleased about it.

Feeling free to love women has revealed a facet of desire that I had not previously noticed. With hindsight I can now see that in my relationships with men my desire was not direct – what I desired was their desire of me. It was narcissistic, constrained. It was confined within the social construction of femininity, in spite of my feminism. It was not autonomous and it was not free. In loving women I am somehow freed to desire directly; to have my own lust; to desire, whether or not I am desired; to want, and not just to want to be wanted.

GILLIAN

I was extremely fortunate and blessed in having a mother who was a very spiritual woman and sent me to Sunday school at a tender age. She had been brought up a Methodist and sent me to a Free Church which stood, literally, next door to a mission belonging to the High Anglican parish church down in the village. Whenever we passed I was told it was 'very Catholic' which meant nothing to me. Some time later the First World War army-hut church which I attended moved itself to the tin mission next door, and we all became more Roman than Rome; indeed so much so that by the time I was a teenager I couldn't understand why they all didn't join the Roman Catholic Church. I decided to become a Catholic when I grew up. As soon as I was able I did so. By then I had been further attracted by the lessons I had learned from history: if Christ indeed founded a church then that must be it. I was also very attracted by the poems of Gerard Manley Hopkins and to John Henry Newman and the Oxford Movement, by which I presume my Church of England church had been influenced.

On becoming a Catholic there was enormous antagonism from my family who tried to cut me off. At the time it was agony, and so sad because we were such a small family. Eventually they got over it and came round. It was a difficult period for me because at about the same time I came to the realization that I am lesbian. I think had Radclyffe Hall not been a devout Catholic I should have proceeded much more warily. Radclyffe Hall has been, and indeed still is, a major influence in my life. It was through her having lived in Holland Street, Kensington, that I discovered the Carmelite Church. Being besotted and wanting to be better than everybody else I decided to join their Secular Order. During my novitiate I began to have qualms that I might be one of those people who, according to the manual, would 'cause scandal'. But then scandal only exists within the perception of the scandalized, and by simply being as God made me I couldn't really see how I could be different from anybody else, so I overcame my scruples.

Over the years my spirituality has broadened and deepened, perhaps to break through the narrow confines of organized Religion with a large capital R. I am now a kind of Theosophical Catholic with Buddhist and Spiritualist overtones! My spiritual life is very rich and I regard myself as fortunate and blessed. How can I regard 'being' as a sin, or indeed the special love I have for a particular person? The church's hang-ups about sex go back to the Greek Stoics and pagan times, and have caused such harm, especially to women.

CHRISTINE

I think that one of the key factors in my confidence about the lack of contradiction between my religious convictions and my sexuality/sexual practice is that only by questioning did I reach a decision to become a Catholic, and it is this faith to which I am committed. I was brought up as an Anglican (middle of the road), but in my teens I began to doubt very much and by the time I left for university I was, I suppose, a kind of humanist (with tinges of atheism). However, religious beliefs and practices still interested me, and I continued to read and think about them (while feeling strongly about humanism and socialism and what seemed to me to be a disgusting 'respectability' and judgementalism about the churches).

My first approach to a priest was in 1974; I was finally received into the Roman Catholic Church in 1977. It was very important to me that I could enter it completely – intellectually and in every other way. I do not see faith as a safe thing, kept in its own world, but as something that should permeate and be in tune with everything else, including one's involvement in political, social and sexual matters. I have never stopped being open to question, and I can never be happy or relax if I haven't thought properly about something. I may give myself a hard time here, but it is important to my peace of mind. And so here I am in 1993, a Catholic who is appalled by much dogmatism and the totalitarianism of the Church, but here I stand; I can do no other.

I suppose that at school I was vaguely aware that I found women more interesting but I was much more set on fire by books and music and what I saw from my window. I wasn't involved with boys at all. This was also true at university in the early 1970s. I didn't really become very sexually aware until my twenties and was involved with some rather unsuitable men. I couldn't be bothered.

Strangely enough, it wasn't until I had set off for Rome (metaphorically) that I became a really sexual being. I had a lot of sexual energy and discovered the joys of masturbation. In my first real lesbian relationship I was both younger and more passionate than my lover and, I suppose, more in need. I was teaching at a Catholic school which was very repressive, and used to look forward to weekends, which weren't! At the same time, she was very angered by my Catholicism, considering it a betrayal. It didn't seem wrong to me despite her articulate attacks, although I felt just as strongly about the nonsense of the rules which did not take any account of the quality of love at all. I could not have become a Catholic if I had been unable to make a distinction between powerful public men making laws and a faith which has gone on (despite it all) through the years. I have simply never been able to consider my sex life a threat to my faith, or the other way around. I think of the conciliar document which refers to the conscience as being able to speak more truthfully than that of authority, and I think of the importance of being true to myself.

I have lived for seven years with Sue. She is a marvellous person and we love each other very much. Sex is obviously part of the relationship but as a full and wide thing. I am capable of feeling guilty about sex, but this is when, for example, I use her and don't consider her. I justify our life together in terms of love, for that is where my faith has its source. Of course, I get fed up with not being able to refer to Sue as others refer to their spouses. I get angry with mention of weddings and those wonderful nuptial masses and masses for golden anniversaries and suchlike. I get fed up of listening to crappy sermons with their analogies to sacrificing mothers and references to marriage, as if we all aspired to it. Sometimes I get so fed up with the 'voices of the Church' that I miss Sunday mass, but end up going again because I'm simply not prepared to let them be an obstacle between me and my faith. Nor am I prepared to despise myself as a sexual being.

There appears to be a close but complex link between spirituality and sexuality. All of the contributors in this section have embraced a kind of spirituality which is very different from mainstream Christianity. It is different, for one thing, in its positive approach to bodiliness. To go back to Deborah's experience for a moment, she speaks of her Christian upbringing as a time when she was 'unaware of the significance of myself as some-body'; she had been encouraged to live a 'spiritualized existence', 'being kept apart from myself and therefore from others too'. Living as a lesbian for her involves an active unlearning of these messages.

It is also a spirituality which emphasizes the need for constant questioning and exploration, and resistance to the imposition of external authority. In her book *Not in Our Name*, Rosie Miles talks to women who have left the church. She discovers that a very important motivation for many is the imposition of a rigid and censorious belief system which is very controlling of women's spiritual development. As I said in my foreword to that book:

The women in this book want a spiritual life that is about doubt; about asking questions, living with tensions, dealing creatively with difference and dissent and being challenged by new theological insights. What they find in the churches is very different.[11]

Lesley draws a clear link between this kind of spirituality and her sexuality: 'It seems to me that I have been able to set off on a rather independent search spiritually because I have had to establish a sexual identity without any guidelines. There were no norms to follow, no parents to talk to, no community to bless us, only a morality to defy.' It is no surprise, therefore, that Rosie's book features a significant number of lesbians. It seems that such women do not leave the Church because it asks more of them than they can give, but because it doesn't ask enough.

Fundamentalism

There is a form of Christianity which is a far cry from the 'no holds barred' explorations thus far described. The inflexible, narrow and authoritarian phenomenon which is religious fundamentalism seems to be growing in power and popularity. Women who discover themselves to be lesbian in this context face a very different set of challenges.

KIRSTY

It's three weeks since I moved out of the house that was my home for nearly three years. Despite my attachment to it and all the good memories, it has been a relief to come here, to find solitude and peace after such traumatic events. My feelings are only just catching up with me, feelings of betrayal, shame and grief.

A few months ago I started a relationship with a woman. She isn't my first lover but this is the first time that I'm 'going for it'! I love Bryony and want to be with her, which is difficult on a regular basis as she lives in France. I decided to tell my flatmates about the relationship but procrastinated. Being evangelical Christians they wouldn't approve, I knew. There was a time when I wouldn't have approved either. But something's happened inside of me lately. I want to live. Being in love is wonderful. I'm 30 and it's the first time I've owned these feelings which I've tried to contain for so long, exploring them rather than constantly fighting myself.

This is the first time I can remember making a decision that I know doesn't have the approval of my church. I'm still not sure if God approves or not, but

I'm taking that risk. I can't tell you how alive I feel surrendering to these longings, but I feel a lot of pain and hurt as well.

I knew my flatmates wouldn't approve of Bryony and me sleeping together when she came on a two-week visit, but I hoped they would capture some of my joy. Some of their comments ran through me weeks after: 'abomination'; 'I think you're doing the wrong thing'; 'we don't want you sleeping together in the house'. I overheard one flatmate talking about 'not knowing what to do' and that the Bible says to 'cast out the immoral person'. I wasn't too worried at the time because I thought that their only objection was to sex in the house.

After some negotiation I agreed to move out for the two weeks. The atmosphere would have been too uncomfortable for us anyway. I rang to ask some friends if we could stay, and they said 'yes' immediately. After I'd explained the situation they were very affirming. I put the phone down and burst into tears. The sobs came from a deep place, the pain of being rejected and the pain of being loved for who I was.

Bryony and I had a wonderful two weeks together. The inconvenience of living away from home was more than bearable, even exciting. I didn't understand the strength of the anger of some friends when I told them about the behaviour of my flatmates. I still believed things would work out at home.

During the second week I began to have doubts. Firstly, my flatmates hadn't contacted me at all. Secondly, when we went round to pick up mail they wouldn't eat in the same room with us, which I found incredibly rude.

By the end of the fortnight I had decided to look for another place to live. My flatmates had had a similar idea. Not only did they not want to live with me, they also said they wanted no further contact with me on the grounds that I call myself a Christian whilst I am at the same time 'a practising homosexual'. They kept saying that they 'hated the sin and loved the sinner', but I find this increasingly difficult to reconcile with their actions.

Looking back on my life, I have experienced 20 years of belonging, activity, purpose, fun, earnest endeavour for God, and the sincere conviction that I/we had answers to all the problems and pain of the world in the Bible and through an ever-deepening relationship with Jesus Christ. But I also had 20 years of feeling that I was never quite good enough or doing enough for God, for the Church. There was always more prayer, Bible study, evangelizing to do. I had a cause I believed in, and I was needed and welcomed, but only as long as I kept the rules.

Being with Bryony is discovering who I am. Christianity has been at the centre of my identity for so long, but despite the hurt I'm glad to have moved on, freed from the obsession with being right or wrong. I no longer identify as a fundamentalist Christian. A whole portion of what I thought was unshakeable belief has fallen away leaving uncertainty, questions and a sense of isolation. I don't know the answers any more. I'm learning to receive love from other people (as opposed to viewing them as potential converts), learning to value them and myself for who we are now.

ULRIKE

Recently, two feminists, one an 'out' lesbian, were asked to lead the women's work in my denomination. This has caused a vigorous discussion and the fundamentalists, in particular, are totally against it. Even though they don't literally say 'this is the Devil's work', the way they react and express their criticism shows that this is what they think.

I myself have a fundamentalist background. As my relationship with Steph developed I had to struggle with my fundamentalist heritage. As you can imagine, the current discussion in my church involves me personally and gives rise to my own inner struggles – not in terms of justifying our relationship to myself (this struggle, at least, is over) but to find arguments to explain my current position to people; to find words for what I feel and know is true and right for my life.

I haven't told my parents about us yet, and only one friend from home knows. She supports us. As for my parents, there are times when I have the feeling that they will accept, if not understand and tolerate, my decision, but I don't yet know when the right time to tell them will be. We will visit them in the summer and see what happens.

I don't want to hurt them. I have often done that in my life. Our faith always brought us together again. But this decision, this step, could destroy that sense of shared faith. In a fundamentalist's understanding, a lesbian relationship is against the law and the will of God. So I might lose them and the rest of my family, because all of them are fundamentalist Christians.

As for me, I know that this could happen, but I have to go my own way. In the whole process of accepting my love for Steph and accepting her love for me, it was not losing God; rather, God was leading me in this direction. On returning to my home in Germany (we've now been separated for several months), I thought that maybe this sense of guidance might disappear, but it has got stronger. God is not meant to be 'fixed' and only available in church laws and fundamentalist rules. I am determined to follow this new way, and I can only hope that it will be not only a challenge but ultimately a liberating discovery for my parents and family.

UTA

When I was in my early twenties I had a very powerful conversion experience in an American evangelical Pentecostal church after a heart-breaking love affair with an American soldier. Some years later I travelled to the USA. In my search to belong, I was looking for a Christian community, and I ended up in a cult-like fundamentalist group, a set-up which to a great extent repeated the patterns of my authoritarian German upbringing. I was not allowed to think for myself or come to my own conclusions. We were worked so hard that we didn't have any time or energy to do a lot of thinking. There was also direct intimidation. We were told that disobedience to the leaders equalled disobedience to God.

But there I met a woman who also had a longing for a sense of connectedness and affection. We were the only single women in the place. I can remember the first time she touched me. It was a touch that expressed all my longing and I responded to her. I had not felt an erotic attraction to women before, but it felt so normal, so exciting and natural. Somehow my longings, which had been repressed for years, met hers and I fell in love.

Every time we 'fell into sin' we felt incredibly guilty and repented afterwards. I don't quite remember how I actually dealt with this internally. All I knew was that I needed her and that she was the only person with whom I could honestly share what was going on for me. The high moral expectations of the place created such hypocrisy in everybody, and denial of the reality of our lives was literally cultivated.

I returned home after two years, to a father dying of cancer. Failing to find employment in Germany, I ended up coming to work in London. Here I struggled for the next two years with the after-effects of my time in the US.

I met another woman at my workplace, where most of the staff are evangelical Christians. We very quickly started to touch and hold each other, telling ourselves that this was some spiritual ministry we were performing for each other which had nothing to do with sexual needs. This went on for some time until I became increasingly aware that I had strong desires for more contact and felt sexually aroused when we were together. Again a lot of guilt came up for both of us, yet there was some sustaining connection between us that broke through all the guilt and doubts. I had never before experienced such a deep sense of connection and intimacy as we were trying to struggle with the issue of our sexual desire for one another. There were lots of tears and anger and we hurt each other a lot, but there was also a ray of hope. This sense of finally being wanted and seen could not be all wrong.

I had a deep awareness of meeting myself in this other woman. I have always had a deep sense of body shame. I received some sense of healing through being able to touch her and also observe her relative freedom about her body. But as with my first lover, she could not deal with her growing desire and sense of guilt, and started to cut me off, which was very painful for me.

At the moment I am taking stock. Who in the world am I? What is my sexual identity? Is it fixed or is it evolving? I still feel that I want something from men (I don't exactly know what), that's why I don't call myself a lesbian, even though sometimes I would be glad if it was more clear cut. What in the world does it mean to be a human being with sexual desires? I do not recognize any form of authority in the traditional sense, but I listen to those with whom I experience a mutual vulnerability. I am learning in a slow and painful way to look after myself and yet stay connected and be vulnerable with a chosen few people, mainly women.

I have made some good contacts with women, particularly in spiritual groups of one or another persuasion. But I feel as though I fall between two stools; uneasy about still being in my questioning phase. One friend of mine said upon hearing that I am seeing a male therapist 'well, that needs to change'. That angered me a lot because it felt like pressure to become 'like us'. All my life I have been told how to see things: what to believe; how to feel; how to act. I don't need that again. I want to find out what it means to be me, not how I can fit into yet another set of rules. I am 36 and I hope I will come closer to finding out who I am, and being able to live from there and be free. And that in the end is what I believe my spirituality is all about.

Fundamentalist Christianity maintains a rigid stance on lesbian and gay sexuality. Same-sex sexual expression is against the will of God. That is non-negotiable. Lesbian women who are conservative Christians therefore face dramatic make-or-break choices. It is interesting to note, however, that these Christian women often interpret their lesbian sexuality (at least initially) within the terms of their faith tradition. It is considered to be the 'will of God' – as part of God's purpose for them – and this is experienced as empowering, even if it does not meet with the approval of the community. In these cases there is a sense in which conservative Christianity is being turned against itself. As with other forms of Christianity, it is important to recognize that the choice is not just between continuing to assent to a particular belief system or leaving it behind. It is far more complicated than that.

Think for a moment about how these forms of Christianity function. Adherents are taught not to think for themselves or make autonomous decisions; they are encouraged to mix only with those whose belief system is identical; debate within the community is squashed, with the power to speak publicly or lead prayers restricted to a tiny minority of (usually male) superior adherents specially chosen for their conformity. As Uta says, disobedience to religious leaders is equated with disobedience to God himself. In leaving behind religious fundamentalism, one leaves all of one's friends and social contacts and (in some cases) one's family too: the whole network of relationships that sustain one's existence. But more than that, one leaves behind the structures of meaning by which one has made sense of the world. It is difficult to imagine losing more, and it is easy to see why the 'healing' option for lesbians as espoused by women like Jeanette Howard[12] is so attractive. It offers an apparent way out of an impossible dilemma. The fact that lesbian women do manage to leave fundamentalism behind demonstrates how crucially flawed is the vision and construction of what it means to be human which such religious structures impose.

It would be tidy and neat to be able to say that the recognition of lesbianism always leads women of Christian heritage towards ambivalence or outright rejection of Christianity. But that would not be an accurate picture. The following experiences show that for some women the reverse can be the case.

STEPH

I consider myself to be a religious person. This is having come full circle; having been raised a Methodist; having had my feminist consciousness raised as a theology student whilst dating an Anglo-Catholic ordinand; having subsequently written a thesis about women's spirituality, cross-culturally, whilst living in an Indian ashram; having thereafter relinquished all connections with Christianity and explored the alternative spiritualities of the women's movement whilst living in a separatist women's peace camp in the USA; having exhilaratedly come out as a lesbian, only to return to Britain where, losing my ideological, supportive community I reached out for a 'normal' (yet profoundly dissatisfactory) heterosexual relationship and became pregnant; having had an abortion that went completely against all that I had lived and breathed in the life-affirming, emphatically non-violent community of the peace camp; having finally loved and lived with a woman who restored my faith in human nature; having been drawn into the lesbian and gay Christian community after years of floundering isolation and cynicism; having been accepted as an 'out' lesbian by an overseas mission organization to work in China; having become aware, in the context of a nation apparently at sea, of religious convictions I never knew I had; having met a fundamentalist Christian woman brimming over with compassion for these people all at sea; having been impressed and intrigued by her intense, personal relationship with Christ; having had my faith in God restored through experiencing the gift of the incredibly deep love that sustains my partner and me during our current separation; and having decisively retrieved my Christian roots from the garbage pile to which they had been consigned.

It's funny but I left the Church as a feminist, yet re-found a niche in the Christian community as a lesbian. That's not to say that I have come to any level of acceptance of all the sexist rubbish, not to mention the homophobic rubbish, but of course that isn't the essence of the faith is it? What I've come to realize is that the core of Christian faith is an awareness of God's love. God is the precious essence of all loving, caring relationships, I think. It's really soul-destroying when people don't recognize God in certain relationships, such as the love between myself and my partner.

JEAN

My perspective is a bit different from many, I think, as I'm a Christian feminist in a committed lesbian relationship – but with the Christian bit being the most recent. Feminism came first, and with that, recognition of my lesbianism. Then, many years later (eleven at least) I experienced a slow conversion process to becoming a Christian. One and a half years ago, I joined the Church of Scotland.

When I was young I had extremely powerful attractions for women and older girls, but at an all-girls school this was fairly standard. However, on leaving school and whilst actively involved first with boyfriends and then with my (now ex) husband (and to whom, in both cases, I experienced powerful sexual attraction), I continued to have erotic dreams and feelings about women.

I eventually met a woman with whom I fell in love and this led to the end of my marriage. There were other contributing factors but that was the key one. The sense of liberation and wholeness that came from that relationship, especially in the early stages, was amazing. I felt I could really be 'me' and was incredibly energized, although my life was extremely difficult, bringing up two small children (my lover had two also and was divorced). Four kids between us was hard work. I know I did a huge amount of growing up in this relationship. So much more, I think, than I would have done had I stayed in the 'patriarchal nest'. My ex-husband is a pretty conventional man, and my life married to him was setting off down that road. I think that was also a spur. It was a very definite statement that I would be me and could not be so within that relationship and context. It was not, therefore, just a sexual thing. My sexual life with my ex-husband had been good at first, tailing off before I met the woman with whom I fell in love. We had been married seven years when we split up.

I am now five years into a difficult, demanding, challenging, unhappy, very happy, relationship with the woman I live with, and whom I regard as my life partner, although it's constantly on a knife edge, and we are still working at lots of issues between us. She is a Christian – though not a particularly conventional one in terms of church attendance. However, she is very well qualified theologically, and so part of our great companionship is around many issues arising from Christian life/ethics/morality, etc. In terms of sexuality I feel more at peace and at one with myself probably than ever before, although sex itself continues to be up and down, according to how the rest of our relationship is – which I think is more or less as it should be.

In the face of what Steph calls 'the sexist rubbish' and 'the homophobic rubbish' it is often difficult to imagine that a lesbian woman could ever find anything positive in Christian spirituality. Yet it seems that we can and do. Earlier in this chapter Sally commented that for her Catholicism's teaching on homosexuality does not vitiate the whole religious tradition. What comes through very strongly in the contributions to this chapter is an amazing level of integrity and courage. These women demonstrate an independence of mind which is evidenced by the strength of their resistance to external pressure. It seems that as lesbians of Christian heritage we are not prepared to despise ourselves or our sexuality – nor have our spirituality defined for us by men in ecclesiastical authority. We exhibit courageous imagination, theological vigour and the confidence to combine the resources of our religious upbringing with the new insights of self-discovery. Although I said in my introduction to this book that the good of the church was not my primary preoccupation, it is nevertheless worth pointing out how much it has lost in actively alienating women like these.

NOTES

1. The Osborne Report, Report to the House of Bishops on homosexuality, unpublished, 1989, para. 61d.
2. *Ibid.*, para. 62.
3. *Ibid.*, para. 71.
4. Ecumenical Press Service, World Council of Churches Central Committee, Johannesburg, South Africa, 20–28 January 1994, press release no. 10 (22 January), p. 1.
5. *Ibid.*, press release no. 23 (18 January), p. 1.
6. *Ibid.*, press release no. 23 (28 January), p. 2.
7. *Ibid.*, press release no. 24 (28 January), p. 3.
8. The Student Christian Movement (SCM) is the oldest student Christian organization in Britain, founded in 1889. It is ecumenical, and committed to an exploratory and critical faith and to its application to social and political action. The Christian Unions which now predominate in British student life originated as a splinter group which seceded from the SCM.
9. Mary Daly, *Outercourse: The Be-Dazzling Voyage.* The Women's Press, London, 1993, pp. 111–12.
10. This debate focused upon John A. T. Robinson, *Honest to God* (SCM Press, London, 1963), and was similar to the debate in the 1980s about pronouncements by David Jenkins, Bishop of Durham.
11. Rosie Miles, *Not in Our Name: Voices of Women Who Have Left the Church.* Southwell Diocesan Social Responsibility Group, Nottingham, 1994, p. v.
12. Jeanette Howard, *Out of Egypt: Leaving Lesbianism Behind.* Monarch Publications, Eastbourne, 1991.

7 lesbian clergy

A TV researcher sent out a circular letter via lesbian and gay Christian networks asking for lesbian and gay priests/deacons in the Church of England to contribute to a documentary. The letter said:

> I would like the programme to feature a number of different gay and lesbian ministers, each of whom could throw a personal light on the dilemmas they are now facing within the Church .... This would be a unique opportunity to place the whole debate about homosexual clergy in a very real and recognizable context, and would show that a priest is a priest whatever his or her sexuality might be ... However, I fully appreciate the difficulties that priests and deacons would face if they were to 'come out' on screen and in most cases it will probably be necessary to protect the identities of the interviewees.[1]

This researcher found it very difficult to find women who were willing to participate in this programme, an experience that is not unusual for journalists seeking lesbian input into programmes about 'Christianity and homosexuality' and, in particular, 'homosexuality and the priesthood'. It seems that the invisibility of lesbians explored in the previous chapter is strongly replicated in the lives of lesbian clergy.

Since media professionals seem to be somewhat perplexed and bewildered by this reticence on the part of lesbian clergy, it is worth exploring it further. Interestingly, I did not have to make special efforts to find contributions from lesbian women who are working, have worked, or hope(d) to work as religious professionals. Such women came forward from a range of denominations: Methodist, Anglican, Baptist and Roman Catholic (from religious orders). The most obvious explanation for this is the perception that as a lesbian myself I am less likely to misunderstand, misconstrue or misuse their material. There are, however, more subtle but no less significant possible reasons. For one thing, the gender neutrality of the researcher's letter gives little impression that he is aware that lesbian experience is very different from that of gay men in this matter (a fact which will be explored in more detail later). In addition, it is possible that my project offered lesbian clergy an opportunity to contribute their insights on their own terms in a way that TV documentaries do not. The two options of appearing either *openly* on TV as a lesbian clergyperson or pastoral worker, or *in disguise*, as though one is ashamed of who one is, are both decidedly unattractive. The latter option is insalubrious and not conducive to the maintenance of self-respect. The former is a foolproof way of opening oneself to annihilation at the merciless hands of the ecclesiastical institution. One cannot fully understand the decisions of lesbian women to remain silent without a clear understanding of that institutional power. Consideration of this power will therefore form the focus of this chapter.

CAROL

We begin with the enlightening case-study of Carol who, in the 1980s, trained to be an Anglican deaconess. At theological college she entered into a relationship with a woman training for the ordained ministry in another denomination. Because they were unwilling to be secretive about the nature of this relationship, the college principal felt it necessary to inform Carol's sponsoring bishop. As a result of his action Carol's career in the Church of England was curtailed before it even began. What follows is some of the actual correspondence which surrounded the case. The first letter is from Carol's theological college principal to her sponsoring bishop:

My dear Bishop,

I fear that a pastoral problem is going to intrude upon my acknowledgement of your so much appreciated letter of congratulations. It is good to be associated with you again even though it is a difficulty which brings us once more into close communication.

A deaconess candidate, Carol, with a very good Cambridge background, was sponsored by your diocese in 198–. She has been such a good student here, so personable and popular and efficient, that she has been elected President of the Junior Common Room for next term.

Her life, however, has been complicated over the past few months by the fact that she has formed a very intense attachment to one of the Methodist women candidates for the ministry. So close is their relationship that the Methodist girl, Barbara, has abandoned the opportunity of a year's training abroad in order to remain at college to be near to Carol. They have both seen me and asked that if possible they may obtain postings next September which would enable them to live together. This is very disturbing because although such relationships between women have not attracted the opprobrium of male homosexuality, there is no doubt that in our prurient times such associations are more likely to cause scandal than they were ten or twenty years ago.

The staff are divided on the matter. Some, like a counsellor attached to the cathedral where she did her placement, feel that we should do everything possible to help them to fulfil their relationship, which has undoubtedly been a great support to them this last year. Others believe that both their Ministries will be ruined if this relationship continues.

We have asked our Pastoral Theology Tutor to give them special care in the early weeks of term. I wonder about the permanence of the relationship, since I would hesitate to classify either as 'homosexual'.

My colleagues feel that I should bring the problem to you in order that we may learn your mind and your opinions as to what should be Carol's future should the friendship persist.

Yours,

G ———

The next letter comes from a woman lay office holder in the first diocese in which Carol sought employment:

My dear Carol,

I hope it has been a lovely Easter and that despite all the problems you are finding a new and re-creating strength of love to give you the confidence and the courage you need. Bless you.

We shall have to advertise that Girls' Friendly Society/Diocesan Industrial Chaplaincy in this diocese. I believe it needs someone with a measure of experience of either parochial or chaplaincy work and the Girls' Friendly Society stresses this. Also, I talked as I promised you, to the Bishop of W———. He is very doubtful whether you could in fact exercise a ministry while living with Barbara in open partnership. The warmth and trust of a college fellowship is so very, very different from the attitudes you would meet in the outside world.

I do hope you have the opportunities to discuss all this with friends whom you trust who are also Gay Christians. I think I told you I have one such very good friend here, and I do listen to him.

The fact that this chaplaincy will also be 50 per cent sponsored by the Girls' Friendly Society is another immense hurdle. I could not, with the best will in the world, recommend you to them as the right person. And this for the reason I have given you above. I believe ministry would prove impossible. You would never be given a chance to be known as the committed, courageous and lovely person you are. All that folk would allow you to be is a cruel caricature and that would be desperately hurtful for all concerned.

There is nothing of comfort in this. But only by being realistic are you going to find the sphere in which God intends you to exercise your very real abilities and insights.

Yours in love,

D———

Carol's reply read as follows:

Dear D———,

Thank you for your letter, read to me over the phone as I am away from home. I think I would have welcomed a meeting with, rather than a letter from you – though I guess time is short and pressures always present. As you say, it was of little comfort to receive.

I would like to speak honestly of some of my feelings, some of which are the fruit of our contact re the W——— job and some of which, no doubt, are accumulating through my various experiences with the Church of England Hierarchy. I struggle with these in order to understand them and to be free of them; increasingly I find the need to search for God in the silences, as I discover the deeply sown seeds of resentment and bitterness within me planted as I have journeyed during the last 18 months. More than anything else I resent the fact that I allow the discovery of loving and being loved, with all the joy and pain that involves, to be overshadowed by fear and prejudice and experience of injustice.

I sense that it was hard for you to write to me and I value that you struggled with your feelings in order to say what you have. I appreciate also that it is hard for one on the outside of an experience to completely understand what it feels like for another on the 'inside' of that same experience.

I think I said before that I find it difficult to claim the label 'gay' for myself; knowing my own sexuality I feel it to be – for want of any better label – bisexual, and I believe such is the nature of most people's sexuality. Those who support Barbara and me by giving love and encouragement, are not those who label themselves 'gay', they would describe their own sexuality as heterosexual probably. We know only one or two gay people well, though I have come to know more since sharing our experience with the college community. I do not believe we need to acquire certain labels in order to comprehend the 'humanity' contained within different relationships.

I fear for the church – as much as it fears for me – and so I try to stay within it to shoulder part of the responsibility involved in the consequences of the church's life. The church finds it easier to pass me by on the other side than I it – and that is part of my pain. I fear for the ghetto mentality of the church as I experience it today, not only in relation to Barbara and me but in so many other areas – lay ministry and women in the church, to name but two. I fear for its lack of vision, for its fake gospel and for its lack of courage and honesty. It asks of the world that it take responsibility for its sins and shortcomings whilst it disowns its own: such witness is seen for what it is – unauthentic and hypocritical. With one and the same breath the church invites me – and all others – to journey in discipleship with all its risk and uncertainties, and then warns that in no way can it partner me on that journey except in 'safe' and 'restricted' terms. To my cost (none of the church's) I have discovered that the way of discipleship means giving up all – all that was previously thought understood and known has been exploded in the gift of loving – to follow Christ.

Those who are called to represent Christ to me in their ministries have failed me: I have been given silence, sympathy, interrogation and many words. Yet I remain unaffirmed in my vocation, without direction because no one dares to speak or to take seriously that which in my God-given being I am.

You, and others, have spoken of choice: between my vocation and my relationship with Barbara. Are all married clergy asked the same question? I doubt it, yet I am sure that many of them have to live with marital tensions which mar ministry in as great a way as possibly my relationship with Barbara could. I deeply believe that ministry by anyone only 'works' well when it draws from a deep source within close, intimate, and loving personal relationships – the two are fully complementary. It is for this reason that our living together is important for both of us: we are not out just to make a point. Necessarily, we realize this involves a deep spirit of discernment when sharing what we are to one another with others. Inevitably at some time or other a trust given to someone will be betrayed and we shall shoulder the consequent hurt and cost of that: the church should be prepared to do so also. It seems to me that there is no need to look to countries overseas to discover an 'underground' church, for one exists in England where a large proportion of church members – both clergy and lay – live their deepest relationships of love and trust 'in secret' for fear of what the church hierarchy might do to them. This 'underground church' fails in its witness also by permitting itself to be 'underground'.

There are choices open to us – all of them hard, all of them ones which we never envisaged ourselves having to make – but the church asks that it be so. We too may join the 'underground church', though having begun a journey it is difficult to forget the country already seen. We may seriously consider the extent of our participation in the church's life in the future, or we may adopt alternative strategies for 'ministry' outside of the 'official' employment structures of the churches. We may, as does the church, keep separate our public and private lives, but that is not the gospel journey we see ourselves travelling upon. Our steps are tentative, our prayers often silent and our faith's vision often cloudy. More than anything else we look forward to the time when we shall be less concerned with our self-identity (at every turn the church's demand of us is preoccupied with this) and more with that of those around us.

I write these words so that you may not neglect to make my experience a part of yourself and thus a part of the church.

I trust that you will find the right person to fill the W—— industrial chaplaincy post and that her work is successful.

Yours,

Carol

Having been turned down for this post. Carol applied for a job as a Higher Education chaplain. She was interviewed and offered the post, which she accepted. On hearing about this, Carol's theological college principal wrote to her:

My dear Carol,

I was so overcome with delight last evening that I am not sure that you fully glimpsed my joy. I should have made you both have a drink – even if there was no champagne, only the dregs of sherry.

Sometime you must tell me about the interview – I know C—— and like him immensely. He produced some of my radio talks and we have close mutual friends.

I hope all goes well for you now. Let me know how things develop. With love and congratulations to you both from both of us.

Yours affectionately,

G——

In order to take up the post of chaplain Carol needed a bishop's licence. The following letter was sent to her from the bishop concerned:

Dear Carol,

To come quickly to the heart of the matter it has become clear to me that it is simply not within my power to license you as Chaplain to the University. I felt this to be so just thinking the matter through after our conversation last week. Since then I have discussed the matter with my colleagues on the diocesan staff and with the Bishop of G—— and Archbishop ——, and I have to say that they have only strengthened me in my belief in the inevitability of this decision. I have come to this decision with sorrow and with a great respect for both you and Barbara. It is fair to you that I try to briefly spell out the thinking that lies behind it.

I think this can be done most easily by trying to give the answer to three questions:

1. What is the official teaching of the Church of England on homosexual relationships? In fact very little has ever been said on this subject. The Church of England has simply accepted the Judaeo-Christian tradition that all such relationships were sinful. This would be supported by scriptural quotation. Significantly, the most recent study of the subject under the chairmanship of the Bishop of Gloucester, though it has aroused a degree of hostility because of its sympathy with homosexuals, even if it had been approved by the Church of England would not, as I understand it, have made it possible for me to give you a licence.

2. What is a true Christian understanding of homosexual love? Strictly speaking, this question is irrelevant to the issue as there is an important sense in which a Bishop has to administer the law as it stands rather than as he thinks it should be. If within myself I had been absolutely convinced that the relationship you have together is one that reflects truly God's love to us, though it would not have made possible my formal approval of the situation, it would have made me feel it right to give you every encouragement that I could. Obviously there is no time here to go into the weighty subject in depth.

But for myself I am increasingly coming to doubt whether the modern identification of human love with divine love is not wrong. An older tradition has over-inclined to see them invariably pulling in opposite directions. Might we not have moved too far in the opposite direction? Many a man and woman nowadays feel it right to abandon their wedded partner for another simply on the grounds that 'we love one another'. I do believe that affection and love is something that every human being needs. But in God's mysterious providence I am not certain that it is something we are entitled to claim for ourselves whatever the price to others or to our possibilities of usefulness to our fellow human beings. In short, I cannot answer this question but I am less certain than most people that the answer is bound to be favourable to your cause.

3. What is the purpose of a Bishop's licence? The Bishop's licence is given to those who are in a teaching position within the Church. It is the outward sign that this person has the Bishop's confidence and can be accepted as a reliable guide in matters of faith and morals. In giving a licence the Bishop is not acting as a private person, he is acting as a representative of the Church of Christ in that area. The single factor that has weighed with me most in deciding that I cannot give you a licence is that I have been able to think of no relevant group of people who would have supported this decision. If I had discussed it with the chaplains for Higher Education, or the Bishop's Council, or the Diocesan Synod or my fellow Bishops, in every case I am certain that the answer would have been NO. For a Bishop to act in opposition to both the law and custom of the Church and the unanimous advice of every representative group in the Church would surely have been an abuse of his position. The Bishop of Gloucester, who has a great deal more sympathy with your situation than most people I think, and is ready to accept that your position is entirely compatible with the Christian religion, was nonetheless quite certain that it would not have been possible for you to do the job of a chaplain once the matter had become known. He felt strongly that people's attitude to you would have been impossible. Others have emphasized to me the possible attitude of parents of students, and this brings me back to the significance of a licence as a sign that a person has the accepted authority of the Church of England as a whole in the work they are doing.

I fear all this will not seem terribly helpful to you. I don't believe that the Church or any Bishop is infallible. We could be wrong. In years to come we may be led to a deeper understanding of these things. We are all answerable ultimately to God alone. I can accept that you may well feel that you have been treated unjustly by me. I only ask that you do not allow any bitterness to hinder your relationship with Almighty God. In calling each of us into his service he promised us that it would be the way of the cross and it can too easily be forgotten that a suffering we have chosen is not really suffering at all.

Yours,

———

Bishop

One week later, this bishop wrote to Carol again:

Dear Carol,

There is no real point in me saying again how sorry I am that things have turned out as they have. I do feel very sad about it but the changed circumstances brought about by the new information that came to us after your appointment does make it inevitable that I withdraw the offer of the post as university chaplain. As outlined in my previous letter, I am not able to license you and without that licence it is not possible for you to be paid and therefore the appointment cannot be proceeded with. I can understand and sympathize with the motives that led both you and your referee to keep from us this information but I cannot see that the result has been other than a considerable degree of unnecessary hurt and distress.

Yours,

———

Bishop

This was Carol's reply:

Dear Bishop,

I have received your letter and note that you withdraw the offer of the post as University Chaplain with the Chaplaincy of Higher Education. I note also that the reason for this (your earlier letter) is due to the fact that you feel unable to license me to the appointment because in my personal life Barbara and I desire to live and share our life together. I would like to state again here that I had been offered the post and already accepted it in writing and that I myself have not withdrawn my application for this appointment.

I would also like to spell out some of my thoughts during the past weeks concerning this job specifically, and my relationship as a woman lay worker to the Church of England in general. I find much of your first letter difficult to reply to because I feel it has little to do with me in my life as I try, somewhat haltingly, to live the Gospel journey to which I feel called. Much of what you say about the authority of the Church and the Bishop's role in administering that authority may make sense in theory, but it exhibits a wide credibility gap in practice.

It is the Christ of the Gospels who gives authority to the Churches and it is He upon whom the Churches called when proclaiming God's salvation from all sin. It seems to me to say more about the nature of the Church and its representatives than it does about the so-called 'sinner', when the Church picks upon certain 'sins' in order to highlight their sinfulness (and these are usually sexual sins as other kinds do not draw the crowds in quite the same way) and proceeds to use such labelled goods so that it may exclude from the power structures and discriminate against those it does not find desirable company. I draw little comfort from the fact that you and others in authority have told me I am 'courageous', 'sincere', 'well qualified', and 'highly suitable' for pastoral and other work in the Church of England, and yet actively discriminate against me for personal choices I have made and at some cost, for living my life in relationship to other human beings and God Himself. To be a Christian is for me a vocation to be a human being in the fullest way possible; for this I need to 'own' my own human nature – you choose to focus on one part of this, the sexual part – and this I have and am trying to do in as honest a way as possible, which involves 'falling short' in much the same way as you yourself share in human sinfulness from day to day. This is the way of the cross as I understand it.

You speak to me as a Bishop and yet you credit me for thinking little about my own Christian discipleship. I am equally aware that 'love' can cover a multitude of sins: I am aware that married couples sin as grievously as do promiscuous same-sex couples, and I too want to witness to the quality of life in human loving rather than the somewhat cheaply bought sensuous encounters in relationships. It is for this reason that Barbara and I refuse to live in secret and to make life comfortable for the Christian communities to which we belong. We have found that 'divine love' has become incarnate in our lives in the love we hold for one another, and have come, not so easily, to receive this as God's gift of Himself to us and to others. We are deeply aware of the cost involved not just for ourselves, but for the Church and those in authority within it, if this gift of God is to be received and witnessed to: perhaps, rather naively, we believed that such a witness might take place within the bosom of the Church's life. We are not witnessing to a 'cause', as you put it, nor are we saying over much about our sexual orientation, and very little about that of others, though over the past few months we have come to see how afraid people are of their own sexuality and how little the Church has to say that is positive about it.

I say to you as Bishop:

What do you have to say to me and to many others that is positive about the complex and rich nature of our ambivalent human, and often sexual relationships?

What do you have to say to God when you choose for ministry in the Church those who are socially acceptable and mostly conformist (at least outwardly) in their sexual, political and religious behaviour when He Himself chose to spend his time with the 'tax collectors and sinners'?

How do you account for the well-known fact that there are many priests in the Church of England who would call themselves 'gay' and yet practise full-time ministry, some of whom are in chaplaincy work in Higher Education, and yet feel able to prevent a woman, and a lay person, from doing the same? In the area of sexual relations, as well as in many other areas of the Church's life, is there to be one rule for the clergy and another for the laity?

How will you prevent a situation like my own recurring in your own diocese? You say that you feel you have been misled by the withholding of 'relevant information', and yet I sent in an application form and attended an interview, both of which failed to ask for such information. In the Church's selection procedures there is no set way of obtaining the information required: the names and sex of people I may come to love or with whom I may choose to have sexual relations; the precise state of my marital relations. May I suggest that such information is 'irrelevant' to ministry, and for you to require such information in the job application procedures is an act of discrimination and a kind of sexual apartheid.

And finally, if the office of Bishop is to be primarily a pastoral rather than an administrative one, what do you have to say to me as someone who feels she has a calling to a full-time Christian pastoral ministry when the Church is saying that I can only do this on its own double-standard terms by denying the presence of the Incarnate God in my own human relationships?

I suspect that there is little to be said on all these matters now that I, whose life's future has been decided by others, have been silenced. The power of self-interest and self-respectability in the Church and its representatives is too strong a drug for anyone to allow a vision of anything other than 'scandal' to form in their imaginations. If nothing else, I have learnt to pray in earnest for the Church to which I belong, for I see that the Gospel it has chosen to preach for itself is not the Gospel at all but a fake and comfortable imitation of it which causes 'scandal' to few.

I hope that if nothing else I leave you with many questions about the credibility of the authority you administer as bishop. Meanwhile I am returning to my place in the pew which, it seems, is my only rightful place in the Church at the moment, though I know that even there I shall find it difficult to carry the hurt and the disillusionment of the past year.

May the Spirit of God go with you.

Yours,

Carol

Finally, Carol's sponsoring bishop adds the following postscript:

Dear Carol,

It is a good many months since we corresponded, but I have been kept in touch with your progress at theological college and have heard from the Principal how very well you have done in the final year of your course.

It makes me all the more sad that, for the reason of which we are both aware, I have not been able to offer you an appointment in this diocese, and the same I understand to have been true of W—— and S——. The Principal has asked whether I might commend you for the Inter-diocesan Certificate, and while I should dearly like to do so, it does not seem honest to take such a step while refusing you a licence.

I can therefore only say that if your circumstances should change in the future and you wanted employment in this diocese, I should be very glad to hear from you. As things are, I am not sure how much you will value my prayers and hopes that you may find fulfilment in another kind of employment: but such as they are, you certainly have them.

Yours,

——

Bishop

Turning to the Gay Christian Movement (as it was then called), Carol received the following advice from an office holder:

Dear Carol,

Thank you for your letter. You ask some very fundamental questions!

It seems to me that there are two levels on which to seek answers. Dividing the levels is in a sense artificial, but to do so may help clarify the issues. First there is the personal level in all aspects of this. You and Barbara both have had and have responded to a personal call to the Christian ministry. You are both in training for what you believe to be God's will for you in your Christian discipleship. Alongside this vocation there has come the loving relationship which you experience each for the other. The first thing you have to do (and I know you are both working on it) is to relate your love for each other with the love and obedience with which you responded to God's call to the ministry. You have to be quite sure in your own minds that the two are compatible. This is not a matter of being gay; it is a question that everyone called to minister has to face – the place of loving personal relationships in that ministry ...

The second level is that of the institutional Church in which you seek to minister. To the best of my knowledge neither the Church of England nor the Methodist Church will at this time ordain anyone who is living openly in a homosexual partnership. That is certainly true for men; I cannot be quite so certain about women. Those men who are already ordained and have 'come out' as gay are tolerated (depending on the diocese or area a bit), so long as there is no open scandal, i.e. so long as no one is scandalized. There is much connivance and consequently some very distasteful dishonesty and hypocrisy, as well as some openness and acceptance. It is certainly a source of embarrassment to church authorities, who consequently will play safe when it comes to appointments. Openly gay couples find it difficult to move at all, let alone get preferment. The majority of homosexual clergy, who are not voluntarily celibate, tread the path of extreme discretion and stay in the closet.

These are the circumstances in which you ask if it is possible to be true to one's personal life/relationships while functioning as a minister/deaconess. The answer is that it is quite possible; indeed I would say it was essential. But you may well find that you will not be allowed to hold any ministerial office in the Church – at any rate for the moment. Whether you find yourselves forced into an either/or situation, or whether you can in good conscience manage a both/and, only you can decide.

Yours,

P——

The first and most obvious thing to notice about Carol's case-study is the male construction of the whole situation. Carol and Barbara are a pastoral 'problem' – an irritant. They disturb a finely balanced impersonal world of male power games where what counts is studying at Cambridge, being president of the 'Junior Common Room' (notice the Oxbridge jargon imported into a non-Oxbridge theological college) and keeping up appearances. The intrusion into this world of two young women of integrity, who take seriously the Christian imperative for honesty and the integration of their self-knowledge with ministry to be 'all that they can be' without compromise, flings the whole structure into disarray and the power figures into frustration. One can almost hear them questioning one another: why didn't these women just play the game? Why hadn't they kept quiet about their relationship? Surely they could have been economical with the truth regarding the exact nature of it? Even the representative of the Gay Christian Movement seems rather confused by Carol's case. Faced with the inadequacy of his usual categories of analysis (designed for making sense of the choices facing gay men) he appears at a loss as to what to suggest.

What kind of ministry is it that will be 'ruined' by a loving relationship such as this one? Where a deep and valuable friendship is said to 'persist' like flu symptoms? Where honesty will be undermining? That's the form of ministry that the men in this correspondence have created and seek to maintain by employing all the power that is available to them. One does catch a glimpse of a certain measure of regret – perhaps even sadness – that they have had to deal so severely with someone they liked and (after a fashion) respected. Nevertheless there is no question that this is a price worth paying to shore up the institution.

The final insult is surely that those who were instrumental in serving the institution claimed that their decisions were designed, ultimately, *for Carol's own good*. They assumed, from their Olympian standpoint, that she would never be accepted by the ordinary people of the Church; that the laity would see her only as a 'cruel caricature' of the person which they, by contrast, could appreciate in all of her multidimensional glory. An interesting theological perspective emerges here, too. 'Only by being realistic are you going to find the sphere in which God intends you to exercise your very real abilities and insights', Carol was told. If I was still in the habit of using religious language I might write an excellent sermon about that. Whatever happened to leaps of faith, to prophetic witness and the foolishness of the gospel? Has the Church of England given up on them?

Those who accuse lesbians and gay men of making a 'big deal' of their sexuality, or of self-ghettoization, would do well to read this correspondence. For Carol's identification as lesbian was precipitated by the ecclesiastical establishment's treatment of her. In the correspondence she calls herself 'bisexual' – and that only for want of a better word.

Readers should know that by the time she had left the Church she was in no doubt about her lesbian identity.

Linked with this, the terminology employed by the bishop who refused to license Carol to the chaplaincy job is instructive. Because, for him, 'homosexuality' is just 'a cause', he assumes that the same is true for those who are lesbian and gay. He seems to confuse 'opinions' with lived reality. This kind of thinking was also prominent in the recent age of consent debate. For many MPs, whether the age of consent was to be 16, 18 or 21 was simply an issue of abstract argument: the debate was just another opportunity to play around with ideas. There was little awareness of the gravity of just what was at stake for gay men (and, indirectly, for lesbians too). And so it is in this correspondence: the bishop ponders Carol's future as though he were doing *The Times* crossword, and concludes with an admission that he could be wrong. Apparently it makes little difference to him. Such is the nature of power. In effect, he sat in judgement on the relationship between Barbara and Carol and found it wanting. He was even able to deny any personal responsibility for this conclusion by saying that he was just following orders: had he consulted various committees and authority figures, he felt sure that they would have taken his view. So sure, in fact, that he didn't even bother to do so.

That same bishop's final sentence is quite astonishing for one charged with pastoral care responsibilities. He says, in effect, that if Carol thinks she is suffering, then this is because of her inferior earthly perception. In the grand Christian scheme of things, apparently, this is not really suffering at all. It is worth bearing in mind at this point that as a result of the actions of this bishop, Carol had no home, no job and no professional prospects in the career for which she had just been trained. From a religious perspective, her whole *raison d'être* in life had been fundamentally called into question and her structures of meaning and value undermined. The only 'solace' this bishop can offer is that her pain is mere illusion.

By way of a postscript, it is worth pointing out that although it is several years since this happened to Carol, no policy changes have been implemented within the Church of England to prevent exactly the same situation arising again. Questions of sexuality are still studiously avoided at the candidating stage, and a policy of duplicity is operated by the church institution thereafter. As I said in Part One of this book, the most recent report from the House of Bishops[2] made a distinction between clergy and laity, urging local congregations to welcome lesbian and gay people (in relationships or not) in the latter category, while reinforcing the ban on sexual activity for lesbian and gay clergy. The bishops assured us that there would be no 'witch-hunts' and no 'prying into the private lives of clergy'. In other words, clergy are still being discouraged from living lives built upon openness and honesty, with an enormous amount of power still concentrated in the hands of individual bishops.

JOANNE

I was disillusioned once I was a curate in a 'middle of the road' C of E parish. I realized that most church members do not want to hear traditional Christian assumptions challenged. There was little opportunity for me to explore the issues which really inspired me – a radical approach to scripture; the rethinking of Christian concepts of the family; sexuality and the role of women. When I did try to introduce such issues, I was met with bewilderment, not only by parishioners but also by some of my local fellow clergy. There were some individuals who shared my concerns, but they were in the minority.

My career lasted only a year. I fell in love with Celia, who was a member of my congregation, and we decided to make the break from our unhappy marriages and make a future together. During the trauma that inevitably followed upon this decision, a number of issues were raised, most of which we can only analyse with hindsight. I had assumed that my resignation would be inevitable, but the pain surrounding it was so great that we could not stand back and look at what was happening to us, and it was a long time before we could think about the issues dispassionately.

At the time we felt that stereotypical attitudes to homosexuality were behind the way in which we were treated, and undoubtedly they played their part: lack of recognition of women's sexuality; blaming the older partner for seducing the younger; inability to take a gay relationship seriously. However, we have reflected on this since in the light of other people's experience. What stands out for us now is the church's embarrassment and pastoral ineptitude about sexual matters generally, and its dishonesty. It might be helpful if I try to explore what the church might have done differently about my situation.

I did not expect to be able to continue in ministry and live with my new partner – I was aware of the lack of tolerance towards homosexuality within the church and was realistic about this. Furthermore, I recognized the element of scandal in what was an adulterous relationship with a member of my own congregation, and although I felt that I had ample grounds to end my marriage, which for me had failed on many levels, I accepted responsibility for entering into the marriage in the first place and did not expect to get off 'scot-free'. To do the church credit, they fully accepted that my marriage was over and would have happily retained my services as a separated/divorced woman. So I cannot say, now, that I feel any anger towards the church about my resignation in itself. The bishop did not demand my resignation when I first told him of the situation, but insisted that I took a month to think before making a decision. In this, too, I now see that he was right. It was a major decision, and no one, not even Celia and I, could at the time have been absolutely certain that our relationship would prove worth the sacrifice. I had to be given the opportunity to change my mind.

The failure was primarily in terms of pastoral care. When I told the bishop that Celia had been 'frozen out' by our vicar, and had received no pastoral care, he explained to me quite seriously that since she had ceased attending services (she had been told that she was not welcome once her relationship with me was known), she was strictly no longer one of his parishioners and pastoral care was not appropriate. He made no other attempt to support her, and her needs were completely ignored. Celia was cast in an almost demonic role, blamed entirely for the whole affair, and attacked quite ferociously, while I was shown love and concern. This placed considerable strain upon our relationship, and, at the risk of being cynical, we believe that the intention was to drive us apart. My husband, who could have been cast as the victim in the situation, received almost no support at all from the local clergy.

The congregation, who knew that something was amiss and had lost one of their clergy and a prominent member overnight, had no opportunity to air their feelings because the subject was not open to discussion. My vicar and bishop were anxious about possible scandal. This resulted in a conspiracy of silence – the congregation were given no reason for our disappearance and thus no opportunity to face up to the situation. Fellow clergy in the deanery were also kept in the dark. Information, some of it inaccurate, filtered through to people by rumour.

I think the church's dishonesty is also a major cause for concern. I have been told by more than one person that, had I simply left my husband, asked for a move to a different parish, and then continued my relationship with Celia 'discreetly', no one need have been any the wiser. This was never an option for me, because I knew I could not demean our relationship by pretending it did not exist. It would also have involved being dishonest with my husband, or asking him to keep quiet about Celia on my behalf, both of which were out of the question. However, I have no doubt that the Church would have preferred it that way. I think it was an embarrassment to them that I made such a clean breast of things – the bishop even admitted that he had never heard a woman express lesbian feelings before.

The support we received during and after this time was from personal friends, most of them Christians and some of whom were clergy, but not from those who had professional responsibility for our care. The experience of other friends, both straight and gay, who have found themselves in similar situations, suggests that this is a common pattern. Enlightened individuals within the church can offer support, loyal friendship, understanding, and deep insight; but for some reason their voices are seldom heard at a hierarchical or public level. Sexuality is still an embarrassment to the church, and those whose behaviour raises sexual issues are themselves an embarrassment.

Joanne's story builds upon Carol's and contributes to our growing familiarization with the dynamics of institutional church politics. Joanne recognizes before 'going public' all the issues which those in authority over Carol urged her to consider. She is aware that she may meet incomprehension or condemnation from her congregation; that her new relationship will 'cause scandal'. It is partly because she is aware of these possibilities that she brings her change of circumstances into the open, expecting, not unreasonably, to be dealt with in a similarly open and professional manner. Her expectations were not met. Some of the issues which emerged in our exploration of heterosexuality are replicated here, in particular the power of information control. It is likely that the damage done to Joanne's congregation was significant, as the authorities displayed a disrespect and a distinct lack of trust in keeping the reality of the situation from them. If the intention of those who dealt with Joanne was to 'protect' her congregation (from the truth), then it is probable that they did more harm than good.

There is another issue here which relates to comments I made earlier in Part Two about sexual violence and exploitation. Joanne's situation contrasts with the examples I gave in that section of male clergy who slept with women congregants in the course of carrying out their parish duties, while remaining, in many cases, married to their wives. This I described as abusive behaviour. Joanne experienced a change in the nature of her relationship with Celia, who was a member of her congregation, and with whom she fell in love. The fact that they were both women does not mitigate the potentiality for an abuse of power in this situation – Joanne was still in a position of clerical authority. The big difference was that Joanne immediately informed those in authority over her that the nature of the relationship between herself and Celia had changed. She did this in the full recognition that she would inevitably lose her job, but in the (not unreasonable) expectation that the best way forward might be explored openly and honestly. Yet the authorities reacted with near panic. This can only have served to discourage others in similar situations (whatever their gender) from taking the same course of action, and it graphically demonstrates just one more way in which the Church actively encourages abusive and exploitative behaviour by discouraging openness, honesty and professional accountability.

It is my perception that the Church of England prides itself on being the 'national' church – open to all and servant of all, irrespective of whether or not people are regular church-goers. This is often cited as one reason why it should remain the established church. Such a claim is significantly undermined by the fact that both Celia and Joanne's husband were denied any form of pastoral care. Surely even a non-churchgoing member of the parish community deserved better treatment than that? Such a bizarre response by the church is probably symptomatic of the discomfort with issues of sexuality which Joanne herself identifies among those who dealt with her case. The fact that Joanne and Celia had embarked upon a lesbian relationship probably exacerbated this pastoral ineptitude. In the cases of both Carol and Joanne the men in ecclesiastical authority seem completely nonplussed by their encounter with lesbianism. Put together, these stories expose a deep level of ignorance about lesbian sexuality.

JENNIFER

These reflections come from within the context of a committed relationship with another woman, and of being a priest in the Anglican Church. In relation to our partnership the main issues seem to be: whether we take on board heterosexual norms as our own, with reference to structures and ethical behaviour; the relevance or otherwise of the Church to our situation; and the resulting effect on my relationship with God.

Our situation has brought out a lot of questions, and the answers are very much 'in process', because by definition there is a dynamic interchange between ourselves, between us and the Church, and between us and God. We have asked what is the meaning for us of fidelity, monogamy, loyalty and whether these are different for us than for a heterosexual couple; do we take on their norm, or are we in a new-found land in some sense?

I think we have found that the issues around loving someone – the lessons, the give and take, the sacrifices and the self-assertion needed – are little different, and that temperamental differences are as common as gender ones might be. In terms of the structures allowed to us, however, there is more of the pioneering element, i.e. working out commitment within a single-sex partnership, agreed but not publicly recognized; if you are not explicitly 'coming out', what do people call you?; we do not wish to be defined by our orientation/practice sexually, and therefore if you don't state it openly, some people are left confused.

I would say that how we live together has occupied far more of our attention than whether or not we should sleep together, which reflects a sense I have that, as Dorothy Sayers puts it, 'God is far less interested in our sleeping arrangements than we think!'

To the extent that the Church rejects or cannot include the ideal of a committed relationship which accepts the physical within the whole, it feels irrelevant; to the extent to which it requires splitting the parts of ourselves rather than advocating wholeness, it feels irrelevant; to the extent that we choose not to be open, we can (in Bernard Lynch's words) still 'be loved for what we are not'.[3] Because we still hope to meet God in the Eucharist, and precisely because we do not wish to isolate the sexual element of our relationship by coming out about it, we remain within, yet inwardly on the fringes, both liturgically and emotionally.

The issue is further complicated by the fact that one of us is a priest, and therefore potentially stigmatized by the fact that though Christian lay gay persons are to be accepted within a Christian community, clergy may love another person of their own sex, but by denying their sexual being. I recently had a very interesting conversation with Bishop David Jenkins who stated that he expected the same sort of standards from his committed homosexual clergy as of any priest in a heterosexual marriage. Although I welcomed his acceptance I regretted the seeming ignorance of what a gay clergy couple would lack in support if their relationship were in difficulty. I also felt that he hadn't taken on board difficulties over 'simple' issues such as holding hands in the street. While this would be perfectly acceptable for his heterosexual clergy, his gay clergy would face censure if they were so to behave. These sorts of dilemmas have not been faced.

In relation to God, without formal structures of recognition and without scriptural authority for our commitment, we live on the frontiers of belief; because we don't 'know' as heterosexual couples 'know', we live by faith that we are loved as we are and in our own integrity, continually returning to our inner truth, since there is no external affirmation, except from open Christians and friends.

I feel that the so-called Christian understanding of marriage is about solidifying and fixing a human institution as ultimately definitive and authoritative in a way that our human experience cannot confirm; it ignores the fact that the spectrum of sexuality and human development is experienced by many as much more dynamic and fluid than those structures would allow, and that this dynamism itself reflects the nature of God more realistically. This is not a plea for licence or impermanence, but for the acknowledgement of a range of contexts within which the qualities of God, such as fidelity, forgiveness, passionate love may be expressed and validated in freedom among others.

It remains true that as women together we have a lower profile than male couples and therefore attract less comment or ridicule. This is ambiguous, because as women we are therefore unseen, but it means that life can be lived relatively normally, for which we are grateful. Because we are aware of the costs, I wonder if our gratitude of one another is sharpened in a way it may not be for a heterosexual couple who can take the relationship for granted in its acceptability.

Differences between experiences of lesbians and gay men

In her reflections Jennifer draws attention to some of the specificities of her experience of loving another woman. She notes differences between her perspective and a heterosexual one, and between herself and gay men. How lesbians and gay men diverge is a theme worthy of further investigation. One contributor reflected upon her involvement with the predominantly male Gay Christian Movement at a time when that organization was debating whether or not it should support the campaign to ordain women in the Church of England. She begins with a quote from Adrienne Rich:

PAT

> Lesbians have historically been deprived of a political existence through 'inclusion' as female versions of male homosexuality. To equate lesbian existence with male homosexuality because each is stigmatized is to deny and erase female reality once again. To separate those women stigmatized as 'homosexual' or 'gay' from the complex continuum of female resistance to enslavement, and attach them to a male pattern, is to falsify our history. Part of the history of lesbian existence is, obviously, to be found where lesbians, lacking a coherent female community, have shared a kind of social life and common cause with homosexual men. But this has to be seen against the differences: women's lack of economic and cultural privilege relative to men;

qualitative differences in female and male relationships, for example, the prevalence of anonymous sex and the justification of pederasty among male homosexuals, the pronounced ageism in male homosexual standards of sexual attractiveness, etc. In defining and describing lesbian existence I would hope to move toward a dissociation of lesbian from male homosexual values and allegiances.[4]

I have been sitting here for a long time now, my mind refuses to focus on the issue. It will mean that I have to put words to what I feel as a woman amongst many men, to what woman-to-woman (as opposed to men-to-men) relationships feel like, to what it means to be Christian but without having a denominational allegiance. I am a woman loving another woman who has been put outside of her church and chosen to stay there. I am a woman who can talk theology but for whom Gospel means different things now.

It is hard for women to live double lives within the churches. We retreat into personal religion, separated from the mainstream and get laughed at for our privatized piety, our prayerful domicile whisperings. It is too painful for us to live close to the ecclesiastical structures. These are men's games, men's fantasies and we have no part except to play our part, scripted and directed by those in power and authority – men. I did not play my part well; I improvised, explored new roles and the play goes on without me. I never even made the first night except as part of the audience. And having been on stage I could never quite believe the actors in the same way as I had done before. For the most part it is ham acting and the spoken words say nothing about my life.

Gay men are saying that the women's issue has nothing to do with them. My liberation as woman who loves women has nothing to do with liberation for men who love men. How separate have our worlds become that you do not realize how many of us live on the edge of the world, your world which you have created for us? And my words cannot mean that much to you until you choose to see as I see my world.

My problem is that I do not have a history as woman. This is hidden away and I must discover women who have written about their public and private worlds so that I can reflect on my own. My personal life as woman loving woman is much more political than yours, for in it I begin to say that maybe men are not essential in my life. Men, in the way they organize public life including church life, have been saying that for years about women, whatever sexual preference claims them. Gay men sometimes say that more forcefully to women than other men, but for lesbians to begin to say that to men is seen to be quite preposterous and intolerable. And in the churches, once again, we upset the divine order of things and trespass where even angels fear to tread.

The issue of women in GCM is a personal one and therefore a political one. Women are considered to be ineffectual because, if lesbian, we have put ourselves outside the churches anyway. If we stay it is a precarious, fragile existence because we no longer know in our own terms who the God is about whom we talk, or the liberation which we know about because we feel it in our gut. And all the time you want us to make statements, to 'come in with you', to make our Christian peace. But I cannot because I want new forms, new creations, and I do not believe that they will rise from the ashes of our present impotent ecclesiastical structures.

The Gospel for me is about contention and risk. It is about lacking credibility because I stop playing the games I am expected to play. It is about laughing because I do not comprehend the world in which I live or the relationships I enjoy. The Gospel is intolerable because when I live it I do not believe people will change or set each other free. But I hope against hope and try to live with my oppression in ways that oppress me least, ever conscious of the ways in which I chain others, even you, to burdensome things.

The issues of women in GCM is an issue of Gospel. For me, to be radical we must put our hearts, feet and mouths in the same place. If we did that, we could not afford the luxury of pontificating about gay liberation in the churches and we should see that the churches offer us a cheap liberation indeed.

I undertake discussion about the differences between lesbians and gay men in the full knowledge that the 'divide and rule' mentality of those who oppose us makes it an uncomfortable task. Nevertheless, I believe such a discussion to be necessary. It is worth remembering that those who oppose us do so because they hate diversity; what they most desire is for everybody to be the same (i.e. heterosexual). It is not surprising, therefore, that heterosexism forces upon the lesbian and gay community a negative construction of our diversity. Part of our subversive task is to recast this diversity as a cause for celebration. Indeed, not to do so may be considered collusion with heterosexism.

Lesbians and gay men differ from one another in all sorts of ways: along lines of gender, race, religion and age, to name but a few. Fundamental mistakes are made when gay men or lesbian women from dominant groups make assumptions about what is common ground for all of us, without a recognition that the structural inequalities which shape society as a whole also apply within the lesbian and gay community – and that our respective social-change agendas will be affected by this. So, for instance, white lesbians and gay men have been brought up with the same levels of racism as any other member of society; gay men have shared in the same process of gender construction as any other man, albeit from a different perspective. The challenge is to recognize and combat these structural inequalities so that collective political action honours the diversity within the lesbian and gay community rather than bringing about fragmentation.

It is not my intention here to address comprehensively how we might go about meeting that challenge. But two points spring to mind which may help. Firstly, we must recognize that outside challenges tend to clarify common ground. Let me take as an illustration my personal response to a recent article by Polly Toynbee in the *Radio Times*: 'I have always found it bewildering that lesbians and gay men get lumped together when they have little more in common than either might have with heterosexuals.' The perspective from which this comment was made becomes clear later in the article:

> The rest of us don't go about identifying ourselves by our sexual proclivities, so I am instinctively suspicious of those who claim to speak for the 'gay community' ... Most of the battles for gay acceptability have been won, though there is still some prejudice. Frivolous arrests by bored policemen in public lavatories still happen occasionally. Judges taking away custody from a woman because she is found to be gay ... affect very few people indeed. They are totem issues to run up a flagpole ... if I were gay, I think I'd find more pressing issues in urgent need of good campaigning energy.[5]

In the face of such ignorance from a heterosexual woman I have to admit that my priority is to focus on the common ground which lesbians share with gay men, rather than upon the differences between us. There is a lesson here about political expediency: that sometimes it pays to minimize our differences and present a united front. Ultimately, however, this can only be effective if everyone knows this is what is going on, and that we are not really all the same. This brings me to my second point: that we need to be aware of the nature of our differences; *that* we are different, and that *how* we are different is constantly changing.

Perhaps a concrete example might help to illustrate this point. Recently, a vast number of lesbians, gay men and our supporters made the equalization of the age of consent for gay men the temporary priority for our campaigning energy. For some (particularly, of course, the young gay men who faced being criminalized by the law as it stood) this issue *really was* of primary importance. Others of us *made it* a priority because we could see its symbolic importance for the whole lesbian and gay community, and its indirect implications for society as a whole. It is crucial that we understand the variety of motivations here. It is important, for instance, that gay men understand that for some lesbians the age of consent is not the issue we care about most in the world, but that we gave our support regardless. It is important because if we are challenging the structural inequalities which shape the lesbian and gay community, this must be a reciprocal arrangement.

The need to appreciate the different agendas and motivations which make up the lesbian and gay community is crucial for those working for change within a religious context. Sadly, Pat's experience was that there was little understanding of gender differences within the lesbian and gay Christian community. That is my experience also.

Let us return to the issue of lesbian clergy by way of example. I have noticed a tendency within the lesbian and gay Christian community to treat lesbian clergy as though their situation were exactly equivalent to that of their gay male counterparts. This has been particularly apparent as the first women priests have been ordained into the Church of England, though the tendency can be seen in other denominations also. The term 'closet lesbian priest' has crept into parlance alongside 'closet priest' (meaning a man). Such terminology obscures the vast differences which separate the two in reality. To begin with, it takes no account of the fact that gay men have been ordained for centuries, which means that to be 'closeted' has totally different implications for men than for women. While I am in no way implying that to be a gay male priest is easy, there are survival networks for men which have been developed over centuries which exclude all women, and there is no reason to believe that lesbians will be welcomed with open arms. No account is taken, either, of the fact that lesbians enter the priesthood in the face of incredible institutionalized discrimination and hatred against them *as women*. Men enter it as normative beings with no questions asked.

Women and men also carry different gender constructions with them into ministry. The survival of lesbians and gay men in such work depends upon an ability to separate one's 'private life' from one's 'public role'. It just so happens that this accords with the social construction of masculinity, whereby men are encouraged to compartmentalize their lives. It is, however, in direct opposition to the social construction of femininity, which encourages integration. That's not to say that every man will find it easy to separate the 'public' from the 'private', or that every woman will find it difficult, but there is likely to be some correlation along gender lines.

Finally, and perhaps most importantly, the symbolic significance of lesbian women is totally different from that of gay men within the Christian construct of reality. Here I turn to Sheila Jeffreys for guidance:

> Man-loving is one rather obvious way in which gay men diverge from lesbians. Gay men desire and love members of the ruling class of men. In this respect gay men are loyal to the basic principle of male supremacy, man-loving. Manhood and masculinity, the symbols and behaviour which denote membership of the political class status of men are celebrated in many aspects of gay male culture.[6]

Nowhere is compulsory man-loving more obviously paramount than within Christianity where (as Mary Daly puts it) God is male so the male is God. And for a celebration of membership of the ruling class of men one need look no further than the antics of those closet gay male priests who demonstrate their misogyny in a variety of ways, not least in their virulent opposition to the ordination of women to the priesthood. It is hardly surprising that lesbian ministers and priests find that it tears them apart to live and work within this context. One contributor expressed her feelings in the form of a letter to God:

JILL

> My quarrel is not with you, but with your Church. I've struggled with this for a long time, but now I think I've reached decision-point. I know it's always been something of a love–hate relationship – that conflict which so many of us feel between the vision of the community of faith, healing and liberating and working for justice, and the reality of vulnerable people struggling in imperfect and restrictive structures. I can live with that conflict; I believe it's part of being human and fallible, and I've always been one to try to work for change from within. But what's kept me going is the knowledge that I've found you in the church in the past, and the conviction that, in spite of all its flaws, you are still to be found there: that your love and healing and liberation come to me through the words, the symbols and above all the people; that the church is your body, your word made flesh, incarnate in those who bear your name.

Part of my anger is that I believe that could still be true – is still true in some parts of the church. But the power of that truth is becoming crushed for me underneath the weight of the church's condemnation of my sexuality as a lesbian woman. I find that the official voices of the church reject, or at best tolerate, the relationship which brings me joy and healing, and the sexuality which is at the core of my identity. I do not believe – and I have never believed, since I first recognized my capacity to love women – that you condemn. I believe that you have made me in your image, and that in the passion and delight, the tenderness and vulnerability, which my partner and I share, your love is mirrored. The church denies that – and what is worse, what amounts almost to blasphemy, denies it in your name. So by doing what I have done so far, by staying, by concealing, by being discreet, I am compromising not only what I am, but my most fundamental and deeply held beliefs about you.

This is a betrayal of myself and of you, and that I think is at the root of my pain. It is also a betrayal of my integrity as an ordained minister. More than 20 years ago I believed you were calling me to ministry. I had a hard job convincing others – even in a denomination that ordained women there was opposition, scepticism – but I was determined. It is now 15 years since my ordination, working out that calling in industrial towns; in the inner city; in chaplaincy; through the leading of worship; pastoral work; the attempts to work out what it means to see you on the side of the poor and the powerless. During that time I have often doubted myself and you and the reality and meaning of that call; and I am increasingly convinced that you do not need or require a special group of people called 'the ordained' – I am sure that has much more to do with our human sense of status and structure and order. But I do still believe in ministry in the widest sense – and I do not believe I can be faithful to that ministry as an official representative of a church which denies value and dignity and human justice to those in loving relationship with someone of their own sex. How can I offer pastoral care and solidarity to lesbians and gay men in the name of a church which condemns their love? How can I lead worship in a tradition which denies blessing to same-sex partnerships and renders them invisible with its constant emphasis on the heterosexual family unit? How can I continue to teach the resources and symbolism of a tradition which has such a distrust of the bodies, the sexuality you have given? How can I uphold moral codes which I believe are based on a deeply flawed ethic? How can I encourage and persuade others to join a church which so blatantly contradicts the core values of the gospel of Jesus? Most of all, how can my ministry have an integrity about it when I am so inwardly compromised?

There are people around me who would like me to stay. There are many who believe as I do that you do not condemn, who don't see my sexuality as a problem, who point to the areas of tolerance and openness within the church. They are caring and genuine; I respect them and they are part of the reason for my continuing loyalty to the church. And there is part of me that would like to be convinced by them, that wants to stay, that wants to say 'The church belongs to us too – we are entitled to be here'. But I have come to feel that I can only do that if I can do so openly and proudly, not allowing others to define the terms by my silence and concealment. Yes, I know there is movement – discussions and reports and working parties and some areas of openness – but I feel the gospel demands more than the extending of grudging, cautious permissions, as if they are doing us a favour by allowing us to exist at all! And there are still such painful, enraging areas of intolerance. When my own denomination withdrew from a conference because the Lesbian and Gay Christian Movement would be there, I felt disowned and excluded – and that I colluded in my own oppression, because my opposition, although expressed, was muted by fear for my own position. When I read in the daily newspaper that a religious publisher [SPCK] had withdrawn a book of prayers and blessings for gay and lesbian relationships,[7] I felt both furious and impotent – a deep grief and anger as if even prayer was forbidden to us, as if they would even deny us access to you because the fear and distrust of our sexuality is so great. At each of these points I have nearly left the church – I have hung on desperately, but the seeds were sown, and over time the decision to leave has become more firmly rooted in my mind.

So why is it so hard for me to leave? I can hear so clearly the voices of my feminist friends, telling me the church is a male-dominated patriarchal institution, the voices of those who say 'Why do you want to belong to a church like that?' echoing my own self-questioning. Partly, I suppose, it is, or has been, loyalty. The church has given me so much in the past, and I cannot deny that, and there are many people within it whose commitment to justice and compassion I respect. Partly it is that I have always belonged – the church is part of me, part of my identity, and has given me a sense of affirmation, of worth, of value. Partly that I still cherish many of the symbols and values of the Christian faith – the conviction that women and men are made in the image of God; the accepting, inclusive love portrayed in the story of Jesus; the presence of the Spirit within and amongst human beings; the core symbols of death and resurrection, of sharing bread and wine. But also, of course, I am scared. Scared about what my family will say, scared of the reactions of other Christians, scared of the impact on my present job and future career, scared of the possible loneliness of looking for worship and spiritual nurture elsewhere.

At one time, perhaps, I would have been scared of losing you. Not any more – I am confident enough that you are energy and love within me, that you can be found outside the church, that you will still speak and love and hold and struggle with me. It feels more perilous to stay; that the picture of you with which I am presented in so much of the church's worship and teaching is so distorted, so far from gospel truth, that I will be in danger of losing all faith if I remain.

It is hard to go. I feel as I imagine a woman in an abusive relationship must feel – knowing I am being damaged psychologically and spiritually, and yet searching for the strength that is needed to move from being a victim to being a survivor. But I know that I will survive – I know that already I am naming you and defining myself in new and liberating ways.

I do not know where I will go, where I will find ways to express my faith in you in communion with others. But I have some clues – in the knowledge of you within me, in the groups of women (and sometimes men) who are searching for a more whole spirituality, in those who share a passion for healing and for justice, whatever name they give it. And you have always told me that the wilderness is the place of discovery, that risk is the way to growth, and that the other side of death is resurrection.

Jill's self-questioning and, finally, her leaving encapsulate a struggle which many lesbian women, clergy or not, undergo regarding their place in the Christian community. Clergywomen embark upon their vocations because they have a vision of the justice-making work which they want to do, and they believe that the church is an appropriate context within which to pursue that work. This belief would seem perfectly reasonable given that the Christian gospel is supposed to be central to the church's life. What these women discover is that the church in its institutional manifestations is an obstacle to the fulfilment of its very *raison d'être*. This in turn raises fundamental questions for women about both the content of their faith and the nature of their Christian involvement. These questions will form the initial focus of Part Three.

NOTES

1. Letter from Mick Grogan of Yorkshire Television to all members of the Lesbian and Gay Christian Movement, undated.
2. A Statement by the House of Bishops, *Issues in Human Sexuality*. Church House Publishing, London, 1991.
3. See Bernard Lynch, *A Priest on Trial*. Bloomsbury, London, 1993.

4. Adrienne Rich, *Compulsory Heterosexuality and Lesbian Existence.* Onlywomen Press, London, 1981, pp. 21–2.
5. Polly Toynbee, *Radio Times*, 6–12 August 1994, p. 24.
6. Sheila Jeffreys, *The Lesbian Heresy: A Feminist Perspective on the Lesbian Sexual Revolution.* The Women's Press, London, 1994, p. 145.
7. Elizabeth Stuart's *Daring to Speak Love's Name: A Gay and Lesbian Prayer Book* was commissioned by SPCK, who then refused to publish the work. It was subsequently published by Hamish Hamilton, London, 1992.

III

Rethinking Spirituality
and Sexuality

8 'why don't you just leave?'

In her celebrated *Scum Manifesto* Valerie Solanas declared: 'The male . . . has made of the world a shitpile.'[1] It might be said that in the particular corner of Christendom in which the women of this book find themselves, patriarchy (with more than a little help from lots of men and quite a few women) has made a similar job of Christianity. It therefore seems pertinent at this point to raise the question which many feminists and members of the lesbian and gay community raise with women who retain any connection, however tenuous, with Christianity: if it's so bloody awful, why don't you just leave it all behind?

A variety of assumptions lurk behind this question. Before going on to explore these in more detail I'd like to make a few preliminary comments.

Often the question about women's continued engagement with Christianity comes from 'within': from other women of Christian heritage who have (or think they have) succeeded in 'leaving Christianity behind' and can't quite understand why everybody doesn't follow suit. I myself have asked the question of women who retain an engagement with Christianity which is deeper than my own. The motivation behind the question is sometimes benign curiosity but more often, perhaps, it is insecurity. If I'm not quite sure that I've done the right thing in attempting to cut myself loose, it makes sense to seek validation of my choices through others. After all, it's always good to have company in the wake of one's ideological decisions, and the more the merrier. Christians certainly feel that, so it makes sense for those who've left Christianity to feel the same way.

An alternative scenario is when the question comes from someone with no religious background whatsoever. In this case it may arise from complete incomprehension, or sometimes (though I stress, not always) the question is offered as a new and exciting insight which cannot have occurred to its recipient. I have experienced both, and in the latter case it is hard not to feel insulted. Intentional or not, the implication can easily be that women who admit to any link with Christianity at all must be either gullible, naive, weak or plain stupid.

I raise this point because Part Three of *Found Wanting* represents an attempt to suggest ways in which we can make sense of and deal creatively with the women's experiences described so far. In this context, it makes sense to remind ourselves that women of Christian heritage who question their place within the tradition are those who are most acutely aware of the oppressive nature of Christianity. Such women do not need to be told that the most obvious and logical solution is to 'jack it in'. We're quite well aware of that. The reasons why this option is neither as logical nor as easy as it first appears will be the focus of this section.

I would like to begin by challenging two notions. First, *that in escaping Christianity we escape patriarchy*. It interests me that religions in general, and Christianity in particular, seem to be isolated from other institutions in our society in what we might call 'exodus discourse'. The question 'How can you be a feminist/lesbian and remain a Christian?' is far more common than 'How can you be a feminist/lesbian and remain: a doctor, a lawyer, a computer programmer, a domestic worker, a school teacher, a member of the Labour Party, a journalist, an engineer?, etc.' Yet the institutions which uphold such forms of vocation, employment or political affiliation are just as shot through with sexism as any form of religion. Spending all day, for instance, communicating in phallocentric terminology about whether a computer is 'up' or 'down' and whether a disk is 'hard' or 'floppy' is hardly a dyke's or feminist's paradise. Neither is working within the criminal-justice system, with all the racism, sexism and heterosexism inherent in the laws that are upheld and the selection of those appointed to apply them. And the same conditions exist in each of the other areas of engagement mentioned. As long as we are conscious, we are encountering patriarchal and sexist forces in our lives. So why do we imagine that leaving one particular manifestation of such forces behind will give us freedom?

In answer to this it is sometimes said that while the other areas of life outlined above are inescapable, religion is an optional extra. But that construction has a very limited application, for it is only among a tiny proportion of secular Westerners that religion is not inextricably linked with cultural identity (and even then the extent to which secular culture can be understood without reference to religious forces is debatable).

This brings me to the second notion that I would like to challenge: *that religion is irrelevant*. British people are rather embarrassed about religious phenomena, perhaps partly because of the popular construction of religion as a purely 'personal matter', like sexuality. The lesbian and gay community is, in general, hostile – particularly towards Christianity, Judaism and Islam. This can be justified in part as a legitimate response to the bigotry and hatred directed at lesbian and gay people from certain fanatical adherents of these traditions, but this does nothing to help those who count both as part of their identity. It's something of a cliché that it's harder for a lesbian to 'come out' as a Christian within the lesbian and gay world than it is for her to come out as lesbian within the Christian community. But if there's even a grain of truth in that (and I think there is), then something is amiss.

I would want to argue, however, that even in our little secularized corner of Western Europe it is a serious tactical error to conclude that religion can be ignored. This is particularly true when it comes to lesbian/gay/sexual politics. Religious motivation behind political change in the UK is a stronger force than we might like to admit. Such motivation can manifest itself in a crude and unsophisticated way, as, for example, in the figure of Stephen Green of the Conservative Family Campaign. He equates his own brand of biblical fundamentalism with objective truth, and his political views with the will of God. No subtlety there. But there are other less obvious examples: Emma Nicholson working against the rights of lesbian women to become mothers; Tony Blair becoming the leader of the Labour Party; Chris Smith coming out as gay in the House of Commons; a majority of the Roman Catholic MPs voting in favour of an equal age of consent; even, perhaps, John Selwyn Gummer trying to make us all eat hamburgers. In all these cases I believe there to be religious dynamics at work. And they all have relevance to sexual politics (yes, even the hamburgers![2]). The simplistic strategy is to conclude that Christianity is the root of all prejudice and bigotry, and to declare that we will have nothing whatever to do with it. But we would do better to be more sophisticated in our analysis.

Religion is poorly understood in our society – particularly, it seems, by those who claim it as justification for their oppressive politics. Take the recent controversy over 'Back to Basics'. As the definitive slogan encapsulating Tory policies, it offered simplistic, so-called 'common-sense values' (listed in single words such as 'neighbourliness', 'honesty' and 'respect') as the tool for a magical transformation of society. The basis for these values was said to be Christianity. Yet what came through most powerfully in the speeches of Tories defending this policy was an infantile grasp of religion, morality and the links between the two. They castigated teachers and clergy for not inculcating effectively the 'right kind' of morality; they implied that religion and morality are interchangeable; and the content of the morality which they proposed was, at best, vague and superficial. From a religious perspective their position was indefensible, for any attempt to impose morality by force is usually counter-productive; and Christians (and religious people in general) have no monopoly on behaving morally.

As if these mistakes were not enough, there is very little that is 'Christian' about the filtering of virtues like 'neighbourliness' and 'respect' through a middle-class mind-set and elevating the results to the status of universal truth. And particularly when we know to our cost that it is possible for a man to appear to be perfectly respectable and neighbourly while beating his wife behind net curtains and closed doors. 'Back to Basics' sounded to me suspiciously like a regressive return to a selective focus upon external appearances.

Belief in the irrelevance of religion has one further disadvantage: it can lead to an assumption that those who are involved with it have nothing to offer to the social-change agendas of sexual politics. A common perception of Christianity is that it offers a cosy escape from the 'real world'. This is hardly surprising given that this perception is actively cultivated by churchmen seeking an excuse for their financial misconduct or pastoral incompetence (or, indeed, their financial incompetence and pastoral misconduct). I hope if this book has shown anything, however, it is that there can be no better grounding for learning how institutions work than observing the churches. A rueful but common remark from women who have left the church is that while within it they learned all that they needed to know about the dynamics of discrimination. The inequalities and oppressions of human community are all there. Church politics is as dastardly and devious as any other kind; surviving within Christianity or disengaging from it are as demanding – intellectually and emotionally – as any other 'negotiation' with institutional power. There is nothing other-worldly or rarefied about the Christian establishment in its varied forms.

Reflections on 'losing faith'

I would like now to attempt to articulate some of the political and religious forces that form the backdrop against which women question their 'faith' or their place within the Christian community. This is vital if we are to understand the complexity which lies behind the apparently simple question posed by the title of this chapter. Firstly, I will focus on 'belief-centred' considerations, beginning with some further reflections from an earlier contributor.

REBECCA

I grew up encouraged to enjoy intellectual arguments with my father, so that, ironically, the fact that the church was wrong about a lot of things never surprised me once I was aware of them. Becoming lesbian was more in this category – the church might condemn me for loving women, so the church, like the law, was an ass. Almost no problem. It wasn't entirely as simple as that, of course, but the secret part of me that believed I was probably damned became the rebel part.

Besides, as I grew up and left home, I was stumbling into some sort of relationship with a deity who suited me, who wasn't male, wasn't even particularly anthropomorphic, but appeared in the brightness of leaves and the patterns of birds in flight, and had a voice, tears and a dry sense of humour. It was tricky sustaining this pantheist streak and turning up at a church most Sundays, but I managed it on and off for years. Because my idea of 'God' really was genderless (partly because I assumed it was still important to be monotheist, and this was the only way I could manage that), I was immune to rhetoric about women 'needing the Goddess'; yet, if I used a pronoun at all, it was a female one. I was becoming feminist without really quite believing that I was an adult woman, so I didn't need a deity to be like me. Some of the spiritual experiences that sustained me were, I suppose, the kind called 'mystical' (though they felt completely natural as well). Other experiences were far less solitary, nurtured by glimpses of the brightness in other people, including the courage of feminists struggling to reinvent their lives.

The Christian feminist movement gave women space to explore not only female but also their own images of God, so it seemed to be what I was looking for. We also commonly identified ourselves as being on the edge of the church, sometimes in exile from it, sometimes in Exodus (as if we had the ark of the covenant and they didn't). The idea was never, or almost never, that the church hierarchy had our tacit approval, or that changing it would be easy. I was never a particularly fervent supporter of the Movement for the Ordination of Women – not hostile, just troubled by an anti-clerical streak which doubted that the lofty ideal of priesthood I'd been brought up to (my father again) was a good thing for human beings of any gender. However, I didn't want to support anti-feminist forces, so I sometimes shut up and tagged along. At different times I also clung desperately to, or meandered rather aimlessly in and out of, Metropolitan Community Church, Gay Christian Movement (as it then was) and Women in Theology, met a few 'radical' male clergy and learned to sound vaguely intelligent about liberation theology, and sustained friendships with separatist women who would have touched none of the above Christian groups with a septic bargepole. I seemed to be on the edge of everything, and never quite to fit, and to be grumpy about it a lot of the time.

After the death of my father, I found myself having, at last, an experience – 'losing my faith' in the sense another friend described as losing something that constricted her like a corset. It happened in a retreat house with my colleagues, in the middle of a discussion about what we as individuals really believed. It became clear to me that these pleasant, well-intentioned men were rather bored with 'God', and much more excited about 'Jesus'.

Jesus – I hadn't really thought about him for ages. I knew he was a nice person, and I'd carefully compiled lists of serious conversations he'd had with women, but what was it I was supposed to find unique about him, anyway? The more I tried to locate it, the more it slipped away. The 'kingdom' seemed like a pointless jargon word for a vision of a more just world that I'd found as convincingly described in all kinds of other places. The line that claims Jesus 'experienced everything we can experience' never did wash with feminists – crucifixion is clearly nasty, but it's not a synonym for everything, and women's potential for pregnancy and childbirth are not incidental. The man was a man. This matters. And salvation, or even atonement, the idea that my relationship with the divine, even when it was muddied by fear or by doubting or hating myself, could undergo some startling one-off change because of a dying god, or dying man, or both, or something – that was crazy. I'd tried hard to trust it at various times in my life, but now it seemed long-gone. The divine broke into my life every now and then, but these were not 'Christ-events'; they wore a wild or a womanly face.

With nothing else much left to lose, I became, after all, a feminist that needed the Goddess. Not necessarily hooked on romantic nostalgia for a matriarchal age, or picking the pleasant, female bits out of any mythology I happen to trip over. There are, for sure, important clues in goddesses from other cultures, if their source is honoured, and they build to a picture where there is a place for tougher emotions, for anger, for grief, for the bloody struggle to give birth. But there are shelves of books by feminists describing how this can be. The story is not always exactly the same, because the deeply personal experiences of different women are not exactly the same – how could they be? For me, the underlying truth is still that brightness of leaves, those tears, that dry sense of humour.

Rebecca's experience raises the question of what is actually meant by a 'loss of faith' or, as she puts it, 'unconversion'. What exactly is going on? I would suggest that there are two distinct possibilities here which are linked, but which nevertheless call for separate consideration.

The first is that what we are experiencing in unconversion is *a loss of meaning*. This reflects my own experience of ceasing to find meaning in the language of Christian doctrine and worship. While the process was gradual, the cumulative effect was a sudden realization that words and phrases which had meant something – had had some resonance with who I experienced myself to be and how I experienced the world – now no longer did so. It is difficult to describe this loss of resonance, because the explanation for why it was ever there in the first place is hard to pin down. Why do people find that gabbling about 'being washed in the blood of the Lamb' or 'being saved through the death and resurrection of the Lord Jesus' helps to make sense of their daily lives?

There is an element of 'mystery' to all this, which is partially but not completely explained by various psychological and sociological theories. And there are various ways of articulating in philosophical terms what is happening. Wittgenstein, for instance, said that 'being religious' means being skilled in the use of religious language – knowing what makes sense and what doesn't; applying the rules of the game. This explains why those who have no experience of the game find it pointless or incomprehensible, but it doesn't really explain why one might end up on the sidelines with one's understanding intact. My problem was that I could – and still can – use religious language in the right way; I can see its internal logic. But, crucially, my heart isn't in it. To coin a religious cliché, the salt has lost its taste, and the rhetorical question is, how can it be restored?

The second possibility is that we cease to assent to the propositions which are considered to define Christianity, or that, alternatively, we assent to propositions which are felt to be incompatible with Christianity. To illustrate the distinction between this and the experience of a 'loss of meaning', let's take as an example the words of the Creed as they are spoken in church: 'I believe in one God, the Father, the Almighty, maker of heaven and earth, of all that is, seen and unseen.'[3] I could have one of two problems with this. I could disagree with it in some way, e.g. by believing that there is no God, or that there is more than one God. On the other hand, it may not be that I actually disagree with it – just that it makes no sense. It leaves me unmoved either way, because it's literally 'nonsense'. There is a third possibility, which is that I have no problem saying that I 'believe in' the Creed, but I discover that my own interpretation of it is rather different from that of the rest of the religious community to which I belong. This is what happened to the Revd Tony Freeman, the Church of England vicar sacked recently for allegedly 'not believing in God'. Actually, he does still believe in God, he just has a different concept of God from that of his bishop and, unfortunately for him, his bishop has more power than he does. He doesn't believe in God as an objective being 'out there', but as a label for that which is within human beings and connects us with one another and the rest of creation.

THE POLITICS OF THEOLOGY

This brings me to the political aspects of 'loss of faith'. What are the boundaries of Christianity and who decides them? Both explanations of what is constituted by a 'loss of faith' are affected by this question, but let's explore the 'loss of meaning' option first.

Much of the language of Roman Catholicism is incomprehensible or meaningless to Protestants, as is the language of Christian fundamentalism to those of a more liberal persuasion. Each religious movement has its own thought-structures, formal or informal, for making sense of the world. If the way in which we create sense departs significantly from that of the tradition to which we purport to belong, then we are expected to go elsewhere. Indeed, it is highly unlikely that one would want to do anything but go elsewhere.

In exploring the second issue – the refusal to assent to the defining propositions of a religion – I would like to utilize a particular case-study. The World Council of Churches Seventh Assembly in Canberra, Australia (February 1991) was a huge gathering of Christians from various major denominations worldwide. An address was given at this event by a professor of theology from South Korea, Chung Hyun Kyung. To give a flavour of her perspective, here are two brief excerpts:

> I come from Korea, the land of spirits full of *Han*. *Han* is anger. *Han* is resentment. *Han* is bitterness. *Han* is grief. *Han* is broken-heartedness and

the raw energy for struggle for liberation. In my tradition people who were killed or died unjustly became wandering spirits, the *Han*-ridden spirits. They are all over the place seeking the chance to make the wrong right. Therefore the living people's responsibility is to listen to the voices of the *Han*-ridden spirits and to participate in the spirits' work of making the wrong right. These *Han*-ridden spirits in our people's history have been agents through whom the Holy Spirit has spoken her compassion and wisdom for life . . .

For me the image of the Holy Spirit comes from the image *Kwan In*. She is venerated as Goddess of compassion and wisdom by East Asian women's popular religiosity. She is a bodhisattva, enlightened being. She can go into Nirvana any time she wants to, but refuses to go into Nirvana by herself. Her compassion for all suffering living beings makes her stay in this world enabling other living beings to achieve enlightenment . . . Perhaps this might also be a feminine image of the Christ who is the first born among us, one who goes before and brings others with her?[4]

Hers was perhaps the most imaginatively and stunningly presented of all the plenary sessions at this conference. But it caused uproar among some delegates, particularly those representing the Orthodox Church, and white male Westerners. This was a predictable reaction, for any attempt to generate female images of Christ has, historically, led to hysteria among men in ecclesiastical power. Perhaps this is because such men are charged with 'imitating Christ' and can't bear the damage that would be done to their masculinity if they were thought to be attracted by the idea of 'female impersonation'.

The objection, on this occasion, was that her theology was 'syncretistic'. This was an interesting and enlightening choice of words. Syncretism refers to the mixing and fusing of socio-cultural and/or religious beliefs which are known to have existed independently. Apparently, the term originated as having the positive meaning of a 'prudent alliance', but was later used as a term of abuse in theological circles.[5] There is no doubt that the word was being used here in its negative sense, the implication being that while her accusers ascribed to a 'pure' form of Christianity she, by contrast, had developed an indefensible hybrid, combining Christianity with the religious beliefs and traditions of her culture.

What was not recognized by her accusers was that their own faith is just as syncretistic. White male Westerners, for instance, subscribe to a form of Christianity which is heavily influenced by a mixture of Western capitalism and Victorian morality. It seems that when a Third World woman brings the traditional religious insights of her culture to bear on Christianity she is being 'syncretistic', but when a rich white Western man draws upon the political and economic thought-forms which underpin the domination of the Third World, the result is normative Christianity.

A similar dynamic also emerges in the debates within the Anglican communion about polygamy. The Western nuclear family pattern of one man and one woman grouped with the offspring of their union has developed as a result of various cultural and economic factors, but it has taken on the mantle of the 'truly Christian'. On the other hand, polygamous family patterns that have endured and developed in African countries, where Christianity was exported as both tool and foundation of colonialism, are considered to be in competition with Christian values. Debates about this are usually couched in terms of whether such 'polygamous lifestyles' should be 'allowed' to continue, or whether a line should be drawn which clearly states that Christians must, by definition, be monogamous.

The major point to be made in the light of these two examples is that the boundaries of Christianity are defined by people – usually men – for particular political reasons. This has always been the case. What Christianity is said to be and what Christianity is said to teach cannot be objectively defined. Every aspect of the faith tradition has a social and political history. This matters, and how it matters will be explored later.

Belief-centred considerations are not the only ones which cause women to question their place within the Christian community. 'Praxis-centred' considerations are important too. By this I mean that women may be alienated as much by who Christianity expects them to be and by how they are expected to behave, as they are by particular theological beliefs. Here are the further reflections of another earlier contributor:

SALLY

I have ceased to be a minister of the Eucharist (I took the role on because I was asked to and felt it was important for women to be seen administering the sacrament, not because of any vocation); I do not go to confession; if I am away from home on a Sunday I do not seek out a Catholic church. I have chosen my parish carefully, preferring a university chaplaincy which emphasizes inclusivity to a more traditional parish. It is important to me that the priest and fellow members of the congregation would be likely to accept and affirm me as a lesbian woman. This has become more important in recent years due to the strident official statements on homosexuality coming from Rome (the 1992 letter against anti-discrimination legislation caused a real crisis of faith), and has nothing to do with my personal circumstances. (I have been in a lesbian relationship since 1982.) I am still a Catholic because my faith is still there. I cannot see myself transferring to another denomination with a more inclusive attitude to women or homosexuality. Either God loves lesbians too (in which case the Church has got it all wrong and must be challenged) or God does not love lesbians or God does not exist. It would not make sense for me to swap a Catholic God for a Non-conformist God, an MCC [Metropolitan Community Church] God or a postchristian God/ess. I am not really interested in God as a theory.

I do not pray regularly, beyond the usual stream of urgent petitions, except at mass. I value the space afforded by that hour each week. Part of me would like a very ordered life – I love saying the psalms and would not be unhappy going to mass every day – but I see this as a temptation to retreat from reality. All that time given to religion would leave much less time for people and, as I feel strongly that there is no point to the religious practice if it is not rooted in the experience of God through the people around one, this would be self-defeating. If I did have more time to spare I think I would still be deterred from daily mass attendance by the enthusiasm of the rest of the congregation to welcome me to their holy elite. I am not happy in church except on the edge. I do not want to be seen as a 'good Catholic'.

Sally has not experienced an 'unconversion' or loss of faith. But she has modified the nature of her involvement with institutional Christianity in the light of her experience as a lesbian woman. Echoes of Sally's situation are apparent in the case of Frances, in the chapter on heterosexual experiences in Part Two: 'We moved on. We still had our mutual love, *and our mutual faith*, but we felt that didn't have any legitimacy. We couldn't walk into a church building and feel we could express it, because we felt that we were out of line with the Church of England ... [my italics].'

By addressing issues of 'belief' and 'praxis' separately, I am not implying that they can be considered in isolation from each other. On the contrary, what comes through from many of the stories in this book is how closely linked they are. A lesbian woman may leave the church because she feels it is an obstacle to her sexual integrity; she may have observed other lesbian and gay people being treated badly; or she may herself have experienced overt rejection. While her primary reason for leaving will be aspects of church praxis, her beliefs are unlikely to remain unaffected. To give just one example, the central Christian teaching about God's unconditional love and acceptance is likely to seem less than wholly credible in the light of the destructive activities of those who claim to be living out such teaching. Almost inevitably, such experiences will have short-term or long-term effects upon her spirituality.

LOSS OR GAIN?

One problem with the 'loss of faith' model is that it tends to have a predominantly negative focus. In concentrating upon what has been 'lost', we risk ignoring the fact that for many women such an experience may ultimately feel like liberation – or at least a stepping stone to a more sophisticated spirituality. Here are a couple of examples of how women discovered the value of resources outside of Christianity. We begin with Paula, whose specific need was to deal with her childhood sexual abuse.

PAULA

Theology rages on as there is debate and discussion as to the place of ethics, morals and women. It is amazing it survives at all, not utterly spent at the hands of those who will not respect its own independence, wisdom and life.

As a woman I gave up on the church and organized religion in despair, as I realized that nobody was interested in what I had to say anyway, and so I went in search of a way of coming to my own elsewhere. I found it through my work with people with profound and multiple learning difficulties. They were not going to tell me whether God was, who Jesus was, and without ever questioning who priests were they began to minister to me. At times I was pulled apart, confronted with an inner rawness I could not stand, at times led towards a gentleness of understanding I could hardly comprehend, but never for a moment did I doubt the truth of what I was experiencing. Two severely disabled women I was closest to died, very young, and have continued to minister, to bring me peace, to break through barriers, to restore hope and healing. Life beyond death isn't even to be argued with on those terms.

And I suppose together we were bound to be dismissed if not ridiculed by the mighty authority of the church, too often pounding on the intellect instead of sounding out the heart. But together we did make a decision on our spiritual journey – we are here whether or not you choose to recognize it. And we are not going to wait for you to catch up and do so. Perhaps in those words the nature of theology takes on quite a new face.

PAULINE

I became interested in Goddess imagery. It didn't turn out to be a sea-change in my spirituality – it was transient, and was, I believe, part of a process of self-integration. For me, now, spirituality is not at root anything to do with anthropomorphizing images, and does not find expression in any sort of liturgy or ritual – Goddess rituals are as unhelpful to me as any others. It's much more to do with my sense of connectedness with the universe, my sense of my life being part of the flow of all life; my sense of the fundamental oneness of everything. This is an experience which comes and goes. It is most nourished by windy mountain tops, deserted cliffs, rough seas, open expanses of countryside, being buffeted by the weather while out walking; and in mutual communicative sex, the loss of body boundaries and ego boundaries. An implication of that is that I have no interest in currently ideologically fashionable sexual practices – multiple sexual partners, S/M and so forth; they seem to me incompatible with the kind of openness and mutuality which nourishes me and, I believe, a wider community. Given all this, my continued connection with the Quakers is perhaps not surprising, though I exist somewhat on the fringe of the Society of Friends as an institution. It is a body of people interested, in the main, in the sorts of questions I am interested in. It has an approach to spirituality within which I can find a space for mine. It is non-doctrinaire, and only partially Christian, with plenty of non-Christian 'space' within it. It has, on the whole, acceptable attitudes to women's issues, and to lesbians and gays. Its attitude to authority is that the individual conscience is the final arbiter. So it provides a context, a place to attach loosely to, where I can pursue my own questions and explorations.

But most of my personal journeying is not dependent on any particular grouping. Other people are, of course, important – but I think I find and meet these people in all sorts of contexts. At the end of the day my only guide to what I do is my inner sense of what is right for me in a particular context, and that includes the other people involved. Desire, the erotic, seems to me to be the motivating energy of life – it is about our depths of connection, of pleasure, of satisfaction, of truthfulness. My connection with the trees and the mountains is no less an erotic connection than that with a lover. And similarly, in this phase of my life I can shape my own spirituality; I can take what wisdom I may find elsewhere, or leave it. I am not constrained by anyone else's prescriptions, and my spirituality is just about being who I am in as whole a way as I can; and this is a journey which continues, does not come to rest at some point. It is about my mind and my body as well as my 'soul', whatever that word means. It has nothing to do with a god who is 'out there'; it is entirely about immanence. It is also highly political – if I experience myself as connected to everything, then the pain in the world is my pain, not as an intellectual idea, but as lived reality. If my connection with the world is erotic, if the world is also my lover, then the world's pain pains me – and I wish to do what lies in my power to heal it.

Connection is not, however, identity. My own sense of the connectedness and positive loss of boundaries possible in a good sexual relationship depends on there also being separateness, autonomy, individuality – sufficient personal space, physically, psychologically, and emotionally; enough breathing space that the togetherness does not become suffocation. This is equally true of the kind of spirituality I have attempted to describe – the sense of oneness and connectedness is of necessity a transient phenomenon, even if it comes frequently. To live a life in the real world it is also necessary to experience separateness, individual identity, differentness. The two aspects need to form a dance together, in relationships, in sexuality, in spirituality.

Now, in my forties, I don't see that Christianity has anything to offer me at all, let alone the dreadfulness of the mainstream denominations. I perceive my spirituality not so much as finding 'a path' as dancing across an expanse of sand, together with many other women, each doing our own dance, but also being aware of, and relating to, the other women's dances. And periodically the tide washes away our footprints, but we carry on dancing – there is nowhere to 'go', but there are many ways of 'being', of carrying on the dance.

Elements of ambiguity

We are beginning to build a rather more complex picture of women's engagement with Christianity. There is ambiguity, in that a loss of commitment to Christianity is not always negative. There is also ambiguity regarding the extent to which it is completely possible. A question which seems to crop up frequently is: how do you know when you've left Christianity behind?

REBECCA

Christianity has been hanging around my life for the whole of it, and for most of that time it has been too close to see properly. I've tried out several versions of it for size, and tried, in-between times, to leave several times before I finally managed it; and since I still work for the church, even that last leaving must seem to many people to be a half-hearted affair.

How it seems to my colleagues, radical Methodist ministers, is something else. Perhaps twice a year we repeat the following exchange. They carefully explain that they want the staff team to 'do theology' together. I carefully explain that (leaving aside the question of what 'doing theology' means anyway) they are not my spiritual community and I'd rather stick to what I am paid to do (running the office). They carefully explain that my views are valuable. I carefully explain that I know they are but it's incredibly important to me to express those views and that vulnerability in other places, not with my work colleagues. Then I spend 48 hours wondering why I ended up in the wrong again. This odd little lobster quadrille has come to say more to me about the bounding self-confidence of Christianity, about what it thinks it has to offer, than anything the more formal churches have ever thrown at me. Even the greedy demand for a bigger piece of me is offered quite spontaneously as a precious gift, a 'vision of community' as they say, certainly never as a rip-off of my spirituality, my feelings and (valuable) ideas.

DEBORAH

I don't miss Christianity in my life at all right now. On the contrary, it's a relief to feel I've escaped from a thought-cage against which I was banging ever more painfully. Yet I haven't escaped entirely and perhaps I never will – I was immersed too deeply and for too long. I'm beginning to believe that 'spirituality' is a construct that can only have gained currency out of a fundamental splitting of human experience into 'body' and 'soul'. If spirituality does have a meaning, I would like to think it's inseparable from embodied immersion in relationships of all kinds. I think that one significant way in which the Christian West has gained violent supremacy in the world today is through that splitting – all those familiar but deadly binary oppositions that shape our lives individually and collectively are derived from that body–spirit dichotomy: bad–good, black–white, female–male and woman–man, emotion–rationality, passion–dispassion, etc. Thankfully, I'm becoming more able to live my life in the border zones – certainly gender-wise, but also in terms of allowing contradictions and complexities within myself and in the world I observe around me. I do sometimes feel cut adrift without the solid certainty of God in my life. But the more I accept responsibility for myself in my entirety, the more secure I feel.

JUDITH

The Christian teaching I received now seems to me to have been narrow and rigid – a matter of absolutes – something to be accepted. Questions could be asked to gain knowledge from the authorities, but disagreement and challenge did not seem possible. In my education, academic exploration of biblical material and church history was acceptable, but personal exploration and spiritual growth were not part of the curriculum.

In spite of the anger which is evident here, there is much in my past which I value. I don't want to give up Christianity altogether – though maybe this is due to nostalgia, and I shall have to acknowledge that I have left it all behind. The church has been a very important part of my life – though a problematic one for most of my adult life. It was a place to make friends locally, and it is difficult to find anything to take its place in that respect – but that is hardly a religious matter (or is it?). I miss friendship and companionship and worship, but have to be true to myself, and cannot be there any more.

I believe that the spiritual is of vital importance in human life, but find difficulty when I try to define that. I feel that I am involved in the/a spiritual search, and for me in recent years, that has been taking place largely in my analysis – i.e. in getting to know myself, the forces that have shaped me, learning to listen to myself – and thus becoming better able to listen to others. I think I wish I could have some mystical experience – but I would distrust it! Mysticism has been neglected (even positively discouraged) by the Church. Maybe it is a capacity in all human beings, which needs to be rediscovered and encouraged.

I now think of 'religious' as meaning 'belonging to a particular religious tradition' with its beliefs, practices, ethics, etc. 'Spiritual' to me is much wider than this – my spirit within is my own individual, personal core – but this spiritual capacity is there in every human being, not just in the 'religious' (and perhaps sometimes there is less of it in religious people than in some others?).

I am beginning to see the dreaded (for me) matter of sexuality as tremendously important, as something which is part of the very fabric of our lives, and as something to which the Christian church has done enormous damage. It needs redeeming, for me and for society. Can the church learn to value, respect it, thank God for it, rejoice in it – in genuine ways – no longer treating it as suspect, dangerous, taboo?

I have been slow to link my difficulties regarding the church and Christianity with the fact of being a woman. Ten years ago, I was one who still said 'but we all know that "men" means "all human beings" '. But gradually feminism and feminist theology have influenced me and made some things more clear. I came to realize that a major reason for my finding church worship meaningless was because of its sexist language, which left me out. I became a supporter of the Movement for the Ordination of Women in order to support women who feel called to priesthood – but have never wanted to see them as priests unless that means other greater changes. It is, I believe, priesthood itself that needs changing or abolishing. Ministry is not that special thing for the few. We are all ministers to one another. Ministry is not a position, but a function in which all must be engaged (all of us being Christ to each other, if you like).

It feels strange to me not to be involved in the church's festivals – I experience a little guilt, a little nostalgia, and a considerable feeling of liberation and relief.

The nature of religion

Drawing upon the women's experiences articulated in this chapter, it is worth pausing to reflect upon the nature of religion. In particular, it is important that we make sense of the creative and liberating aspects of 'losing faith' and the ambiguity which surrounds it, and that we understand the link which I drew earlier between belief and praxis. My initial focus, therefore, will be upon what construction of religion is being resisted by these women.

Religion is commonly reduced to some combination of two predominant aspects: a collection of so-called objective propositions about the universe or the divine, and a set of rules about how human beings should behave. A problem with Christianity is that both its protagonists and its opponents seem to wish to reduce it to various manifestations of either or both of these things. Any attempt to say that you cannot be a true Christian and also live as a lesbian (or a gay man) is a prime example of the reduction of Christianity to an ethical code. And when it comes to the formulation of the 'objective propositions' which one has to believe in order to claim the label 'Christian', God is a popular target. Most commonly, we are asked to believe that God is 'a being' who 'exists' (somewhere 'out there'); that the only correct imagery for envisaging God is male; and that 'He' exists in some complex and incomprehensible relationship to 'His Son' and a rather less tangible intermediary called a 'Holy Spirit'. I over-simplify, but you get the picture.

In her book A *History of God*, Karen Armstrong criticizes attempts to define and describe God, and the impulse to make assent to such definitions a compulsory prerequisite of religious adherence. Indeed, she goes further, saying that such an approach is antithetical to real religion:

> God has indeed been used in the past to stunt creativity; if he is made a blanket answer to every possible problem and contingency, he can indeed stifle our sense of wonder or achievement. A passionate and committed atheism can be more religious than a weary or inadequate theism.[6]

This is important, for it means that there are other ways – perhaps more authentic ways – of being religious, including being Christian, ways which do not prioritize the need to assent to particular doctrines or behave in an externally prescribed manner. Another theologian, Don Cupitt, affirms this approach:

> Today, an individual's Christian faith is the outcome of a personal reading, interpretation and appropriation of text. By 'text' I mean everything that the Christian receives – and it is all made of signs. It is scripture and liturgy, doctrine and instruction, myth and symbol. This mighty flowing river of signs does not have just one true pre-established Meaning, out-there. It gets a meaning as it comes to life in me. I take it in, and its chains of interconnected signs enter my sensibility, evoking and channelling a play of feeling and so becoming interwoven with my life. I appropriate the text, make it mine and actualise it – and this is a creative activity, inevitably different in each person and different each time.[7]

This vision of religious commitment is primarily about undertaking a creative quest rather than a descriptive or disciplinary one. Its concern with questions of ultimate meaning and value distinguishes it from other fields of human endeavour, but it also shares much in common with these – politics, art and music, for instance. This alternative understanding of what religion is all about puts the questions of women who live in tension with Christianity in a different perspective. What if the 'unconversion' experiences described in this chapter are not stories of losing religion at all, but reflect the discovery of a form of religion which is more authentic. than the forms of Christianity that they left behind? That this is indeed what might be going on is borne out by the fact that the women concerned do not speak of wanting to leave behind all forms of spirituality and any possibility of a religious outlook on life. As Karen Armstrong reminds us, such reconfigurations of the nature of religion itself – particularly with reference to our conceptions of God – have a distinguished history:

Ever since the prophets of Israel started to ascribe their own feelings and experiences to God, monotheists have in some senses created a God for themselves. God has rarely been seen as a self-evident fact that can be encountered like any other objective existent. Today many people seem to have lost the will to make this imaginative effort. This need not be a catastrophe. When religious ideas have lost their validity, they have usually faded away painlessly: if the human idea of God no longer works for us in this empirical age, it will be discarded. Yet in the past people have always created new symbols to act as a focus for spirituality. Human beings have always created a faith for themselves to cultivate their sense of wonder and ineffable significance of life.[8]

It is wise, at this point, to make clear that this creative form of religious endeavour must be a communal project if it is to accord with a feminist social-change agenda. Mere individualism, or a renegotiation of Christianity only in order to feel better about ourselves, is not what is being discussed here. Not that feeling better about oneself is a bad thing – but feminist religious perspectives must go further. In short, they must be political. The words of Linda Hurcombe sum up much of our discussion to date:

A God for women will be imaged from remembered history as well as radical new perspectives, from a new and unassailable comprehension of our own sexuality; it will not come prepackaged as a drug or apocalyptic cult, or even the siren song calling for a return to earlier goddess religions. In her wonderful poem, *Sappho's Reply*, Rita Mae Brown says:

'You who have wept in direct sunlight,
who have hungered in invisible chains,
Tremble to the cadence of my legacy:
An army of lovers shall not fail.'

Who is in charge of reclaiming and reinventing God? We, the army of lovers, in the teeth of patriarchy. The road to heaven is paved with good invention.[9]

Concluding reflections on 'leaving'

In the discussion so far I have pointed out that in escaping Christianity we do not escape patriarchy – although it is an understandable mistake to equate the two. I have also explored the whole concept of what it means to 'lose faith', particularly considering the power politics which lie behind constructions of boundaries between 'belief' and 'unbelief'. This led in turn to a consideration of religion as something more imaginative and complicated than a mere set of objective propositions about God, or an unambiguous ethical code. Let us return now to the original question: why not leave Christianity behind?

I would like to add two more initial comments. Firstly, it is necessary to understand that the context in which we face the choice inherent in the question is culturally specific. The expectation behind the question is that we make choices about 'remaining Christian' or 'jacking it in' in the same way as we would expect to make any other consumer choice. Some people do 'shop around', replacing religious commitment to one tradition with religious commitment to another, but this makes no sense to those for whom culture and religion are inextricably linked. Our free-market-inspired, postmodern ethos brings us 'choices' which are meaningless in other parts of the world, and to those within our own society for whom a religious community is necessary for identity and survival. That's not to say that the question is trivial or immoral, it is just to put it in perspective.

Secondly, there is a sense in which religious identity cannot be dispensed with at will by anyone. This is true for those of us who are what sociologists of religion call 'once born', that is, the religious background of our upbringing forms an ineradicable part of who we are. It is true, in a different way, for people who are 'twice born' – those who have undergone a more dramatic conversion process. Religious identity is implicated in a person's morality and values; motivation and temperament; political understanding and commitments; consciousness of race, class and gender; and social networks and contacts. It cannot just be dismissed.

In the light of all this, my conclusion is that our original question is an unhelpful one. It is founded on a poor understanding of the nature of religious identity, and it forces us to adopt a self-definition which is essentially reactive. Our preoccupation becomes whether we should associate or dissociate ourselves from a patriarchally defined religious tradition, when what is wrong is the definition itself. What we need to do is sidestep the choices which this dilemma offers to us. We need to find ways of responding which are neither positive nor negative, because the agenda itself is not ours. In short, we need what Mary Daly calls a 'Transcendent Third Option'.

The story of Mary Daly's invention of this concept is told in her philosophical autobiography, *Outercourse*. In 1971, she was invited to give a sermon at Harvard Memorial Church. As the first woman to have such an 'honour' extended to her, she was faced with a dilemma: accept the invitation and thereby assume the role of 'token woman' in a misogynistic institution; or turn down the 'opportunity' and pay the price of being silenced. Her solution was to preach 'an "Exodus" sermon which was in reality an anti-sermon, a clarion call to leave that whole scene – the Church with its sermons and token women preachers'. The result was that 'hundreds of women and some men said No both to assimilation and to erasure of Feminism by stampeding out – smiling and proud of ourSelves'.[10]

Lesbian and feminist women also face a dilemma. For 'leaving Christianity behind' is a form of collusion with the unimaginative, anti-religious and fundamentalist forces which use the power afforded by their political supremacy to define who God is, what Christianity is, and what is ethical and unethical. Yet not to leave is also a collusion with the forces of patriarchy, for our precious energies are wasted in trying to 'change things from within', or even in just holding on to a basic belief that we have a right to exist. Continued engagement of any kind could be interpreted as legitimation of what patriarchal Christianity stands for.

So what might a 'Transcendent Third Option' look like in this context? Firstly, there will be a plurality of options and this is valuable. In response to a question as to why she remains at Boston College, where the religious foundation has treated her particularly badly, Daly replies:

> I was choosing to Fight/Act (Stand my Ground) at that precise location on the Boundary between Background and foreground where the demonic patriarchal distortions of women's Archaic heritage are most visible and accessible to me, where my Craft can be most effective in the work of Exorcism – reversing the reversals that blunt the potential for Realizing Ecstasy.[11].

There's something wrong when lesbians and feminists tell one another – directly or by implication – what 'battles' we should be fighting. Surely the more ground we cover between us in our actions of resistance, the better and more comprehensive our overall analysis becomes. This is not to say, of course, that constructive criticism has no place, quite the opposite. But the criticism will focus on how we go about our work, not whether or not we should be bothering in the first place.

The 'Boundary locations' where we choose to 'Stand our Ground' will depend on our personal history and experience, for these shape where our passions lie, and we are most effective when we are most passionate. On the specific issue of how lesbian and feminist women deal with a Christian heritage, it strikes me as important that we pay attention to what Christianity has done to us. I have noticed how strong ideological pressure to 'leave Christianity behind' can be counter-productive if it encourages us to take short cuts in our assessment of this. In my experience, we are reluctant to talk about the damage Christianity has caused us, and we certainly don't want to admit that there was ever anything positive in it. We adopt a linear model of 'leaving', whereby we think we can 'close the Christian chapter' of our lives if we try hard enough. Then we hate ourselves if we feel so much as a twinge of longing to sing a Charles Wesley hymn or watch *Carols from Kings* at Christmas, wrongly imagining that this is proof that we have failed fully to purge patriarchal Christianity from our hearts and minds. This model serves to cut us off from the positive aspects of our history and identity, and ultimately to impede our liberation.

In conclusion, perhaps our feminist grammar should make 'should I stay or should I go?' a non-question. To be unduly concerned with it is a waste of precious revolutionary energy. It plays into the hands of those for whom one's relationship with established Christianity is the most important issue. As this book has shown, there is too much political work to be done – 'justice-seeking' work as theologian Mary Hunt would put it[12] – for this to be our focus. There will be times when engagement with the Christian community is appropriate for those with the option, and there will be other times when disengagement is better. The demands of the work will clarify for us which is which. For those of us with a Christian heritage, perhaps the politically pragmatic answer to the question 'Are you Christian?' is 'I am and I am not', and the answer to 'Have you left Christianity behind?' should be, 'I have and I have not – whatever serves the cause of sexual justice'.

NOTES

1. Valerie Solanas, *Scum Manifesto*. Matriarchy Study Group, London, 1983, p. 4 (first published in 1968 by Olympia Press, Paris).
2. See Carol J. Adams, *The Sexual Politics of Meat*. Polity, Oxford, 1990.
3. From the Nicene Creed.
4. Chung Hyun Kyung (South Korea), 'Come Holy Spirit, renew the whole creation: an introduction to the theological theme'. World Council of Churches Seventh Assembly, Canberra, Australia, 8 February, 1991, Document PL 3.3, pp. 2, 7.
5. See the entry 'Syncretism', in Alan Richardson and John Bowden (eds), *A New Dictionary of Christian Theology*. SCM Press, London, 1983.
6. Karen Armstrong, *A History of God*. Mandarin, London, 1993, p. 433.
7. Don Cupitt, *Radicals and the Future of the Church*. SCM Press, London, 1989, p. 13.
8. Armstrong, *A History of God*, p. 456.
9. Linda Hurcombe, 'A God for women', *Rouge*, issue 13, 1993, p. 19.
10. Mary Daly, *Outercourse: The Be-Dazzling Voyage*. The Women's Press, London, 1993, p. 186.
11. *Ibid.*, p. 284.
12. See, for example, Mary E. Hunt, *Fierce Tenderness: A Feminist Theology of Friendship*. Crossroad, New York, 1991, pp. 143ff.

9 the sexual future

The experiences of the women in this book have shown that issues which may at first sight appear to be discrete are, in fact, closely connected. The invisibility of, and discrimination against, lesbians cannot be understood separately from the assumed inevitability of heterosexuality and the idealization of marriage, in which singleness is seen as a transient state for women, a condition of anticipation of 'something better'. In Western Christianity the idea that men and women are 'made for each other', destined to live a particular kind of life together as 'man and wife', now overshadows all our relational ethics.

An older perception was that the primary purpose of human life was communion with God, and that human intimacy constituted a potential threat to wholehearted contemplation of the Divine. That exerted an oppressive influence on human sexuality all of its own. But now, it seems, heterosexuality is fast becoming *the means* to achieve communion with God. Mainstream Christianity is in danger of making an idol of heterosexuality, and of making 'belief in' marriage a condition of belonging. It has been the purpose of this book to demonstrate that such an approach is founded upon the definitions of powerful men as to the true nature of Christianity and sexuality, and that this is inimical to women.

In this final chapter my aim is to outline some of the considerations we might bear in mind when attempting to build a sexual future which is not based on idolatrous heterosexism. I stress that these are only suggestions – not a new set of answers – for I believe that the first priority is to gain an awareness of the questions.

Being some-body

Of all the school assemblies I sat through, and of all the conversations I had with my friends before and during them, there is one which I remember in particular. I was sitting with Helen, which was unusual. She was a friend but not a close friend, partly because I was rather in awe of her sensitivity and intelligence. As we sat there we watched another girl, Sarah, walk across the dining room to take her place at a nearby table. Sarah was, and had always been, painfully self-conscious and shy. She walked awkwardly with downcast eyes and a permanent blush. Helen watched her in puzzlement then said, laughing, 'She looks like she's ashamed to be herself!' Her laughter was born of incomprehension rather than ridicule, and I was struck by her comment because it seemed that she was articulating something which went beyond Sarah's condition and had a wider application for all of us as 16- or 17-year-old young women.

This school was rather unusual in that it was a state-run co-educational boarding and day school (with a strong Christian ethos, incidentally). I was a boarder for the sixth form only, and wondered at the neurotic world into which I stumbled. The school was awash with young women dieting compulsively, exercising compulsively and working compulsively. Here was manifested a collective and feverish dissatisfaction with who we were as young women, and it seemed to go unnoticed among those in charge. 'Going too far' was frowned upon (attempting suicide or going on shop-lifting sprees in the nearest city), but the rationale behind the behaviour itself seemed to accord with the institution's perception of what was psychologically normal for young females. Helen's comment helped to reassure me that self-annihilation through silence, starvation, overdose or overwork was after all ridiculous – and not the way things had to be.

A major aspect of feminist and womanist thought/action has been to affirm women as physical, space-taking, noise-making and sense-loving beings. And to affirm that herein lies our resistance to a patriarchal society that would erase any aspect of ourselves that is not male-constructed and constricted. Theologians Carter Heyward and Beverly Harrison see this as a route to liberation:

> The very womanly flesh we learn to despise is the source of our redemption – from material and spiritual bondage, from self-loathing and from our contempt for women in general. As feminists attempt to show, the possibility of women's liberation is seeded in women's self-respect, a revolutionary act

because it embodies a challenge to fundamental assumptions about womanhood which have been espoused both by the church and by Western societies for two millenniums.[1]

In her definition of 'womanist' ('A black feminist or feminist of color') Alice Walker includes 'A woman who loves other women, sexually and/or nonsexually' alongside the following unequivocal affirmation of bodiliness:

> Loves music. Loves dance. Loves the moon. *Loves* the Spirit. Loves love and food and roundness. Loves struggle. *Loves* the Folk. Loves herself. *Regardless.*[2]

Toni Morrison also gives voice to the revolutionary necessity of loving that which racist constructions of society believe to be despicable:

> Love your flesh ... flesh that weeps, laughs, flesh that dances on bare feet in grass. Love it. Love it hard. Yonder they do not love your flesh. They despise it ... *You* got to love it, *you!* ... This is flesh I'm talking about here. Flesh that needs to be loved ...[3]

Remember Deborah's words in the last chapter: 'I'm beginning to believe that "spirituality" is a construct that can only have gained currency out of a fundamental splitting of human experience into "body" and "soul". If spirituality does have a meaning, I would like to think it's inseparable from embodied immersion in relationships of all kinds.' The subversion here is in working against the construction of physicality/sexuality as having meaning only in opposition to spirituality, which in turn has been constructed as being in opposition to 'the political'. These feminist and womanist perspectives bring all these aspects of human life back into an inseparable relationship. The personal is the political, and the spiritual encompasses and is encompassed by both.

It is insights like this which have led to a theo-political (where theology and politics overlap) trend towards reclaiming the 'erotic' as an essential energy for bringing about political change. Audre Lorde's famous essay, 'Uses of the erotic: the erotic as power', has been a major influence. Here is an extract:

> The very word *erotic* comes from the Greek word *eros*, the personification of love in all its aspects – born of Chaos, and personifying creative power and

harmony. When I speak of the erotic, then, I speak of it as an assertion of the lifeforce of women; of that creative energy empowered, the knowledge and use of which we are now reclaiming in our language, our history, our dancing, our loving, our work, our lives . . .

The dichotomy between the spiritual and the political is also false, resulting from an incomplete attention to our erotic knowledge. For the bridge which connects them is formed by the erotic – the sensual – those physical, emotional, and psychic expressions of what is deepest and strongest and richest within each of us, being shared: the passions of love, in its deepest meanings.[4]

There is a link here with our consideration in the last chapter of where we choose to 'stand our ground', for the issue is a practical one of where our energy for political action comes from, and how it equips us for action. A common reaction which I have encountered, usually from middle-aged men involved in Christian-based social and political action, is an accusation that because I 'major' on sexual politics issues I must be 'obsessed with sex' (in their words). This interests me. These men think that sexual politics is a specialist area which is of little significance in their own campaigns to combat racism, poverty, unemployment, the arms race, etc. Occasionally, they may feel duty-bound to do a special article or conference on gender-based perspectives such as 'women and racism' or 'homeless women'. These represent for them discrete themes, and masculinity is rarely problematized. They think sexuality is about 'sex' and that gender is a separate issue. They could learn much from Audre Lorde and those who have been influenced by her: theologians Carter Heyward and James Nelson, for instance, have taken up her ideas. They show that a radical reshaping of Christian sexual theology is crucial to justice-making in its widest sense. Carter Heyward has this to say:

Lovemaking turns us simultaneously into ourselves and beyond ourselves. In experiencing the depths of our power in relation as pleasurable and good, we catch a glimpse of the power of right relations in larger, more complicated configurations of our life together. Good sex involves us more fully in the struggle for justice – as, or with, people of color, women, differently abled people, ethnic and religious minorities, elderly people, and other earthcreatures.[5]

And James Nelson underlines the importance of this 'erotic' power:

> Of particular importance in our time is the reclaiming of the much-neglected, much-feared erotic dimensions of love. Fearing that to embrace eros would mean a sanctification of the selfish quest for our own satisfaction, we have too frequently collapsed all meanings of love into agape.[6] We need to recapture a vision of the divine eros as intrinsic to God's energy. God's own passion for connection, and hence also our own yearning for life-giving communion and our hunger for relationships of justice which make such fulfilment possible.[7]

Audre Lorde's thinking could be invaluable to the Christian social-justice campaigners, for it helps explain why passion is a better motivating force than guilt, and why earnestness without aesthetics does not inspire participation.

It is worth pausing, however, to consider this concept of the reclamation of the 'erotic' in more depth, for it is not without its potential problems. The dynamics of racism and sexism and the interaction between these two forms of oppression mean that for a womanist to state that she 'loves her flesh' constitutes a different kind of resistance from when the same words are spoken by a white middle-class feminist. And a white man will in turn need to appropriate the activity differently to ensure that it becomes a form of resistance to oppression rather than a form of collusion with it. It is important to point this out because 'the erotic' lends itself to misappropriation by apolitical and essentialist forms of mysticism. It might be interpreted, for instance, as signifying that aspect of ourselves as sexual beings which is free from the political and social forces which have shaped every other aspect of who we are. It is my sense that this is emphatically not what is meant by Carter Heyward or James Nelson, both of whom are astute about the social construction of gender and sexuality. Nevertheless, we are on dangerous ground if our appropriation of 'the erotic' becomes a new quest for a 'pure essence' of ourselves which, if we can only locate it, will prove to be the key to self-knowledge and self-understanding. We must beware of making 'the erotic' a privileged signifier of who we are.

This caution against any temptation to posit 'the erotic' as a new value-free, universalist and unifying theological concept is born out in the following excerpt from an article by Carol Adams:

> Comments by Kwok Pui-Lan are a helpful counterpoint to the feminist theological claim that posits the erotic as liberatory:
>> Ever since the Afro-American poet and writer Audre Lorde published the classic article, 'The Uses of the Erotic: The Erotic as

Power' feminist theologians such as Rita Nakashima Brock and Carter Heyward are excited about the possibility of talking about God and the power of the erotic. But strangely enough, the language of the erotic is noticeably missing in the theological construction of Afro-American women, and feminist theologians from other parts of the world find it difficult to speak about the power of female sexuality . . .

Asian women find it embarrassing to talk about sex and the erotic not only because decent women are not supposed to raise those issues in public, but also because many of our sisters are working as prostitutes in the hotels, nightclubs, bars, disco joints, and cocktail lounges in the big cities like Manila, Bangkok, Taipei, Hong Kong and Seoul .... The magnitude of the international flesh trade and the courageous action of these women's groups challenges us to rethink the connection between the language of the erotic, the control of the female body, and power over women in its naked and symbolic forms.[8]

We do best to regard articulations of the value of the erotic as provisional wisdom, because there is much we do not know about women's experience of sexuality. This is particularly true regarding the effects of the various forms of violence to which we are subjected. Heterosexist assumptions currently operate as obstacles to an honest and open discussion of the impact of these upon our sexuality. For instance, one young woman commented to me that she found it impossible to be open both about being lesbian and about being a survivor of sexual abuse. The widespread assumption that heterosexuality is equatable with psychic health and lesbianism with psychological damage forms the political backdrop against which pastoral and political work is carried out in this sphere. While the predominant starting point within the churches is that human healing and wholeness includes heterosexuality as a necessary ingredient, it is hard to know where work to combat the effects of violence against women can begin. Certainly 'breaking the silence' is particularly risky for survivors of violence who, in being open about their sexuality and personal relationships, risk fundamental misinterpretation of their stories by those of a heterosexist mind-set. That such work has begun, and that lesbian women appear to be disproportionately represented in its execution, is an issue deserving of closer analytical attention.

What these models of health fail to appreciate is that heterosexuality in its institutional forms is itself problematic. Lesbian feminists from

Christian and secular spheres identify the eroticization of dominance and submission as a central cause for concern. Sheila Jeffreys expresses it thus:

> Heterosexuality is the institution through which male-supremacist society is organised and as such it must cease to function. It is difficult to imagine at this point what shape any relationship between different sexes would take when such a relationship was a free choice, when it was not privileged in any way over same-sex relationship and when it played no part in organising women's oppression and male power. In such a situation, when heterosexuality was no longer an institution, we cannot yet be sure what women would choose.[9]

And Heyward and Harrison describe how Christianity has compounded the inequalities of institutionalized heterosexuality:

> Patriarchal heterosexism is founded less upon deep male heterosexual desire than upon men's use of women's bodies as a means of public social control. In this situation, women have no body rights, no moral claim to our bodies as self-possessed. In Christianity, woman is equated with flesh, body, but Christian women have no integrity of embodied selfhood; no authoritative voice in determining where we put our bodies/ourselves, with whom we share our bodies/ourselves, where we put our embodied energies, time, talents. *Women in Christianity are meant to live for others.* The inability of so many women even to imagine that they should be well-treated in a relationship with a man or that they deserve physical and emotional pleasure is conditioned by the demand that we have our being for others.[10]

There is agreement too that the subversive response to this predominant construction of heterosexuality is to prioritize the 'eroticization of equality'. It is conceded that this is no small task, for it involves a cultural revolution in the way we construct sexual desire. As Sheila Jeffreys points out, what is 'sexy' is defined by situations of dominance and submission, preferably with violence thrown in. Heyward and Harrison agree:

> In such 'eroticization of domination', sexual desire is linked with either oblivion or self-assertion. It would be ahistorical and naive to imagine that *anyone's* eroticism in this culture could be untouched by this dynamic. Feminists such as Valverde and Linda Gordon insist that the 'eroticization of equality' must be understood as a historical project of feminism. They

acknowledge, however, that this project is necessarily long term, so securely fastened in our society, and our psyches, is the felt need for a sexual mediation of relational power to confirm our superiority or subjection in relation to others, whether for a moment or a lifetime.[11]

It's at this point that lesbian and gay sexuality is sometimes appropriated as a panacea for inequality. Certainly there are plenty of potential resources for analysis in lesbian and gay relationships; resources which remain untapped because anti-gay and anti-lesbian discrimination promote the assumption that heterosexuals have nothing to learn from us. Since the big issue of gender inequality is missing in same-sex relationships, they would seem to be a logical place to start as we seek to visualize what eroticized equality would look like. On the other hand, as Heyward and Harrison point out, we have all received the same societal conditioning whether we be lesbian, gay, heterosexual or bisexual. As such, critical assessment of relational patterns within same-sex relationships is also necessary.

With reference to the specific need to assess power differentials between women, Mary Hunt has said:

My sense is that parallel power dynamics apply though we have been less explicit as a culture in spelling them out, and need to do so now. Women have learned in patriarchy to pay attention to power imbalances and to safeguard those who are vulnerable ... Differences of race, class, age, sexual integrity, professional status or some other considerations may apply, but the point is that equal attention needs to be paid to the power imbalance even if it is not caused by gender. This is simply feminist common sense, the clear admission that gender is but one of many structural categories which condition power.[12]

At this point important questions arise about the nature of equality. It is sometimes assumed that what feminists mean when we talk about the need for equality in relationships is that two people must be absolutely the same in every conceivable way in order for an intimate relationship and/or sexual contact between them to be justified. It is convenient to assume this, for its impossibility means that the call for equality can be construed as unrealistic and therefore as worthy of dismissal.

The ways in which any one individual has power or lacks it are complex, involving issues of personal resources and constitution together with social pressure, restriction and privilege. Add to this the fact that all of these will be constantly changing as a result of social interactions and material conditions, and it becomes clear that equality could never be a simple notion. I find it unhelpful to employ a model which posits equality as an entity which is either 'there' or 'missing' in a relationship, as though it were a static characteristic emerging from particular external conditions. I prefer a model of equality as something which is created and negotiated rather than discovered. Seeking equality in relationships is therefore about making decisions which aim at the mitigation of actual or potential differences in power and resources. It is crucial to note, however, that this will involve an astute political realism about the nature of power in its institutionalized forms. Ignoring institutional power or simply wishing it away is a sure way of exacerbating inequality rather than overcoming it.

Conclusions

I began this book with a critique of the Christian concept of complementarity between male and female. To that earlier criticism must be added the fact that the concept represents a significant obstacle to the equality-generating process which I have just advocated. Complementarity promotes what we might call a 'Jack Sprat' model of 'equality' in which male and female are designed to make up for one another's deficiencies, rather than inspiring one another to overcome them. It thereby encourages acquiescence in structural forms of gender difference. In so far as lesbian and gay sexuality and relationships have subverted traditional gender stereotypes they may well offer constructive pointers towards equality in relationships.

Deference to complementarity also encourages a reliance upon external appearances when it comes to assessing relationships. But our conclusion at the end of this book must be that things are not always what they seem. To distinguish a good relationship from a bad one takes much more than checking for the presence of a marriage certificate and the involvement of a particular combination of genders. A new and more demanding form of discernment is necessary.

Some church people and politicians portray this change as a movement from the good old days of moral objectivism to a slide into the chaos of moral relativism. I would resist this analysis. What has happened, I think, is that we now recognize that moral relativism is all we ever had, but that some people had the power to portray their subjective judgements as objective fact, as 'the way things should be' or as 'God's will'. There was comfort for some in the hierarchical universe in which everyone knew their place; hence the calls that we return to it. Such a return is impossible, but it would also be damaging. For this is the kind of objective morality that has kept women beaten by their abusive husbands in intolerable situations, chained by rules which state that 'divorce is wrong at all times and in all places'; it has forced lesbians (and indeed all women) to deny the positive value of our love for each other; and it has no place in its world-view for single women whatsoever.

This old form of objective morality was imposed from without, preached to us by various mouthpieces of the Divine, those moral 'heroes' described here by Carter Heyward:

Heroes have brought us causes and crusades, flags and battles, soldiers and bombs. As our liberators and leaders, popes and presidents, bishops and priests, shrinks and teachers, mentors and gurus, heroes have brought us pipedreams and smokescreens and everything but salvation. And this, I am persuaded, is because we tend to search everywhere except among ourselves-in-relation for peace.[13]

Objective morality was also upheld as the only escape from individualism, as though silencing the one in favour of the many or oppressing the minority for the sake of the majority was the only way of dealing with human diversity. Ongoing discussion about morality and values must be a corporate project, but to achieve that it must also be inclusive. As we have seen, when it comes to the development of its sexual ethics, Christianity has excluded many people's experience – particularly that of women.

Like many of the women in this book, I am convinced that unquestioning obedience to rules which have been externally defined is no longer an appropriate way of exercising our moral agency. But we must not reject one set of authoritarian answers only to embrace a new one. There is no point in swapping jaded heroes for new and exciting ones, male ones for female ones, or even heterosexual ones for lesbian ones. We have to get rid of the concept of heroes altogether. The new sexual ethics which we will forge will be astute about power – its structures and dynamics; cognizant of life as it is experienced in the midst of power relations; realistic about limitations whilst also able to inspire us to exceed them; and committed to provisionality. But such thoughts towards a new sexual ethics deserve separate attention. That's the task that lies ahead.

NOTES

1. Carter Heyward and Beverly W. Harrison, 'Pain and pleasure: avoiding the confusions of Christian traditions in feminist theory', in Joanne Carlson Brown and Carole R. Bohn (eds), *Christianity, Patriarchy and Abuse: A Feminist Critique*. The Pilgrim Press, Cleveland, OH, 1989, pp. 157–8.
2. Alice Walker, *In Search of Our Mothers' Gardens: Womanist Prose*. The Women's Press, London, 1983, pp. xi–xii.
3. Toni Morrison, *Beloved*. Picador, London, 1988, pp. 88.
4. Audre Lorde, 'Uses of the erotic: the erotic as power', in *Sister Outsider: Essays and Speeches by Audre Lorde*. The Crossing Press, New York, 1984, pp. 55–6.
5. Carter Heyward, *Touching Our Strength: The Erotic as Power and the Love of God*. Harper and Row, San Francisco, 1989, p. 4.
6. In the Christian tradition, 'love' has been understood to be of different types: agape, philia and eros. Agape involves seeking the welfare of others as in Jesus' commandment to 'love your neighbour as yourself' (Matthew 22:39).
7. James B. Nelson, *Body Theology*. Westminster/John Knox Press, Louisville, KY, 1992, pp. 23.
8. Carol J. Adams, 'Towards a feminist theology of religion and the state', *Theology and Sexuality Journal*, edition 2, Sheffield Academic Press, March 1995, citing Kwok Pui-Lan, 'The future of feminist theology; an Asian perspective', *The Auburn News*, Fall 1992.
9. Sheila Jeffreys, *Anticlimax: A Feminist Perspective on the Sexual Revolution*. The Women's Press, London, 1990, p. 316.
10. Heyward and Harrison, *Christianity, Patriarchy and Abuse*, p. 157.
11. *Ibid.*, p. 150.
12. Mary E. Hunt, review of *When Boundaries Betray Us*, by Carter Heyward (Harper, San Francisco, 1993), *Theology and Sexuality Journal*, edition 2, Sheffield Academic Press, March 1995.
13. Heyward, *Touching our Strength*, p. 11.

appendix
resources and
reading **l**ist

Useful organizations

Britain and Ireland School of Feminist
Theology
c/o The Lodge
Cook Rees Avenue
Neath
West Glamorgan SA11 1JT
Tel. 01792 842752

Catholic Women's Network
c/o Eileen Davidson
Walbottle House
Walbottle
Newcastle upon Tyne NE15 8JD

Center for the Prevention of Sexual and
Domestic Violence
1914 North 34th Street
Suite 105
Seattle
98103-9058
WA, USA
Tel. (001) 206 634–1903

Centre for Feminist Studies in Theology
University of Manchester
Oxford Road
Manchester M13 9PL
Tel. 0161–275 3601/3595

Christian Survivors of Sexual Abuse
BM CSSA
London WC1N 3XX

Institute for the Study of Christianity and
Sexuality
Oxford House
Derbyshire Street
London E2 6HG
Tel. 0171–613 1095

Lesbian and Gay Christian Movement
Oxford House
Derbyshire Street
London E2 6HG
Tel. 0171–739 1249

Network of Ecumenical Women in
Scotland
Scottish Churches House
Kirk Street
Dunblane FK15 0AJ
Tel. 01786 823588

Student Christian Movement (Women's
Network)
Mary Burnie House
Westhill College
14–16 Weoley Park Road

Selly Oak
Birmingham B29 6LL
Tel. 0121–471 2404

WATER
(Women's Alliance for Theology, Ethics
and Ritual)
8035 13th Street
Suites 1, 3 and 5
Silver Spring
MD 20910
USA
Tel. (001) 301 589–2509

Websters
(meeting place and spirituality resource
centre for women)
6A Midford Place
Tottenham Court Road
London W1P 9HH
Tel. 0171–388 0026

Women's Church Resource Group
15d Hill Street

Glasgow G3 6RN
Tel. 0141–331 2693

Women Priests for Wales
The Secretary
Oerle
Trefeglwys
Caersws
Powys SY17 5QX
Tel. 01686 430626

Women, Religion and Violence Working
Group
c/o 16 Sandyford Place
Glasgow G3 7NB
Tel. 0141–221 2259

World Council of Churches (Women's
Desk)
150 Route de Ferney
1211 Geneva 20
Switzerland
Tel. (0041) 22 791 61 11

selected reading list

Christianity and Child Sexual Abuse, by Hilary Cashman. SPCK: London, 1993.

Christianity and Incest, Annie Imbens and Ineke Jonker, Burns and Oates: London, 1992.

Christianity, Patriarchy and Abuse: A Feminist Critique, edited by Joanne Carlson Brown and Carole R. Bohn. The Pilgrim Press: Cleveland, OH, 1989.

Daring to Speak Love's Name: A Gay and Lesbian Prayer Book, by Elizabeth Stuart. Hamish Hamilton: London, 1992.

Fierce Tenderness: A Feminist Theology of Friendship, by Mary E. Hunt. Crossroad: New York, 1991.

Heterosexuality: A Feminism and Psychology Reader, edited by Sue Wilkinson and Celia Kitzinger. Sage Publications: London, 1993.

An Intimate Wilderness: Lesbian Writers on Sexuality, edited by Judith Barrington. The Eighth Mountain Press: Portland, OR, 1991.

Is Nothing Sacred?: When Sex Invades the Pastoral Relationship, by Marie Marshall Fortune. Harper and Row: San Francisco, 1989.

Journeys by Heart: A Christology of Erotic Power, by Rita Nakashima Brock. Crossroad: New York, 1992.

Lesbian Ethics: Toward New Value, by Sarah Lucia Hoagland. Institute of Lesbian Studies: Palo Alto, CA, 1990.

The Lesbian Heresy: A Feminist Perspective on the Lesbian Sexual Revolution, by Sheila Jeffreys. The Women's Press: London, 1994.

Lesbians Talk: Making Black Waves by Valerie Mason-John and Anne Khambatta. Scarlet Press: London, 1993.

Moving Heaven and Earth: Sexuality, Spirituality and Social Change, by Lucy Goodison. The Women's Press: London, 1990.

No Longer a Secret: The Church and Violence Against Women, by Aruna Gnanadason. Risk Book Series: World Council of Churches: Geneva, 1993.

Outercourse: The Be-Dazzling Voyage, by Mary Daly. The Women's Press: London, 1993.

Resurrecting the Body: Feminism, Religion and Psychoanalysis, by Naomi Goldenberg. Crossroad: New York, 1993.

Sex and God: Some Varieties of Women's Religious Experience, edited by Linda Hurcombe. RKP: London, 1987.

Sexual Violence, the Unmentionable Sin: An Ethical and Pastoral Perspective, by Marie Marshall Fortune. The Pilgrim Press: Cleveland, OH, 1983.

Sexuality and the Sacred: Sources for Theological Reflection, edited by James B. Nelson and Sandra P. Longfellow. Mowbray: London, 1994.

Silence in Heaven: A Book of Women's Preaching, edited by Heather Walton and Susan Durber. SCM Press:, London, 1994.

Sister Outsider: Essays and Speeches by Audre Lorde. The Crossing Press: Trumansburg, NY, 1984.

Speaking of Christ: A Lesbian Feminist Voice, by Carter Heyward. The Pilgrim Press: Cleveland, OH, 1989.

Touching Our Strength: The Erotic as Power and the Love of God, by Carter Heyward. Harper and Row: San Francisco, 1989.

Trauma and Recovery: The Aftermath of Violence from Domestic Abuse to Political Terror, by Judith Lewis Herman. Basic Books (HarperCollins): New York, 1992.

A Troubling in My Soul: Womanist Perspectives on Evil and Suffering, edited by Emilie M. Townes. Maryknoll, NY: Orbis Books: 1993.

Women and Bisexuality, by Sue George. Scarlet Press: London, 1993.

Women Talk Sex: Autobiographical Writing on Sex, Sexuality and Sexual Identity, edited by Pearlie McNeill, Bea Freeman, Jenny Newman. Scarlet Press: London, 1992.

RESOURCE GUIDES

Discussing Sexuality: Workshop Resources for Christian Groups, by Alison R. Webster. Institute for the Study of Christianity and Sexuality: London, 1994.

The F-Word: A Resource Guide to Fundamentalism, edited by Caroline Bailey and Martin Davies. GRAFT: Manchester and SCM Publications: Birmingham, 1993.

God Made Simple: An SCM Basic Guide, by Alison R. Webster. SCM Publications: Birmingham, 1989.

Intimacy and Sexuality, Christian Action Journal, summer 1993, edited by Alison R. Webster for the Institute for the Study of Christianity and Sexuality.

Just Love: An Introduction to Theology and Sexuality, edited by Alison R. Webster. SCM Publications: Birmingham, 1988.

index